Dalet Amot
Halachic Perspectives

HALACHIC PERSPECTIVES

RABBI ARI N. ENKIN

gefen פן
publishing house בית הוצאה לאור
JERUSALEM ◆ NEW YORK

Layout: pushingtheenvelope.ca
Cover Design: Moshe Handel

ISBN 978-965-229-409-8
Edition 1 3 5 7 9 8 6 4 2

Gefen Publishing House Ltd.   Gefen Books
6 Hatzvi St.   600 Broadway
Jerusalem 94386, Israel   Lynbrook, NY 11563, USA
972-2-538-0247   1-516-593-1234

orders@gefenpublishing.com
www.israelbooks.com

Printed in Israel   *Send for our free catalogue*

"And the people of Beit Shemesh...rejoiced!" (Shmuel 1 6:13)

To Shayna
and our children:
Shira Ilana
Eitan Maurice
Tehilla

L'orech yamim tovim, amen.

with love,
Abba

CONTENTS

Letters of Approbation XI
Foreword XIII
Acknowledgments XVII
Introductory Thoughts: The Importance of Studying Halacha XIX
Abbreviations and Sources XXIII

PRAYER AND SYNAGOGUE 1
Prayer 3
Chazzanim 6
Synagogues 8
The Mechitza 11
The Ten Commandments 13

FOOD AND MEALTIME 17
Mealtime 19
Table Manners 20
Kosher Bread 22
Eating Bread 24
Eating Fish and Meat Together 27
Bishul Akum 30
Chalav Yisrael 32
Chadash 34

SHABBAT AND HOLIDAYS 37
Shabbat Zemanim 39
Erev Shabbat 41
Kiddush and Havdala 44
The Melacha of Gozez (Shearing) 47
Brushing Teeth 50
Muktza 53
Amira l'Akum 55
Eruvin (Tzurat Hapetach) 57
Korban Pesach 60
Shabbat Erev Pesach 62
The Mitzvot of the Seder 64
Working on Chol Hamoed 66
Sefirat Ha'omer 68
Lag ba'Omer 70
The Three Weeks 72
Tisha b'Av – Torah Study 73
Elul Customs 75
Omens and Symbolism 78
Judgment Day 80
Kapparot 82

Kol Nidrei 84
Sukka Construction 86
Traveling during Sukkot 88
Simchat Torah 91
Electric Menoras 93
The Shamash 95
Eating during Chanuka 97
Adar I and Adar II 99
The Fast of Esther 101
Matanot La'evyonim 103
Mishlo'ach Manot 105
Purim Meshulash 107
Purim and Chanuka 109

WOMEN AND FAMILY **113**
Kol Isha 115
Mikva 117
Intimacy 119
Women's Hair Covering 121
Childbirth 123
Adoption 126
Divorce 128
Marriage 130
Intermarriage 133

INTERPERSONAL ISSUES **137**
Using First Names 139
Lending Money 141
Charity 143
Waiting Your Turn 145
Returning Lost Objects 147
Handicaps and Blemishes 149
Lifespans 151

INDIVIDUAL CHOICES **155**
Birthdays 157
Secular Studies 159
Tax Evasion 162
Gambling 164
Careers 166
Pets 169
Cosmetic Surgery 171
Vegetarianism 173
Appearance and Attire 176

ISRAEL **179**
The Land of Israel 181

The Israel Defense Forces 183
Hallel on Yom Ha'atzmaut 185
Second Day Yom Tov in Israel 187
Speaking Hebrew 190
Beit Shemesh 192
Eilat 193
Gaza 195
The Golan Heights 197
Lod 199

MYSTICAL AND SUPERNATURAL **203**
Predictions 205
Halloween 207
Demons 212
Dreams 214

MORE MITZVOT **217**
Writing a Sefer Torah 219
Travel 221
Birkat Ilanot 224
Shechita 225
Shatnez 228
The Beit Din 230
The International Dateline 232
Geniza 234

END OF LIFE ISSUES **237**
Bikur Cholim 239
Euthanasia 241
Funerals 243
The Death of the Wicked 245

OTHER **249**
Cruelty to Animals 251
The Humanity of Shechita 253
Music 255
Ruth 257
Rabbeinu Gershom 259
The New Sanhedrin 261
Spices 263
Medicine 265

APPENDIX **269**
Talmudic Quotes to Live By 271

About the Author 277

ב״ה

מתתיהו ברויד
Michael J. Broyde
1428 LaChona Court
Atlanta, Georgia 30329

כ״א מרחשון, תשס״ו

Rabbi Ari Enkin has written a wonderful sefer on a wide assortment of halachic issues. This is a wonderful sefer in three distinct ways.

Firstly, it is extremely well written, and presents halacha in a concise manner that is easy for anyone to understand.

Furthermore, the wide assortment of issues that this sefer addresses is certain to provide every reader with something of interest.

Finally, and most significantly, this sefer manages to combine both the ethical as well as the technical, in a way which offers an excellent glimpse into the workings of Jewish law. As this sefer shows, halacha is not merely and exercise of permitted or prohibited, but rather a process which takes into consideration many external factors before arriving at a conclusion.

This sefer is truly a worthwhile contribution which will no doubt assist those in the English speaking world in better appreciating and observing Jewish law, and by extension, the will of God.

מתתיהו ברוד

Michael J. Broyde
Rabbi, Young Israel of Toco Hills, Atlanta
Dayan, Beth Din of America

XI

Founding Rabbinical Advisor
HaRav HaGaon Aryeh Leib Berenbaum, זצ״ל

בס״ד

כ' חשון, תשס״ו
November 22, 2005

Dear Rabbi Enkin, shlita,

I would like to thank you for offering me the privilege of reviewing some of the manuscript from your upcoming book "Dalet Amot: Halachic and Aggadic Perspectives", which deals with over one hundred contemporary issues from the perspective of Halacha and Aggada.

The issues you present are very timely and relevant to the average person. Your presentation of Halacha and Aggada, in a light and engaging manner is a compelling method of teaching. You have simplified even the most complex concepts making them easily understandable.

You have successfully shown how a person can integrate so many mundane and routine matters into a life of Avodas Hashem. This is a reflection of your Yiras Shamayim and your overwhelming desire to educate others.

It is my opinion that this book is a valuable and welcome addition to the world of halacha study. I am delighted to offer my warmest blessings and full endorsement to this work. The clarity of such a book has much value for both beginners as well as advanced scholars who will undoubtedly make use of the many references you provide.

May you merit to see your upcoming book "Dalet Amot" warmly received and well circulated amongst Klal Yisrael,

With Torah blessings and warmest regards,

Rabbi Daniel Channen
Director, Issur V'heter
Pirchei Shoshanim Semicha Program

FOREWORD

"I will thank Hashem with all my heart." – Tehillim 111:1

Baruch hatov v'hameitiv shehecheyanu v'kiyemanu v'higiyanu

lazman hazeh – hashir v'hashevach l'chai olamim.

The Sefer Chassidim teaches that the opportunity to write a book is both a special blessing, and, at the same time, an obligation.[1] In fact, he writes that a person who has something constructive to publish, and doesn't do so, is to be considered a robber whose knowledge is unlawfully acquired. Similarly, the Pele Yoetz[2] instructs us to share what we have learned with others through the publishing of books, specifically books of halacha. I am humbled to have somehow been found worthy of this *siyata d'shmaya*.

The title of this book is derived from a Talmudic passage that has always intrigued me. We are taught that "from the day that the Holy Temple was destroyed, the Holy One blessed be He has nothing in His world except the *dalet amot* [literally, "four cubits"] of halacha." Keeping in mind that in rabbinic literature, the term *dalet amot* refers to automatic acquisition of anything that is found in a person's immediate custody, we can suggest that through the study of halacha we truly connect with the Holy One blessed be He.

As the Talmud teaches, with the option of dwelling in the Temple no longer available, God chose to dwell within the realm of halacha. This would seem to suggest that the study of halacha is somewhat equal to the presence of a fully functioning Temple! In fact, Rabbi Hershel Schachter teaches that when we dedicate all of our activities towards the service of God, which can only be perfected through the study of halacha, then even our mundane

---

1   *Sefer Chassidim* 530.
2   S.v. "Sefer."

daily routines can be comparable to the service of the high priests in the Temple![3]

It is this idea that encapsulates the essence of this work. We must sensitize ourselves to an awareness that anything a Jew does is intimately bound with halacha. There is nothing in life or even in our seemingly mundane routines that does not have halachic significance or halachic value – everything we do is part and parcel of serving God. While the world of Torah study is filled with many inspirational texts, it is only through the study of halacha that God is directing us in the path we are to follow. Indeed, when we pray, we are talking to God, but when we study, God is talking to us.

That being said, while this book contains many of the major issues that are dealt with in the Shulchan Aruch, it also deals with, and perhaps more importantly so, issues that are *not* to be found in the Shulchan Aruch. This book endeavors to show that everything from birthday parties to cruises, from showering[4] to sleeping[5] – all our decisions, actions, and seemingly trivial routines – are an inseparable component in our service of God.

Each chapter in *Dalet Amot* consists of a six-hundred- to eight-hundred-word essay. The intention was to keep the entries short and sweet, and, at the same time, to provide an information-packed review of every topic. While there is certainly much more that could have been written on each topic, our sages have taught us that it is simply not humanly possible to completely cover any one subject, and therefore, I didn't even try.[6] Much effort was made to present material that is original, slightly unusual or unfamiliar, entertaining, and ultimately inspiring. Although some readers may disagree with some of the authorities or perspectives presented in

---

3   As discussed by Rabbi Herschel Schachter at http://torahweb.org/torah/2002/ parsha/rsch_lech.html.

4   Once when Hillel was departing from his students, they said to him, "Master, where are you going?" He replied, "To perform a mitzva." They asked, "Which mitzva would that be?" He replied, "To take a shower." They asked, "Is that a mitzva?" He replied, "Absolutely! If in the theaters and circuses, the images of the king must be kept clean, how much more so is it the duty of man to care for the body, which was created in the image of God!" Vayikra Rabba 34:3.

5   OC (*Orach Chayim*) 3:6, 4:16, 240:17.

6   Rashi, meforshim, Kohelet 12:12.

this work, be sure to recall the Chida, who taught that one should never hesitate to publish a book out of fear that others may disagree with the material.[7]

Considering that this work endeavors to provide a wide range of halachic opinions on each issue, I would like to take this opportunity to invoke the essentials, "ground rules" of sorts, of *"shivim panim laTorah* (there are seventy faces to the Torah)"[8] and *"eilu v'eilu divrei Elokim Chaim* (these and these are the words of the living God)"[9] – every halachic opinion and perspective is just as legitimate as the other.[10] In fact, the Talmud teaches us that rabbis would be well advised to follow the example of Hillel, and to first share the opposing rulings of their colleagues prior to issuing their own.[11]

Moreover, the Talmud states, "A single verse can have several interpretations,"[12] which further demonstrates that there is no single halachic authority who alone possesses the true and exclusive path to serving God. If God is infinite, then there must be an infinite number of legitimate ways to serve Him. The fact that different segments of the orthodox community emerge with different practices[13] should be of no consequence to anyone. To this majestic diversity let us praise each other with *"ish al machanehu v'ish al diglo* (each man according to his camp and banner)."[14]

I would like to emphasize that nothing in this book should be acted upon in practice without first consulting one's rabbi, *no matter how definitively it is written.* Take for example, the entry on travel, where I write, "Never, but never, polish your shoes on the day of a trip – it's considered bad luck and even dangerous for one's journey." While this and other such rulings throughout the book may be drawn from some of the most eminent sources, they are not

---

7   Cited in the introduction to *Miyam Hahalacha* by Rabbi Yona Metzger, second volume.

8   Bamidbar Rabba 13:15.

9   Eruvin 13b.

10   Rashi, Ketubot 57a, s.v. *"Ha kamashma lan."*

11   Eruvin 13b; *Sefer Chassidim* 15.

12   Sanhedrin 34a.

13   Often mistakenly referred to as "standards."

14   From the Friday night zemer "Kol Mekadesh Shvii." See also http://torahweb.org/torah/2004/parsha/rwil_naso.html.

always binding halacha. If you do notice on the day of departure for a trip that your shoes are so dirty that you would come to be ridiculed – then of course, polish them! Only an expert scholar can be relied upon to advise one on priorities within halacha, and when certain halachic rulings are to be waived in light of other considerations.

As no one is immune from making mistakes,[15] I request that readers who find errors kindly call them to my attention in preparation for future editions of this work. On this subject, the Pri Megadim is reported to have said that if even only three halachot from his printed work were accurate, then the entire publication would have been worthwhile.[16]

There is hardly anyone who can master the entire body of Torah literature, nor be flawless in the observance of every single mitzva. We should strive to be especially meticulous in at least one mitzva, as well as most proficient in a specific area of Torah study.[17] More than three times each day, the Jew prays, "May it be Your will, Hashem our God…to grant us *our share* in your Torah." While many interpretations have been offered to this frequently repeated petition, I would like to suggest that this prayer is actually a personal request for God to ignite within each of us a passion to delve, enjoy, and find satisfaction and proficiency in a specific area of Torah study and mitzva observance that appeals to us most. In this way, each of us can establish our own personal *dalet amot*.

Awaiting the Mashiach and the rebuilding of the Holy Temple,

Ari Enkin
Beit Shemesh
October 2007 /Cheshvan 5768

---

15   Rashi, Tehillim 19:12.
16   Cited in the introduction to Rabbi Yona Metzger, *Miyam Hahalacha*, second volume.
17   See Shabbat 118b.

ACKNOWLEDGMENTS

The journey of bringing *Dalet Amot* from its original rough notes to what you are now holding in your hands has a been a process of continual nurturing over quite some time. There are many people who have extensively assisted me throughout the many revisions this manuscript has undergone. Indeed, for fear of leaving someone out, I have chosen to refrain from mentioning anyone by name. They know who they are and may this latest and improved version bring them much *nachas*.

I would like to take this opportunity to thank Ilan Greenfield and the competent staff of Gefen Publishing House for taking a warm and encouraging interest in my work. I hope that this book becomes the beginning of a beautiful relationship.

I would like to take this opportunity to acknowledge and thank my primary employer, Mr. Jonathan Abeles, CEO of Cheerfully Changed Financial Services Ltd. For the past two years I have served as the manger of the Modiin branch of this unique Olim-focused enterprise. Although my title sounds intricate and does involve some major responsibilities, there is however a tremendous amount of free time which allows me to pursue my academic pursuits. Believe it or not, this book was both researched and written in its entirety during Cheerfully Changed work hours. In the spirit of "the guest does more for the host than the host does for the guest (Midrash Ruth Rabba 5:9, Vayikra Rabba 34)," may this sefer bring Jonathan and the entire staff much nachas.

Similarly, I would like to acknowledge and thank the administrators of the somewhat anonymous website Hebrewbooks. org. This invaluable website contains over twelve thousand Torah books which are available for free at the click of a mouse button. It would not have been possible to properly or efficiently prepare this book while at work were it not for this blessed resource. There is an unexplainable thrill to be able to have web browsers open to the *Shulchan Aruch, Kaf Hachaim, Aruch Hashulchan,* and *Kitzur Shulchan Aruch* and quickly being able to compile the various views on a halachic topic. "They are to be credited with the merits of the public! (Avot 5:21)"

Acharon, acharon chaviv, I would like to pay tribute to my loving and caring wife, Shayna, who stands by my side and with tremendous *mesirat nefesh* enables our children to enjoy the greatest possible atmosphere and attention. The only beracha any marriage truly needs is to merit to always be true *re'im ahuvim. Sheli v'shelachem shelah hu.*

INTRODUCTORY THOUGHTS:
THE IMPORTANCE OF
STUDYING HALACHA

- From the day that the Holy Temple was destroyed, the Holy One blessed be He has nothing in His world except the *dalet amot* of halacha.[18]
- "God loves the gates of Zion more than all the tents of Jacob"[19] – this teaches us that God loves the places that excel in halacha more than all other places of prayer and study.[20]
- One should always conclude with words of halacha when taking leave of a friend.[21]
- When two scholars make an effort to sharpen each other's minds by debating halacha, the Holy One blessed be He helps them to reach the correct halachic conclusions.[22]
- When two scholars listen to each other's views in halacha, the Holy One blessed be He listens to their voices.[23]
- Who is deemed a scholar who may be appointed as a communal leader? Someone who can be asked any halacha and reply.[24]
- "The word of God"[25] – this refers to halacha.[26]
- The essence of Mishna study is to learn halacha.[27]
- The academy of Eliyahu taught: Whoever studies halacha every day is assured a place in the World to Come.[28]

---

18   Berachot 8a.
19   Tehillim 87:2.
20   Berachot 8a.
21   Berachot 31a.
22   Shabbat 63a.
23   Shabbat 63a.
24   Shabbat 114a.
25   Amos 8:12.
26   Shabbat 138b.
27   Kiddushin 49a.
28   Megilla 28b.

- "And God is with him"[29] – this means that the halacha is as he says.[30]
- "You shall build your house"[31] – these are the halachot.[32]
- Be sure to learn halacha more than anything else, particularly the entire Shulchan Aruch. Everyone is obligated to study halacha every day of his life without exception.[33]
- Whoever fails to teach someone halacha is as if he robs him of his heritage.[34]
- Whoever learns from someone even a single halacha must treat that person with respect.[35]
- Every person who merits to learn one halacha inherits an entire world.[36]
- "You shall study all of His statutes"[37] – these are the halachot.[38]
- Who is truly a scholar? One who learns halacha.[39]
- The study of Shulchan Aruch banishes thoughts of idolatry.[40]
- Those who are able to study for only three or four hours a day...should study halachic rulings.[41]
- A person's main study should be in halacha in order that he know how to conduct himself.[42]
- The smart man says: I will learn two halachot today, and two halachot tomorrow, until I finish them all.[43]
- The one who learns halacha and then reviews it is far

29   Shmuel I 18:14.
30   Sanhedrin 93b.
31   Devarim 22:9.
32   *Tosefta Sota* 8.
33   *Sichot Haran* 29.
34   Sanhedrin 91b.
35   Avot 6:3.
36   *Tikunei Zohar.*
37   Shemot 13:10.
38   *Mechilta Beshalach.*
39   Talmud Yerushalmi, Moed Katan 3:5.
40   *Sefer Hamidot* 3.
41   YD (*Yoreh Deah*) 246:4; Shach, *Mishna Berura* 155:3.
42   *Mishna Berura* 155:9.
43   Vayikra Rabba 19:2.

superior to the one who learns halacha but then neglects to review it.[44]

- It is far better to study in pairs rather than alone, for if one of them forgets a halacha, the other will be there to remind him.[45]
- We must ensure that women know halacha.[46]
- Be sure to review halacha with those who are not as knowledgeable as yourself.[47]
- The study of Shulchan Aruch along with the rulings of modern-day authorities is a daily obligation just like prayer and tefillin.[48]
- One's main focus in study must be in those areas that lead to practice.[49]
- The wise man knows that he should sacrifice himself to learn halacha in depth…it is the most beloved service before God and even greater than prayer.[50]
- It is an obligation to be proficient in the Orach Chaim section of the Shulchan Aruch.[51]
- One should endeavor to complete one's studies for rabbinical ordination prior to marriage.[52]
- One who desires to appreciate the greatness of the Creator, let him study aggada, for through it you will get to know Him and cling to His ways.[53]
- One who has mastered aggada but not halacha has not even tasted the flavor of wisdom…. One who has mastered halacha but does not know the teachings of aggada has no taste of the fear of God.[54]

---

44   Kohelet Rabba 4:9.
45   Kohelet Rabba 4:14.
46   *Sefer Chassidim* 313.
47   *Sefer Chassidim* 946.
48   *Pele Yoetz*, s.v. "Dinim."
49   Introduction to the *Mishna Berura*.
50   Chazon Ish, *Emuna u'Bitachon* 3:19.
51   *Yesod Hashoresh v'Haavoda* 6:5.
52   *Shaarei Halacha u'Minhag* (Chabad) 4:33.
53   Sifrei, Eikev 49.
54   *Avot d'Rabbi Natan* 29.

ABBREVIATIONS AND SOURCES

The following abbreviations for sections of the *Shulchan Aruch* (the primary code of Jewish law) are used in this book:

YD – Yoreh Deah
EH – Even Ha'ezer
OC – Orach Chayim
CM – Choshen Mishpat

Note also that all Talmud references are to Talmud Bavli (the Babylonian Talmud), except where Yerushalmi (the Jerusalem Talmud) is specified.

PRAYER AND SYNAGOGUE

PRAYER

Prayer, or better put, a unilateral and private audience with God, is a very serious occasion, not to be dismissed lightly. In this discussion we'll examine some of the interesting ideas surrounding prayer in general, as well as Pesukei d'Zimra, Shemoneh Esrei, and Tachanun in particular.

When taking to prayer, one should be sure to be dressed appropriately – at least within the basic parameters of proper dress and dignity as befitting local standards. For example, if appearing before dignitaries without socks is unacceptable in a certain place, then one should be sure not to do so when praying, or even entering a synagogue. In Israel, however, where dressing without socks is certainly acceptable, then one is permitted to pray in such attire, as well.

Regardless of where one lives in the world, prayer should always be recited while facing Jerusalem.[1] Should one not know the direction of Jerusalem, one should focus intensely on God's presence, and that will suffice.[2] Alternatively, one who wishes to become wise should pray towards the south, and if it's wealth one seeks, pray facing north.[3] Be sure to always look into your siddur when praying, and not at other worshippers. We are taught that one whose eyes gravitate around the room while praying is an ignoramus.[4] Keep your eyes focused in your siddur!

Pesukei d'Zimra, which is the preliminary component of the morning prayers, is focused on praise for God, and is considered to be very special. Accordingly, we are taught that one should be as careful with the recitation of Pesukei d'Zimra as one is careful with counting money.[5] The opening blessing of Pesukei d'Zimra is

---

1   Rabbi Hershel Shachter reports that the Rav's father, Rabbi Moshe Soloveichik, who lived near Yeshiva University, would avoided davening there because the beit midrash did not face east.
2   OC 94:1; *Mishna Berura* 3:9; *Kitzur Shulchan Aruch* 18:10; *Aruch Hashulchan* 94:8; *Sefer Chassidim* 18.
3   Bava Batra 25b.
4   *Pele Yoetz*, s.v. "Sefer"; *Sefer Chassidim* 18.
5   OC 51:8; *Mishna Berura* 20.

the Baruch She'amar, which, according to tradition, was received directly from heaven. Although one may find slight variations in the different versions of Baruch She'amar, all versions contain exactly eighty-seven words, the numerical value of the word *paz*, meaning "gold," referring to the value of these prayers. The central praise of the Pesukei d'Zimra is of course the Ashrei psalm, which is to be recited three times every day. One who does so is assured a place in the World to Come.[6]

Unfortunately, Pesukei d'Zimra is often marginalized when worshipers are in a rush and many individuals assume for themselves the authority to omit selected portions of it. Make no mistake, the only time Pesukei d'Zimra may be shortened is in order to arrive at the Shemoneh Esrei at the same time as the congregation.[7] Even under such circumstances, there are many authorities who still oppose any shortening of the Pesukei d'Zimra. At no other time should any shortcuts be taken in the prayers.[8]

During the Shemoneh Esrei, the silent prayer, one's feet should be together to resemble the stance of the angels.[9] While many people attribute our custom of reciting a silent prayer to the precedent set by Chana when she prayed for a son,[10] this actually may not be the case. The Talmud's explanation for this practice is that, ideally, we should be audibly confessing all of our sins during the section of the Shemoneh Esrei where we request forgiveness from transgressions. However, in order not to embarrass people whose sins were likely to be heard by the worshipper beside them, it was decreed that the Shemoneh Esrei become a silent prayer.[11]

There is an almost mystical dread associated with the arrival of Tachanun, the prayers for penitence. Admit it. Whether it be an ordinary weekday morning – certainly a Monday or Thursday morning – or even after Mincha, Tachanun is often an unwelcome

---

6   Berachot 4.
7   *Mishna Berura*, OC 52:1.
8   Ibid.
9   OC 95:1.
10   Shmuel I 1:10–15.
11   Sota 32b.

arrival. This may perhaps be due to the fact that some authorities have ruled that the recital of Tachanun is optional.[12]

Tachanun is an important part of the davening, with some authorities considering it as an extension of the Shemoneh Esrei.[13] The formal name for Tachanun is *nefillat apayim* (falling on one's face). Indeed, when in the presence of a Torah scroll, one is to recite Tachanun with one's face resting on one's arm.[14] If no Torah scroll is in the area, Tachanun is to be recited sitting up or standing. Common custom in Yerushalayim is that Tachanun is always recited with the head down.[15]

While everyone is very excited to see a newly married man enter the synagogue, thereby exempting the congregation from reciting Tachanun, it should be noted that this may not be ideal. Indeed, some authorities recommend that a groom refrain from attending synagogue services during the week following his wedding in order to allow for the congregation to recite Tachanun.[16] Furthermore, there is no obligation for a groom to make his presence known in the synagogue and thereby cause the cancellation of Tachanun.[17]

Finally, we should be sure not to belittle or marginalize the Aleinu prayer which is recited at the conclusion of all services. Aleinu is actually adapted for daily use from the High Holiday liturgy. I have even heard interpretations that the entire prayer service is simply one gigantic preparation for the recitation of Aleinu.[18]

Prayer is a special moment of personal engagement with God. Not only is it a biblical mitzva,[19] but it is worth noting that the rabbis of the Talmud were envious of those who could find the time to pray all day long![20]

---

12   Tur, OC 131.
13   Rema, OC 131:1; *Mishna Berura* 1.
14   Rema, OC 131.
15   Cited in *Tefilla K'hilchata* by Rabbi Yitzchak Fuchs, chapter 15.
16   *Mishna Berura* 131:20.
17   Ruling of Rabbi Chaim Pinchas Sheinberg cited in *Tefilla K'hilchata*.
18   See *Mishna Berura* 132:8.
19   Devarim 11:13.
20   Berachot 21a.

CHAZZANIM

The chazzan, also referred to as the *ba'al tefilla* or *shaliach tzibbur*, is no less than the acting representative between the congregation that has appointed him and our Father in heaven. There is an entire codification of laws and customs as to who is worthy of being appointed to such office and the procedures to be followed. These rules are especially relevant with regard to the High Holidays.

For starters, we should ensure that the individual chosen as the chazzan is well known as both a Torah scholar and one who engages in a variety of good deeds. It is also considered ideal that the chazzan be over thirty years old, as well as married with children.[21] With such a profile, it is likely that the chazzan will be a more mature, responsible, and pious individual. A bearded chazzan is also considered advantageous. Nevertheless, as long as an individual is desired by the congregation, objections need not be raised.[22] It goes without saying that the chazzan must be properly dressed from the perspective of both modesty and dignity. Many halachic authorities frown upon a chazzan with short sleeves.[23]

As is known, chazzanim often indulge in extensive, excessive operatics and other musical pieces at various points in the prayers. A chazzan who does so in order to impress himself upon the congregation or for other self-aggrandizing motives is not worthy of the position and should be removed. However, chazzanim who do so for no other motive besides their love of God and with the intention to beautify the prayers before Him are to be praised.[24] Even so, excessive renditions for any purpose are to be discouraged. One should note that Rabbi Moshe Feinstein, along with most other authorities, rules that a chazzan should not repeat any words of the

---

21　See *Be'er Heitev* 581:7.
22　*Kitzur Shulchan Aruch* 128:7, Rema, OC 581:1.
23　Rabbi Tzvi Yehuda Kook cited in *Miyam Hahalacha* 1:23. See also *Yaskil Avdi* 7:1, hashmatot; Rambam, *Tefilla* 5:5. Wearing gloves while praying is also unadvised; see Rashi, Pesachim 57b; *Sefer Chassidim* 18.
24　OC 53:11; *Sefer Chassidim* 129.

prayers, even for the sake of "fitting them into the tune."[25] Indeed, in some situations, a chazzan who repeats any words should be removed from his post.[26]

One who is mourning for his closest relatives should not be appointed as chazzan on a Shabbat or yom tov, particularly during the shiva period.[27] Even one who is within one year of a parent's passing or within thirty days of the passing of other close relatives should not serve as a chazzan for the High Holidays.[28] This is because one who is in mourning is seen as one who has been the subject of unfavorable decrees, and, hence, may not be successful in arousing Divine mercy for the congregation.[29] Of course, should there be no alternative, a mourner may lead services.[30] Additionally, one who is contracted to serve as a chazzan or is otherwise committed to a congregation would be permitted to honor the arrangement and lead the services.[31]

As mentioned, the chazzan is the one who represents the congregation before God. He must keep in mind at all times that he is acting on behalf of the congregation, and intends to discharge all of their religious obligations.[32] It is also encouraged to secure a chazzan from a distinguished family, as it is known to assist in having prayers accepted.[33]

An interesting issue for discussion is how it is possible to pay a chazzan for services rendered on Shabbat and holidays. It is seemingly not in the spirit of the sanctity of the day, and unbecoming of the individual. Interestingly, many authorities take no issue with a chazzan, or anyone else for that matter, receiving payment for Shabbat "work" when it is related to a mitzva, or

---

25   *Igrot Moshe* 2:22. See Yabia Omer, OC 6:7 for further sources on this issue.
26   Berachot 33b; Maharam Shick, OC 31; *Aruch Hashulchan*, OC 338:8.
27   *Kitzur Shulchan Aruch* 128:8
28   *Magen Avraham* 581:4
29   *Pri Megadim*, cited in Rabbi Chaim Binyamin Goldberg, *Mourning in Halacha* (Jerusalem: Mesorah, 1991), p. 318.
30   *Magen Avraham* 581:4.
31   *Aruch Hashulchan* 581:4.
32   Rema, OC 581:1.
33   Rashi, Bereishit 25:21.

performed on behalf of a community.[34] A better alternative is to arrange a chazzan's contract in such a way that it encompasses the entire gamut of chazzan-related duties, and not merely the Shabbat component of his work. With such an arrangement, the chazzan is not being paid for Shabbat work specifically, but rather to fulfill the role of a chazzan in all that it entails throughout the entire week.[35]

The office of the chazzan is one of great importance and should not be dismissed lightly. He who is chosen to lead our prayers may just make the difference as to whether or not they are accepted.

S Y N A G O G U E S

When it comes down it, a synagogue isn't really needed in order to hold prayer services. Services can be held in virtually any place, from a community hall to one's home basement. Nevertheless, common custom, and for good reason, is to build beautiful synagogues as exclusive edifices in which prayer is the primary focus. Indeed, it may just be that prayer is only heard by God when conducted in a synagogue.[36] If, however, a synagogue isn't truly needed, is building a synagogue actually a mitzva?

According to the Rambam[37] and most others, yes, it is a mitzva based on the verse "And they shall make for Me a Sanctuary and I will dwell in their midst."[38] Other authorities, however, assert that while building a synagogue is a great thing to do, it does not qualify as one of the binding mitzvot of the Torah. They counter that the verse quoted above actually refers to building the Temple in Jerusalem, and not to other places of prayer. Everyone agrees, however, that synagogues are imbued with extreme sanctity, and that reverence must be shown for them.

---

34   Rema, OC 306:6; *Mishna Berura* 33.
35   OC 306:4; *Mishna Berura* 24.
36   Berachot 6a.
37   Mitzva #20.
38   Shemot 25:8.

One of the many institutions for exhibiting proper reverence for a synagogue is to ensure that men and married women have their heads covered when in the building, at least while in the sanctuary.[39] Although it is preferable for non-Jewish men to cover their heads as well, it need not be imposed. In fact, contrary to popular misconception, halacha does not even require asking a non-Jewish visitor to a synagogue to tuck away religious symbols, such as a cross worn on a necklace.[40]

Here's an incentive to encourage visits to the synagogue: any money found lying around a synagogue is for the finder to keep.[41]

One should never depart from a synagogue in a hurried manner.[42] We should be certain to stand in the synagogue at the required times, especially when the Torah is paraded.[43] Don't sit near the door of the synagogue,[44] nor at the back[45] – find a place in the middle, and never get into an argument with someone over seating arrangements.[46] So important is it to show exclusive devotion to nothing but God while in a synagogue, there are some authorities who go so far as to forbid kissing one's own children in a synagogue, lest it detract from this exclusivity.[47]

This idea of showing reverence for a synagogue has far-reaching halachic implications, with authorities explaining that one must revere a synagogue as one reveres God.[48] Even sitting idle in a synagogue is a great mitzva.[49] Running through a synagogue sanctuary or otherwise using it as a shortcut is considered so inappropriate that it could lead to a shorter lifespan.[50] It goes

---

39 Kiddushin 31a; note: this should of course be ideally practiced always!
40 Har Tzvi, OC 1:86.
41 Bava Metzia 24a.
42 Berachot 6b.
43 *Mishna Berura* 146:17; strictly speaking, standing is not required when the ark is open. See *Shaarei Tzion* 146:18.
44 Berachot 8a.
45 Berachot 6b.
46 *Sefer Chassidim* 759.
47 Rema, OC 98:1; *Kitzur Shulchan Aruch* 13:1; *Yechave Da'at* 4:12; *Sefer Chassidim* 255.
48 *Kitzur Shulchan Aruch* 13:1.
49 *Kitzur Shulchan Aruch* 13:3.
50 Megilla 27b.

without saying that lightheaded activities are forbidden within the sanctuary. Even funerals should not be held within the sanctuary itself.[51] Rather, the place should be reserved exclusively for prayer and study.

Eating within the synagogue sanctuary is strictly forbidden unless directly attached to a mitzva such as a *seuda shlishit* (third Shabbat meal), and on condition that it remains modest.[52] Sleeping in a synagogue is also considered unbecoming, and if for some reason one feels the need to do so, one should sit in the furthest pews.[53] Always be sure to attend your synagogue regularly – God gets angry when you're not there.[54]

Other rooms in a synagogue building besides the actual sanctuary are not considered to have any particular holiness, and therefore most activities would be permissible in these areas. If, however, other rooms are also used for services, then they too should be accorded reverence even when used for something else.[55] Some synagogue committees conduct a stipulation ceremony of sorts, prior to the construction of a synagogue, to publicly declare that certain rooms of the synagogue will remain for ordinary uses.[56]

Never leave someone alone in the synagogue – be sure to wait for him to finish his prayers and then to leave together.[57] Some authorities advise against going to pray in the synagogue if you fear that you may end up chatting with friends during the services.[58] The renowned Vilna Gaon once wrote that with all the *lashon hara* (forbidden, literally "evil" speech) spoken in a synagogue, one is likely better off praying alone at home![59]

Finally, it is certainly worth mentioning that if there is one thing that we can and should learn from our Christian neighbors,

---

51   Megilla 28a.
52   *Kitzur Shulchan Aruch* 13:4; *Biur Halacha* 151, s.v. "v'ayn"; *Igrot Moshe*, OC 1:45.
53   *Kitzur Shulchan Aruch* 13:4.
54   Berachot 6b.
55   Chatam Sofer, OC 28.
56   OC 151:11; *Mishna Berura* 32.
57   Berachot 5b.
58   *Kaf Hachaim* 151:8.
59   Cited at: http://www.pirchei.co.il/specials/gra/gra.htm.

it is respect for our places of worship and proper behavior during services.[60]

THE MECHITZA

As an orthodox rabbi, I consider the mechitza to be a vital component of synagogue life. Without it, public prayer would be more challenging, particularly as it would relate to women's attendance at services. Of course, the mechitza refers to the physical separation between men and women in orthodox congregations during prayer services. It is not merely an architectural invention, but rather a parcel of our history, as we will see.

Our first encounter with the concept of mechitza is found on Noah's ark. As Noah's ark enjoyed the designation of being a holy place, similar to that of a synagogue sanctuary, men and women were separated to ensure reverence and celibacy.[61] Additionally, when the Jewish people gave praise to God after crossing the Red Sea, men and women worshipped separately.[62]

The Talmud introduces the mechitza as having been a necessary addition to the Holy Temple in order to deter what was becoming excessive levity during services.[63] Its original construction was in the form of a balcony, which was the predominant form the mechitza assumed right through to the twentieth century. Some suggest that it was because the mechitza had been so accepted and even taken for granted in Jewish life that it did not even necessitate its own section in the Shulchan Aruch. Our prophets teach us that in the messianic era, mechitzot will continue to remain an integral part of synagogue construction.[64]

The purpose of the mechitza can be viewed in one of two ways. One approach is that the mechitza is to block out any sighting of

---

60   *Sefer Chareidim* 9:19.
61   Rashi, Bereishit 7:7.
62   Rashi, Shemot 15:21.
63   Sukka 51a.
64   Zecharia 12:12.

women, lest it cause men to think inappropriate thoughts during prayer.[65] Although one can argue this case in the reverse, the argument carries more weight within the male realm. Another view sees the mechitza as primarily ensuring that men and women are simply not praying in the same physical domain.[66] Because of the different approaches, opinions as to the height and appearance of the mechitza vary from three feet of even transparent material right through to eight-foot-high opaque structures.

Whether mechitza separation is needed for events such as weddings and the like is subject to much debate among the orthodox authorities. It is noted that in biblical times, many families would gather together to celebrate the Pesach seder, which included many prayers and rituals, and that no mechitza was ever required.[67]

There is also evidence to suggest that during the Talmudic period, weddings were always celebrated with mixed seating.[68] Common custom today is not to demand a mechitza at such events. Nevertheless, there are orthodox authorities who do insist on a mechitza for weddings and similar affairs.[69] Yet others suggest a compromise approach at ceremonial events – not requiring the actual presence of a mechitza, but merely ensuring separate seating.[70]

Halachically, a mechitza may only be truly necessary in the presence of two or more women. For example, in the event that only a single woman is present during a prayer service, a mechitza would not be essential.[71]

The subject of mechitza is one that commands reverence and respect, and should not be hastily dismissed. It has been with us from the earliest of times, and we are told that it will be the way of the future as well. Regardless of whether you personally agree with

---

65   *Igrot Moshe*, OC 1:39-44.
66   The view of Rabbi Yosef Dov Soloveitchik; see *Bnei Banim* 1:1, 2.
67   *Igrot Moshe*, OC 1:41.
68   Pesachim 86a.
69   *Kitzur Shulchan Aruch* 149:1.
70   *Seridei Aish* 2:8; *Bnei Banim* 1:34, 35.
71   Rabbi Michael Broyde, Shmuel I 1:12.

it or not, the concept should allow us all to reflect on the sanctity of the synagogue.

THE TEN COMMANDMENTS

The highlight of synagogue services on Shavuot morning is undoubtedly the reading of the Ten Commandments. At that time, an announcement is usually made in order to awaken any dozing congregants to stand for this special reading.[72] It is even read with a different cantillation, known as the *ta'am elyon* (the "higher" cantillation), which fuses the entire recitation of the Ten Commandments into a single verse.[73]

During the times of the Holy Temple, the Ten Commandments were actually read every single morning prior to the recitation of the Shema.[74] An attempt was later made to have the Ten Commandments similarly recited every morning in the rest of Israel as well, but this initiative was quickly overturned.

Why was the proposal of reciting the Ten Commandments every morning rejected? It was because the heretics of the day were using this emphasis on the Ten Commandments to argue that it is only these ten commandments that matter in Judaism, and that the rest of the 613 mitzvot are of much lesser importance.[75] Indeed, throughout history there have been many attempts to make the Ten Commandments a daily recitation, with a number of authorities even calling it "a requirement."[76] None of these efforts ever bore fruit due to the explanation above.

Not only was the initiative rejected, but some authorities even legislated a ruling actually forbidding a daily recital of the Ten Commandments! Nevertheless, numerous authorities encourage

---

72   It is not halachically required to stand during routine Torah readings although some people choose to do so. OC 146:6.
73   *Magen Avraham* 494.
74   Tamid 5:1.
75   Berachot 12a.
76   Yerushalmi Berachot 1:5.

individuals to recite the Ten Commandments privately when possible,[77] in addition to a variety of other meaningful readings that seem to have fallen into disuse.[78]

Based on the issues raised above, one can certainly question the legitimacy of the popular custom that calls for enhanced decorum when reading the Ten Commandments on Shavuot, as well as in the Torah portions of Yitro and Va'etchanan, where it also appears. With the requirement for the congregation to stand and the distinctive manner in which it is read, why is it that we're not concerned that people today will come to mistake the Ten Commandments as being more important than other parts of the Torah? We don't stand when reading about Shabbat or other fundamental mitzvot!

Halachic authorities offer a number of reasons to justify the ancient custom of distinguishing between the reading of the Ten Commandments and most other Torah portions. For starters, standing is appropriate for this special reading because the Jewish people were in fact standing when the Ten Commandments were first given at Mount Sinai. By standing, we are merely reenacting history, not necessarily offering added importance to the reading.[79]

Furthermore, considering that the reading of the Ten Commandments is meant to inspire one to connect with God, it makes the occasion a fitting one to stand. All agree that it is forbidden to sit while the Ten Commandments are read in a synagogue where the custom is to stand. To do so would appear as a sign of rejection or exclusion from the obligations of the Ten Commandments. Some congregations have the custom to stand from the start of the aliya in which the Ten Commandments appear, so as to minimize the attention that rising only immediately prior to the reading would arouse.[80]

Make no mistake, while the Ten Commandments – the only Torah portion to be written by "the finger of God"[81] – legitimately

---

77   OC 1:5; *Mishna Berura* 16; *Aruch Hashulchan* 1:22–29.
78   Such as the Six Remembrances, the Thirteen Principles of Faith, and even Korbanot (the daily sacrifices).
79   Shemot 19:7.
80   See *Igrot Moshe*, OC 4:22.
81   *Igrot Moshe*, OC 32:16.

occupy a prominent place within the Torah, we must not forget that the entire Torah is one complete, as well as Divine, instruction manual for mankind, in which every passage is just as important as any other. Our Torah has 613 mitzvot, every one of which was given at Sinai as well.

FOOD AND MEALTIME

MEALTIME

There's no denying that Judaism revolves around food, particularly elaborate meals. Whether it's Shabbat, yom tov, or a simcha, Judaism often appears to be one long eating marathon. It is fitting to equip ourselves with the various guidelines that apply during meals, especially meals that are major components of our halachic observances.

It is important to know that according to Jewish law, any meal that does not contain bread is not considered a meal at all – merely a snack! Say you were in a kosher Chinese restaurant bursting from a meal complete with soups, eggrolls, chicken and vegetable dishes, stir-fried meat, fortune cookies, etc. – according to halacha you merely ate a snack (albeit a big one), and not a meal. Hence, the formal "bentching," grace after meals, need not be recited. Therefore, bear in mind that whenever a "meal" is called for in Jewish law (i.e., Purim, Pesach, Shabbat), bread must be served. It is also considered essential to drink something during a meal.[82]

When beginning a meal that includes bread, the ritual hand washing must first be performed, followed by the Hamotzi blessing, which is to be recited while holding the bread with both hands.[83] Answering "amen" after someone else's blessing, whether at the start of a meal or at any other time, is a really big mitzva.[84]

Food should never be stored under one's bed due to the demons and other impure spirits that enjoy congregating down there.[85] And finally, if one sees food lying on the ground, it should not simply be ignored, but rather one must pick it up, unless of course one is apprehensive of the consequences of any possible witchcraft.[86]

---

82   OC 170.
83   OC 167:1.
84   Berachot 47a; *Sefer Chassidim* 18.
85   Pesachim 112a; there are authorities who are of the opinion that the prohibition does not apply if under the bed is a finished floor. See *Darkei Teshuva* 116:37; *Kaf Hachaim*, YD 116:42–44. This leniency should not be relied upon and food should never be stored under a bed. *Sefer Chassidim* 458.
86   *Mishna Berura* 171:11.

While sharing Shabbat and holiday meals with others is important, we are, however, advised not to eat our meals in the company of strangers.[87] One should be sure never to stare at others while they're eating, and always to behave with proper table manners.[88] Sharing drinking glasses with others is considered inappropriate behavior,[89] as is drinking from a bottle. It is also forbidden to eat in a bathroom.[90] If you need to sleep during your meal, don't worry, it's understandable.[91]

As can be seen, meals are a major aspect of our way of life with their own set of responsibilities. Our tables are considered Divine altars, and with the proper reverence, truly an opportunity to connect with the Creator.

TABLE MANNERS

Table manners are an essential component of Torah-true Judaism. Indeed, the Talmud is replete with references and instructions on how, when, where, and of course what we are supposed to eat. The Persians are known to have exemplary table manners worth emulating.[92] So essential are proper table manners to being a good Jew that the Yom Kippur confessional includes a beat on the chest for misbehavior in this area. Let's take a closer look.

---

87   OC 170:20.
88   *Kitzur Shulchan Aruch* 42:13; OC 170:4; *Sefer Chassidim* 50.
89   OC 170:16; *Mishna Berura* 37; *Sefer Chassidim* 111. We are to be careful about spreading our germs. There is an interesting parallel in a Talmudic passage: R. Yossi and R. Yehudah were eating porridge out of the same bowl, one with his dirty hands and the other with a utensil. The one eating with the utensil said to the one eating with his hands: "Until when will you keep feeding me your excrement?" The one eating with his hands said to the one eating with bark: "Until when will you keep feeding me your saliva?" The lesson: to be considerate of hygiene and germs, especially as it affects others. Nedarim 49b, cited on the Hirhurim.com website by Rabbi Gil Student.
90   OC 3:2.
91   OC 178:7.
92   Berachot 8b.

Dining times are delineated by the Talmud according to class and personality.[93] Members of each class are advised as to when they should first sit down to eat every day. Look out for your category: If you happen to be a cannibal, then it is recommended that you partake of your meal within the first hour of every morning. If you're a thief, better you should eat during the second hour. If you're rich, it is recommended that you dine in the third hour of the day. If you're just a simple ordinary Jew, you should be eating during the fourth hour. If your occupation is one that requires you to work with your hands, then you should try eating in the fifth hour. Finally, if you are an aspiring Torah scholar, you should eat your meal in the sixth hour of the day. Regardless of when you do decide to eat, it should be at a set time every day.[94] Women should allow their husbands to partake of the bread at a meal first – it'll ensure the wives themselves won't overeat![95]

Meals are supposed to be held with family and other loved ones rather than alone, as King Solomon says: "Better is a meager meal of vegetables with love than a rich luxurious meal without love."[96] Eating in public, however, is considered to be in poor taste.[97] Furthermore, we mustn't eat until we are stuffed, but rather just enough so that we are no longer hungry.[98] Indeed, overeating is a grave sin.[99] One is also obligated to say *divrei Torah* (Torah thoughts) at least once during the course of a meal.[100] Be advised that drinking hot liquids and eating warm bread Saturday nights has secret healing powers.[101] One should only eat when hungry and only drink when thirsty.[102]

---

93   Pesachim 12b.
94   Yoma 75b.
95   Shabbat 140b.
96   Mishlei 15:17.
97   Kiddushin 40b; some authorities even discourage restaurants based on this!
98   Pesachim 114a.
99   Eruvin 83b.
100   Avot 3:4.
101   Shabbat 119b.
102   *Sefer Chassidim* 127.

It is strongly advised to begin your day with nearly breakfast,[103] and eating well protects one from the weather.[104] We should wait some time after eating before beginning any exercise.[105] Our eating should exceed the amount we drink,[106] and never drink out of the same cup as someone else – it could kill you.[107] We should also not drastically change our diet, as it can lead to severe intestinal disorders.[108] It goes without saying that wasting food is a serious sin.[109]

Eating should never be a rushed event – take your sweet time.[110] The Talmud recommends that we not slice bagels or meat upon our hands, as the blood that gushes from such a wound may spoil or otherwise ruin the taste of our food.[111] Additionally, a guest should never serve food to the children of the host, lest there be a lack of food for other guests.[112] Never stare at someone when they're eating.[113] Be advised that it is prohibited to invite people for a meal if it is known in advance they will not be able to attend.[114]

It is a well-known teaching that our tables are compared to the altar of the Temple, so the next time you sit down to a meal, just think of all the mitzvot that you're able to do!

KOSHER BREAD

There is an interesting, lesser-known clause in the laws of kashrut that often goes undetected, or otherwise not properly observed.

103　Pesachim 112a.
104　Ibid.
105　Shabbat 129b.
106　Megilla 12a.
107　OC 170:16; *Mishna Berura* 37; *Sefer Chassidim* 111.
108　Nedarim 37b.
109　Devarim 20:19.
110　Berachot 54b.
111　Berachot 8b.
112　Chullin 94a.
113　*Kitzur Shulchan Aruch* 42:13; OC 170:4.
114　*Kitzur Shulchan Aruch* 63:5.

It is, however, described in great detail within the Talmud and Shulchan Aruch, making it important practical halacha for every Jew, and certainly so for establishments producing kosher food for the public.

A little-known fact: for bread to be considered kosher, regardless of its ingredients, it must be parve. This means that it may not contain any dairy or meat ingredients whatsoever.[115] Under most circumstances, it is simply prohibited to bake a dairy or meaty loaf of bread. This enactment was put in place lest we come to eat dairy bread within the course of a meat meal (or the reverse). This was, in fact, a genuine cause for concern. For example, there was a custom in Europe to bake the challa bread for Shabbat with meat gravy, and to bake a special dairy bread in honor of the Shavuot holiday, and hence, there was always the worry of where any leftover bread could find itself.

If, for whatever reason, you feel compelled to bake a loaf of bread with meat or dairy ingredients, there are some rules that must be followed in order to ensure compliance with the halacha.

First of all, the bread one bakes must be "very small."[116] The reason for this restriction is that we are confident that such a small amount of bread will not remain in the home long enough – likely not even past the meal it was intended for – to possibly come into contact with foods of the opposite type. What is considered as being "very small"? Some of the opinions on this issue include an amount that can be eaten at one sitting,[117] an amount that will be eaten in one day,[118] or an amount that will be eaten within twenty-four hours.[119]

There are other grounds for exemptions as well – namely, if the type of bread (or bread-like food, e.g., muffins) one is baking is simply never eaten together with meat, then one would be permitted to knead such a dough with dairy products.[120] Many kashrut

---

115   Pesachim 36a; YD 97.
116   Rashi, Chullin 38a.
117   YD 97:11.
118   Rema, ibid.
119   *Aruch Hashulchan*, YD 97:4.
120   *Pitchei Teshuva* 97:3.

organizations do indeed certify cakes, donuts, croissants, and English muffins as kosher even if they contain dairy ingredients.

Another option is to make it clear through distinguishing marks that the bread is dairy, such as having cheese protrude from it, an odd shape, or the like.[121] Industrial kashrut practices do not allow for dairy breads to be prepared in their common forms, and then to merely stamp "dairy" on the packaging to alert consumers as to its status. Such an arrangement is not considered halachically acceptable, and has led to documented cases of "accidents" occurring.

Some may suggest that if one is a vegetarian, and thus won't possibly come to eat bread with meat, then one should be permitted to bake dairy breads as normal. Sorry, the answer is no. Rabbinical ordinances are enacted for the entire community, regardless of whether the particular situation will affect every single individual.[122]

The issues discussed here are all associated with the concern of accidentally confusing milk with meat. Eating milk products together with meat products is a severe prohibition based on three biblical admonitions; we would be well advised to take meticulous care in observing this mitzva.

EATING BREAD

B read. Glorious, soft, warm, freshly baked bread. As with all pleasures in life, Judaism insists on certain character-building measures before indulging in even something so simple, and this Atkins nightmare is no exception. Let's review some of the well-known mealtime customs.

For starters, along with the privilege to enjoy bread comes the duty to ritually wash one's hands before partaking, a practice instituted

---

121   *Aruch Hashulchan*, YD 97:7.
122   Cited by Rabbi Howard Jachter at: http://www.koltorah.org/ravj/Dairy%20Bread. htm.

by none other than King Solomon himself.[123] So connected is the washing of the hands to the eating of bread, that no interruption between the washing and the Hamotzi blessing is permitted.[124] If one did speak out or otherwise interrupt between the Hamotzi blessing and having at least tasted some bread, the blessing may have to be repeated in certain instances.[125] One who is meticulous regarding the washing of the hands before eating bread is assured that the Satan will not harm him.[126]

The ritual hand washing is accomplished by pouring a generous[127] amount of water from a vessel, known as an "antil" in rabbinic parlance,[128] upon one's hands either once,[129] twice,[130] or three[131] times, depending on one's custom. Israeli soldiers in combat are exempt from the ritual hand washing before meals.[132] One must ensure that the hands are completely dry before proceeding with the Hamotzi blessing,[133] unless, of course, you had the luxury of using a mikva to wash your hands.[134] If, for whatever reason, you are unable to personally wash your own hands, it is permissible to ask anyone, even an idolator, for assistance.[135]

So regulated is the procedure of eating bread that even after one has recited the Hamotzi blessing, one is not to merely bite into the bread arbitrarily. Our sages ordained that the first bite following the blessing should be at the choicest part of the bread (the middle).[136] When eating in a group, the blessing over bread should be recited first by the oldest or most distinguished person present.[137]

---

123   Shabbat 15a.
124   Berachot 42a.
125   OC 167:6.
126   Yerushalmi Berachot 6:1:1.
127   OC 158:10.
128   *Sefer Chassidim* 58; hence the wording *netilat yadayim*.
129   OC 158:1; *Mishna Berura* 37.
130   *Mishna Berura* 162:21.
131   Minhag Chabad and some other Chassidim; see *Beit Yosef,* YD 69.
132   Eruvin 17a.
133   OC 159:12; *Sefer Chassidim* 58.
134   OC 159:13, *Mishna Berura* 158:46.
135   OC 159:11.
136   Tur, OC 167; Derech Eretz Zuta 6.
137   Derech Eretz Rabba 7:1.

The procedure for "making Hamotzi" over an actual loaf of bread, as is done on Shabbat, is a little trickier, as there are views within halacha that consider even the act of slicing bread to be an unnecessary interruption between the blessing and the eating. Some authorities recommend that the loaf be at least superficially sliced before reciting the blessing. Others say that this is unnecessary, and that cutting the loaf after the blessing is considered the normal course of eating, and is not a prohibited interruption.[138]

We are encouraged to grasp the bread with all ten fingers when we recite the blessing upon it, in order to recall the ten mitzvot associated with the baking of bread.[139] When slicing bread to pass out to fellow diners, one should not cut too small a slice lest one look stingy, nor should one cut too large a piece lest one look like a glutton, but rather a piece that is just right.[140] Bread should be dipped into salt before biting into it, in order to remember that sacrifices on the altar were always accompanied by salt.[141] According to kabbala, the bread should be dipped into salt three times.[142] If your bread is already tasty without salt, or the salt would ruin your bread, you can forgo the dipping ceremonies.[143] Alternatively, you can dip your bread in sugar.[144]

Leftover bread is to be treated respectfully. If, for some reason, bread remaining from a meal will not be put to further use, it should be wrapped in its bag and then respectfully placed in the garbage.[145] Abusing or otherwise treating food in an undignified manner – such as for example hanging your bread on a hook[146] – can lead to poverty.[147] Bread should preferably never be thrown.[148] One should never put bread directly into another's hand – it's considered a sign

---

138   OC 167; *Kitzur Shulchan Aruch* 41:3.
139   OC 167:4; *Kitzur Shulchan Aruch* 41:5.
140   *Kitzur Shulchan Aruch* 41:4.
141   Vayikra 2; Rema, OC 167:5. Some authorities are lenient today as most breads
       contain some salt in the dough.
142   *Shulchan Aruch Harav* 167:8.
143   Tosafot, Berachot 40a; *Mishna Berura* 167:38.
144   *Minchat Chinuch* 119.
145   *Vezot Habracha* p.18.
146   Pesachim 111b.
147   OC 180:4.
148   OC 171:1; *Mishna Berura* 167:88, 171:9.

of mourning and the manner in which one is to serve those who are sitting shiva.[149] Bread should simply be passed or placed in front of the other diners.

The importance and centrality of bread was recognized by the Talmud long ago. In fact, indulging in some bread each morning will serve as an antidote for at least thirteen troubles.[150] So the next time you prepare to bite into some bread, remember, it's not just some wheat and water in your hand – it's a piece of Torah living.

EATING

FISH AND MEAT TOGETHER

Although modern-day medicine and science may beg to differ, the sages of the Talmud were under the impression that eating fish and meat together is extremely dangerous to one's health.[151] In fact, in those days, there was actually a dermatological condition that was believed to be caused by eating fish and meat together. The rabbis therefore prohibited the consumption of such mixtures, a practice which continues to this day.[152] This ban applies to fowl as well.[153]

Clearly, however, today this is not the case.[154] Some try to reconcile this medical contradiction, claiming that what was unhealthy in those days may not be in ours.[155] In fact, in Talmudic

---

149   *Mishna Berura* 167:90.
150   It will protect against the heat and cold, against winds and demons, instill wisdom, affect one to triumph in a lawsuit, enable the study and teaching of Torah, cause one's words to be heard, retain scholarship, serve as an antiperspirant, attach a man to his wife to the exclusion of all other women, kill the worms in one's intestines, expel jealousy, and induce love. Bava Metzia 107b. See also Bava Kama 92b.
151   Pesachim 76b. Note: the Rambam mysteriously omits any mention of a prohibition on eating fish and meat together.
152   YD 116:2.
153   *Pitchei Teshuva*, YD 116:2.
154   See Bereishit Rabba 34:13, 60:10.
155   *Magen Avraham*, OC 173:1, *Aruch Hashulchan*, YD 116:10.

times it was believed that rotten fish was good for you![156] Without delving into the commentary, it is worth noting that Rabbi Avraham Maimonides, son of the renowned Rambam, advises us not to rely on rabbis for medical advice.[157]

It is important to note that this prohibition is unlike the one forbidding mixing milk and meat. Here, it is merely forbidden to eat fish and meat at the exact same time, or in immediate succession. A waiting period, however, is not necessary. This would logically extend to restrict baking dishes with these two types of foods in the oven at the same time, unless both pots are well covered, lest any tastes, via the steam, spread from one to the other. The dishes used for eating them, however, may be interchanged, and hence there is no need for special "fish dishes."[158] With regard to the use of knives for chopping foods, it is considered acceptable, for example, to use a clean meat knife to slice onions that will be cooked with fish. Even if fish and meat were actually cooked together in the same pot, although the food may not be eaten, the pot retains its kosher status.

Some communities are incredibly strict about this practice, and even require the washing of hands[159] between fish and meat courses, as well as the mouth.[160] The washing of the mouth is considered "accomplished" by merely swishing some fine scotch or other beverage around in one's mouth. Indeed, it is required for individuals to somehow "cleanse" the mouth in between fish and meat, even by merely eating some other food in between.[161]

Common custom requires one to use a clean or different piece of silverware when switching from fish to meat at the same meal, due to the residue that may remain on the utensil. Both foods, however, may be on the table at the same time.[162]

---

156 Tosafot, Moed Katan 11a.
157 Cited in the introduction to *Ein Yakov*.
158 As with any parve food. See Taz to YD 95:3 for more on this.
159 OC 173:2.
160 *Kaf Hachaim*, YD 116:3.
161 Note: drinking water with fish is not recommended; Tosafot, Moed Katan 11a.
162 YD 95:3; Taz, *Yabia Omer*, YD 6:9.

All of these rules pose serious concerns to lovers of Worcestershire sauce, a popular steak sauce that includes anchovies in its ingredients. The resolution of this problem is actually quite interesting. You may be aware that in Jewish law, anything less than one-sixtieth of a mixture is considered insignificant and nullified. For example, if a tiny drop of milk fell into a big pot of chicken soup, the chicken soup will remain permitted, as the milk content would be less than one-sixtieth. So too, there are Worcestershire sauces in which the anchovy content is so small that it is considered insignificant and permitted to be used with steaks.[163] Sadly, Lea and Perrins brand Worcestershire sauce contains large anchovy content and may not be used for steaks!

On a related topic, there are also certain Sephardic and Chassidic communities that prohibit eating fish and milk together (e.g., lox and cream cheese).[164] While this custom is really only an added stringency, the mixture of fish and milk, too, was at one time considered dangerous to one's health.[165] This is, of course, no longer the case today and all mixtures of fish and milk are permitted, including frying fish in butter.[166] One last cautionary note to fish connoisseurs: tuna or salmon that come from the Atlantic Ocean will not taste the same as those from the Pacific Ocean.[167]

Again, while there may be measures within Jewish practice that don't seem to have much relevance within today's world of health concerns, let us keep in mind that "a danger to life [no matter how small] is even stricter than Torah prohibitions."[168]

---

163 Although it may be suggested that there remains a prohibition of *ein mevatlin issur l'chatchila* (one may not intentionally cause a forbidden food to become permitted through nullification), some authorities permit one to consume such a food when a) all products being combined are inherently kosher on their own and b) the bittul is being done by a non-Jew. A full discussion of this issue is beyond the scope of this work.

164 *Beit Yosef*, YD 87:3; *Shach*, YD 87:5; *Pitchei Teshuvah*, YD 87:9.

165 *Pitchei Teshuva*, YD 87:9; *Darkei Teshuva* 116:43. See *Darkei Moshe* to *Beit Yosef*, YD 87.

166 *Shach*, YD 87:5; *Taz*, YD 87:3, *Aruch Hashulchan*, YD 87:15.

167 Rashi, Bereishit 1:10.

168 YD 116:5.

BISHUL AKUM

Even though a food product may contain exclusively kosher ingredients prepared with completely kosher utensils, don't automatically assume that such food may be consumed. The status of kosher food is sometimes disqualified by a rabbinical decree in the event that a non-Jew was involved in cooking the food. This lesser-known enactment of the sages is known as *bishul akum* – food cooked by non-Jews. Its remedy is known as *bishul yisrael* – food cooked by a Jew.

There are two primary explanations as to why the prohibition of bishul akum was instituted. One approach is that it is intended to limit our interaction with our non-Jewish friends and neighbors, and, by extension, curb the chances for intermarriage.[169] Indeed, think for a moment – if Jews were meticulous in nothing else but keeping strictly kosher, intermarriage would be drastically reduced, as social interaction – the bulk of which always revolves around food – would be virtually eliminated!

A second reason for the prohibition of bishul akum is suggested from a practical perspective. The parameters of bishul akum are such that it ensures more of a Jewish presence around food preparation and thereby limits the chances of non-kosher food or food preparation practices inadvertently disqualifying the food.[170]

The rules of bishul akum, however, do not completely preclude all non-Jewish participation in the cooking of kosher food, as bishul akum is subject to many exemptions and qualifications, as will be discussed.

For starters, the rules of bishul akum only apply to foods that are "suitable for the table of a king."[171] Considering that corn flakes and potato chips would likely not be served during a state dinner at the White House, there would be no kashrut concern in terms of who prepared these products. It goes without saying, of course, that the raw ingredients themselves must be certified kosher. So too,

---

169   Avoda Zara 35b.
170   Rashi, Avoda Zara 38b.
171   Avoda Zara 38a.

foods that could have otherwise been eaten raw, and the cooking is merely in order to be able to enjoy these foods warm or soft, are also not subject to any bishul akum prohibitions. Therefore it is perfectly in order for a non-Jew to prepare your coffee, since water, the main ingredient, is regularly consumed "raw."[172] With the advent of sushi, some authorities remove all fish from bishul akum restrictions since it is becoming very popular to eat fish raw.[173]

Modern amenities have awakened many creative applications to the bishul akum regulations. For example, the prohibition of bishul akum only applies if the entire cooking process was performed by a non-Jew. If, however, a Jew contributed to the cooking process in even the minutest fashion, the food will not be subject to bishul akum restrictions. Therefore, rabbinical authorities have ruled that if a Jew merely turned on the pilot light of an oven or ignited the stovetop cooking grates, it is considered sufficient participation of a Jew in the cooking process to remove any bishul akum concerns.[174] Some authorities extend this leniency of the pilot light to include even the internal light bulb of an oven![175]

Although more than this basic introduction to bishul akum is not possible here, this should have been enough to convey the importance and wisdom of such a decree intended to prevent intermarriage. If Jews were uncompromising in the rules of kashrut (and therefore avoided parties, lunch meetings, and other social gatherings where non-kosher food is served), intermarriage might just not be at the top of the crises affecting world Jewry.

---

172   *Yechave Da'at* 4:42.
173   See *Shevet Halevi* 9:16 where it is ruled that the popularity of sushi does not remove fish from the restrictions of bishul akum. He rules that the issue depends on both a) one's personal eating habits and b) the custom of society.
174   Rema, YD 133:7.
175   The ruling and practice of Rabbi Moshe Heinemann, Baltimore, MD.

CHALAV YISRAEL

While milk may seem to be a completely innocuous and naturally kosher food product, fit for immediate consumption just like fruit and vegetables, upon closer examination, this may not be the case. You see, way back in the Talmudic era, it was quite common, for a number of reasons, for farmers to mix various types of milk together, including that from non-kosher animals.

Fearing that non-kosher milk would enter the milk supply, and, by extension, into the kosher home, the rabbis forbade the consumption of any milk whose milking was not supervised by a Jew.[176] Milk without such supervision was called *chalav akum* and forbidden, while kosher milk was known as *chalav yisrael*, milk of a Jew, and permitted.

In recent decades, rabbinical authorities have reexamined and reevaluated this ancient rabbinic decree. With this new assessment, many questions have arisen, such as: What if a dairy farm only has kosher animals on its fields, thereby negating the possibility of non-kosher milk being mixed in? Is such a decree required in countries such as Canada and the US, where the dairy industry is government-regulated and supervised to ensure that only cow's milk is the content of products sold as "milk"? With the hefty fines levied on farmers who would violate the "100 percent cow's milk" requirement, it is highly unlikely that any farmer in these countries would risk mixing other milk into the production.

Historically, there were many authorities who would not hear of allowing any exceptions or leniencies for permitting "regular" milk.[177] In recent years, however, there have been several authorities who did allow for some easing of the restrictions. Rabbi Chizkiya Disilo, known as the Pri Chadash, went so far as to allow all milk that came from a farm that simply did not raise any non-kosher milk-producing animals.[178] In more recent years, the most eminent of authorities to deal with the permissibility of consuming

---

176   Avoda Zara 35b.
177   Chatam Sofer, YD 107.
178   *Pri Chadash* 115:6.

unsupervised "regular" milk as found in our supermarkets was the late Rabbi Moshe Feinstein.

Rabbi Feinstein felt that the government regulations and other industrial practices currently in place in the US adequately ensure that no milk other than that from a cow is sold on the market. He argued that modern-day standards are assurance enough for alleviating the concerns of the rabbis of the Talmud. Indeed, such milk is to be deemed completely and unquestionably kosher. He further reasoned that a farmer would be so embarrassed to be exposed as one who was cheating and tampering with milk that this was also grounds to dismiss concerns of any mixing of non-kosher milk. It is worth noting, however, that Rabbi Feinstein did recommend purchasing specially supervised kosher milk when possible, and many people are stringent about this.[179]

It goes without saying that cheese, butter, yogurts, and other dairy products must be produced under kosher supervision at all times for a variety of reasons, including the addition of many additives to food products which require kosher supervision in their own right. It is important to note that in the many countries where government supervision of milk does not exist, it would be absolutely forbidden to consume anything but certified kosher milk, as per the original Talmudic requirement.

In conclusion, we see that the common custom of not being strict regarding "kosher certified" milk is with reliable basis. Where kosher chalav yisrael milk is as easily and as readily available as common milk, there is no doubt that it should be given preference. There is a famous advertising slogan that "milk does a body good"; knowing the issues and history surrounding the consumption of kosher milk will no doubt "do a soul good" as well.

---

179   *Igrot Moshe*, YD 1:46–49.

CHADASH

There is a lesser-known, frequently overlooked mitzva of the Torah that is inherently bound with the laws of kashrut, the focus of which seems to emerge every spring. Along with the many agriculture-related precepts of the Torah such as the sabbatical year, separation of tithes, and others, there exists a mitzva known as *chadash* (literally, "new"), which prohibits us from making use of wheat and other grains that took root after Pesach, until the next year. We are permitted to use only *yashan* (literally, "old") grain for our baking needs.

The Torah instructs us: "And you shall eat neither bread, nor parched corn, nor green ears, until the day that you have brought an [omer] offering to your God. It shall be a rule for all generations."[180] To better explain: wheat that has taken root after Pesach may not be used until after the following Pesach, when the annual *omer* offering is once again brought. This prohibition applies to wheat, barley, rye, oats, and spelt.

Getting down to business, how is this mitzva to be observed today? Although hardly noticeable, in Israel chadash is meticulously observed. In fact, making use of wheat from the current year renders the bread, cake, and other foods made from this grain forbidden to be eaten. Outside of Israel, however, few people pay attention when shopping in the supermarket's baking aisle as to when their flour was grown and ground. Indeed, as will be explained, there are many authorities who rule that this mitzva of using only "old" grain is not binding outside of Israel. Furthermore, although the Torah does say that this mitzva is to be observed "for all generations," the Mishna, albeit with some dissent, seems to assert that the rules of chadash apply only inside the Land of Israel and only to wheat that was itself grown there.[181]

Truth be told, however, most authorities rule that the prohibition on chadash grain applies everywhere, and at all times, regardless of

---

180   Vayikra 23:14.
181   Kiddushin 37a.

where the wheat was grown.[182] Others rule that chadash is indeed prohibited outside of Israel, but it is rather a rabbinical requirement and not a biblically mandated one.[183] Historically, keeping the mitzva of chadash throughout the years of exile, especially in Europe, proved quite difficult, and hence, leniency was the norm.[184]

The most famous argument in favor of leniency comes from sixteenth-century Poland, where Rabbi Joel Sirkes, known as the Bach, notes that almost the entire Diaspora was lenient in their approach to chadash.[185] He further justified the leniency towards chadash by demonstrating that the mitzva does not apply to grain that was grown in a field owned by a non-Jew. The Bach's approach to the issue became virtually mainstream throughout all the years of the Diaspora.[186] In fact, Chassidic folklore claims that God had notified the Ba'al Shem Tov that the mitzva of chadash does not apply outside of Israel, and that all grains and wheat in the Diaspora may be purchased and consumed without regard to when they were grown.[187]

Although one is to be commended and even encouraged to make the effort to observe the mitzva of chadash, it will continue to remain a negligible practice in the Diaspora.[188] What is worth taking the time to appreciate, however, is that with the return of Jewish independence and sovereignty over the Holy Land, the Torah is now that much easier to appreciate and better uphold in its entirety.

---

182   Rambam, *Hilchot Ma'achalot Assurot* 10:2; OC 489:10.
183   *Aruch Hashulchan*, YD 293:5.
184   Taz, YD 293:4.
185   YD 293.
186   See *Mishna Berura* 489:45; *Aruch Hashulchan*, YD 293:18.
187   Cited at: http://www.koltorah.org/ravj/chadash.htm.
188   *Biur Halacha* 489.

SHABBAT AND HOLIDAYS

SHABBAT ZEMANIM

At one time or another, you have likely faced some confusion with regard to the timing of both the commencement and conclusion of Shabbat. Terms such as "early Shabbat" and "Rabbeinu Tam zeman" may have had you wondering what happen to the good ol' sunset and three-stars calculations as to when Shabbat begins and ends. Let's examine some of the issues and their background.

For starters, Shabbat does have a limit as to how early it can be ushered in. It goes without saying that one may not recite kiddush on Friday morning and then begin Shabbat at such a time. Doing so is completely meaningless. The earliest one may commence Shabbat is known as *plag hamincha*, which is one and a quarter halachic hours[189] before sunset. Although there are other opinions that would permit commencing Shabbat even earlier than this time, it is not a normative practice.[190] Many families choose to make early Shabbat when the days are long in the summer and the children would otherwise be sleeping at the proper time Shabbat comes in. Doing so allows for the family to enjoy the Shabbat dinner together. Shabbat is formally commenced with the lighting of the candles,[191] recitation of the Ma'ariv prayers,[192] the recitation of Kiddush, or by personal declaration, whether verbal or even mental.[193]

Although commencing Shabbat early is a great mitzva,[194] this mitzva is fulfilled when even accepting Shabbat a mere few seconds before the actual time.[195] This actual time is, of course, sunset. Even sunset is not completely accurate, as it's only once nightfall

---

189   Known as *sha'ot zemaniot*. A halachic hour is one-twelfth of the total amount of time between sunrise and sunset (or dawn and nightfall according to other calculations); thus the length of a halachic hour varies seasonally, being shorter in the winter and longer in the summer.
190   *Aruch Hashulchan*, OC 263:19.
191   Rema, OC 263:10.
192   *Mishna Berura* 261:28, 31.
193   *Mishna Berura* 261:21.
194   Regarding whether accepting Shabbat early is a biblical or rabbinical mitzva, see *Bi'ur Halacha* 261:2, s.v. "Yesh."
195   *Bi'ur Halacha* 261:22; *Igrot Moshe*, OC 1:96.

has arrived that it is truly Shabbat according to all opinions.[196] That's right – from the perspective of most classical texts, *melacha*, forbidden labor, can be performed right up until dark, although no one does so today. Again, common practice is that Shabbat begins at sunset, namely, when the sphere of the sun recedes below the horizon.[197] Note: if you lack a watch or are otherwise unsure when sunset is, simply observe where the roosters are sitting; if they're resting on residential rooftops then sunset has arrived.[198] According to Rabbeinu Tam, even though the sun has set beneath the horizon it is still considered to be day for all halachic purposes. He claims that there is a second sunset which takes place about fifty-eight minutes later, at which time Shabbat would commence according to him.[199]

Although we are obligated to begin Shabbat at sunset and not wait until nightfall, there are a number of leniencies that are employed between these two time periods, a period known as *bein hashmashot*. These include the permissibility of asking a non-Jew to do a melacha either for mitzva purposes,[200] or in a situation of possible financial loss.[201] A fascinating, lesser-known opinion is that of the Yereim, who says that bein hashmashot, and by extension, all Shabbat restrictions, begins fifteen minutes *before* sunset.[202] It may just be out of consideration for this position that women make every effort to light the candles before this time, namely, at least eighteen minutes before sunset.[203]

The issue of when Shabbat actually concludes and when Havdala is to be recited is a matter of debate as well. The most elementary of measurements as to when Shabbat concludes is the well-known

---

196   OC 261:2.
197   This is the authoritative view of the Gra, cited in OC 261:2; *Mishna Berura* 261:23.
198   Shabbat 35b.
199   Tosafot, Ibid. 35a, s.v. "Trei." Note that according to Rabbeinu Tam Shabbat also ends later than most other authorities rule.
200   OC 261:1.
201   *Mishna Berura* 261:16.
202   *Sefer Yereim* 274.
203   Other opinions include having women light Shabbat candles ten, twenty, and forty (this latter opinion being the custom of Yerushalayim) minutes before sunset. See *Igrot Moshe*, OC 2:6 for more on this.

"appearance of three medium-sized stars."[204] In reality, though, this assessment is of little relevance, as everyone today relies on the pre-calculated times as they appear on our calendars. Based on the appearance of the stars requirement, various opinions have come up with a variety of calculations as to just when this is. Some rule that Shabbat ends at forty minutes after sunset, some require waiting fifty or sixty minutes after sunset, and yet others require that seventy-two minutes elapse.[205]

The above discussion is but a very brief summary of the various opinions as to when Shabbat should commence and conclude. Be sure to seek competent rabbinical advice as to which opinions you should follow.

EREV SHABBAT

While writing numerous pieces on Shabbat observance may very well be a welcome addition to this work, it would likely not be especially trailblazing or revolutionary. What may be unique, however, is not a chapter about Shabbat observance, but rather one on the observance of Erev Shabbat – namely, Friday rituals. There is an entire array of laws and customs we are urged to follow in order to maximize our Fridays and our preparation for Shabbat. We regularly label Jews as *Shomer Shabbat* (Sabbath observant) or not; how about a *Shomer Erev Shabbat* category as well?

A Shomer Erev Shabbat Jew is one who anticipates the arrival of Shabbat every week. This is, in fact, a biblical obligation. One should even refer to Friday in relation to Shabbat. For example, it's better to say "I am going to get a haircut on Erev Shabbat" instead of "I am going to get a haircut on Friday." This is in keeping with the spirit of the custom of reciting the daily song where we refer to each day in relation to Shabbat. For example, Monday's song begins with: "Day two in relation to the Shabbat."

---

204   Rambam, *Hilchot Shabbat* 5:4.
205   Discussed in *Igrot Moshe*, OC 4:62.

The word *erev* actually means to "blend," referring to Friday, which is actually a blend between the holy and the profane, a weekday with a Shabbat flavor.[206] Work should be minimized on Fridays in order to allow for plenty of time to properly prepare for Shabbat.[207] One should also make sure not to overeat on Fridays in order to ensure a hearty appetite for the Shabbat dinner.[208] Indeed, one of the reasons that weddings should not be held on a Friday is lest people not be hungry for the Shabbat meal after having enjoyed the wedding feast.[209]

When buying food for Shabbat, it is most appropriate to verbally state to oneself that the food is for such purpose.[210] Indeed, one should endeavor to do something every day of the week in honor of Shabbat, as did Shammai in the Talmud.[211] In fact, it is one of the few things one is permitted to do even before one has prayed.[212] It is actually considered a great mitzva to taste the food for Shabbat on Friday to ensure that it is tasty.[213]

It is also a big mitzva to shower late in the day Friday, in honor of Shabbat.[214] It is also written that this mitzva of showering can only be fulfilled with warm to hot water – cold showers don't count.[215] Jewish tradition suggests proper procedures when in the shower.[216] The order of what to wash first when showering is as follows: head, face, chest, right arm, left arm, right leg, left leg.[217] This pre-Shabbat wash is known in kabbalistic circles to assist in removing sins from one's soul.[218] Taking a dip in the nearest and cleanest mikva is also recommended.[219] One should arrange for hair and nail cuts on Erev

---

206   *Ta'amei Haminhagim* 250.
207   *Mishna Berura* 251.
208   OC 249:2.
209   *Mishna Berura* 249:9.
210   *Mishna Berura* 250:2.
211   Beitza 16a.
212   *Mishna Berura* 250:1.
213   *Aruch Hashulchan* 250:4.
214   *Mishna Berura* 260:1.
215   OC 260:1; Biur Halacha, s.v. "Bechamin."
216   For pre- and post-shower etiquette, see Derech Eretz 10.
217   *Mishna Berura* 260:1.
218   *Ta'amei Haminhagim* 249.
219   *Kitzur Shulchan Aruch* 72:12.

Shabbat, but when you do cut (or bite) your nails, make sure that none of the clippings remain on the floor, as it is known to cause miscarriages.[220] It's best to burn your nail clippings, but burying them is acceptable as well. It is recommended not to cut one's hair or nails on Rosh Chodesh.[221]

The home should be meticulously cleaned Erev Shabbat in honor of Shabbat.[222] Taking a nap Erev Shabbat is considered proper, in order to allow one to receive Shabbat fully awake and with strength.[223] You should don your nicest finery late Friday afternoon in honor of Shabbat.[224] Indeed, one should wear these clothes until at least after Havdala Saturday night.[225] If you plan on being a guest at someone's house over Shabbat, you must be sure to arrive early enough on Friday to ensure your hosts will be able to properly prepare for your Shabbat needs.[226]

Fridays allow us to infuse mundane and weekday activities with honoring and preparing for the holiest day. It is best to minimize one's work schedule and to use as much of Friday as possible in order to prepare for Shabbat.[227] Some great rabbis were known not to open their mail Fridays lest its contents cause them worry or depression over Shabbat. Others honor Shabbat by ensuring that the Shabbat table is set early in the day; some even set it on Thursday nights. To each his own.

Think about it. There's a way to honor Shabbat every day of the week, especially Fridays. Try becoming a Shomer Erev Shabbat Jew.

---

220 Mo'ed Katan 18a; *Mishna Berura* 260:6. The reason for this is that before the sin of the forbidden fruit, Adam and Eve's garments were made of fingernails. After they sinned God took away this Divinely manufactured clothing. Since it was Eve who was responsible for this loss, our fingernails – which recall these clothes – could potentially cause damage to women.

221 *Rabbi Yehuda Hachassid* 48.

222 OC 262:1; *Sefer Chassidim* 149.

223 *Sefer Or Haner,* cited in Yitzhak Buxbaum, *Jewish Spiritual Practices* (New York: Jason Aronson, 1994).

224 OC 262:2, 3.

225 *Mishna Berura* 262:8.

226 *Mishna Berura* 249:3.

227 *Sefer Chassidim* 121, 122.

KIDDUSH AND HAVDALA

One of the more beloved, family-oriented Shabbat inauguration rituals is certainly the recitation of the Kiddush around the table on a Friday night. Contrary to popular belief, the recitation of Kiddush is actually a biblical obligation upon men and women alike.[228] That being said, however, if one has already inaugurated Shabbat through the recitation of the evening prayers, or even by merely greeting someone with "Shabbat shalom,"[229] Kiddush would then assume the status of a rabbinical obligation. The Shabbat morning Kiddush, by contrast, is an entirely rabbinical creation.[230] Gazing at the Shabbat candles during the Friday night Kiddush, as well as glancing at the wine in the goblet, are recommended practices known to assist in improved eyesight.[231]

Kiddush should be recited promptly upon returning from the synagogue, as it is forbidden to eat or drink anything prior to reciting Kiddush, or at least hearing it from someone else.[232] Nevertheless, halachic authorities who are mystically inclined recommend not reciting Kiddush during the first hour of the night because that's the time when demons are dominant.[233]

As is well known, all breads and bread products must be covered when Kiddush is being recited.[234] Among the reasons for this practice is that the bread represents the manna that fell from heaven and it, too, was covered. Additionally, we cover the bread in order not to "embarrass" it, as bread usually receives the first blessing of a meal, not wine. Some families have the custom to sit during the Kiddush, while others stand. Every person should continue in their family tradition. Should one lack wine, the Friday night Kiddush may be recited over the challa bread.[235]

---

228 Rambam, *Hilchot Shabbat* 29:1.
229 Rabbi Akiva Eiger, OC 271.
230 *Mishna Berura* 271:8, 289:3.
231 *Mishna Berura* 271:48.
232 *Mishna Berura* 271:1.
233 *Shulchan Aruch Harav* 271:3. Some interpret this as the first halachic hour of the night, others suggest not reciting kiddush between 6 and 7 P.M. year round.
234 *Mishna Berura* 271:41.
235 *Mishna Berura* 271:41.

The Kiddush cup should be clean[236] and beautiful, containing at least 4.4 ounces of wine or grape juice. Red wine is preferable, but white wine may be used as well.[237] Although it is preferable to drink the majority of the cup, merely a cheekful is all that need be consumed.[238] The required amount of wine to be drunk may be divided amongst all those present.[239] Although for the Shabbat morning Kiddush a 4.4 ounce wine cup should be used as well, many have the custom of reciting the Kiddush on a "shot glass" full of scotch or other liquor. Since a shot is the standard portion when partaking of such a beverage, it is permitted to recite the Shabbat morning Kiddush on such if so desired.[240]

While we're on the topic of wine and alcoholic beverages, I'd like to share a fascinating explanation[241] for the well-known custom of preceding the blessing on wine on Shabbat with the words *savri, maranan* or *birshut*, depending on one's custom. One of the explanations offered for this practice is that throughout Scripture, wine has been discovered to be both a positive and negative substance. It has been the source of blessings, but also that of curses. For example, the Torah's first encounter with wine is in the story of Noah, just after the flood. Noah becomes exceedingly drunk, and as a result of a series of unfortunate events, he curses his son and grandson. In this instance we see wine associated with misfortune and death. Therefore, the word *savri*, meaning "with your permission," is used to demonstrate to everyone that we are about to drink wine, but only with the purest of intentions. Indeed, it is actually a prayer that no harm should come from the upcoming drinking session. Furthermore, Sefardim customarily answer *l'chaim* (to life) after hearing the *savri*, to acknowledge and contribute to the wish that nothing negative come from the current gathering.

Similarly, it is customary to always precede sipping one's alcoholic beverages with the word *l'chaim* should anyone else be present. This is because wine and other alcoholic concoctions were provided to

---

236   OC 271:10, 183:1.
237   *Mishna Berura* 272:10.
238   OC 271:13.
239   OC 271:69.
240   *Maharsham* 1:175.
241   Cited in the *Derisha*. See also *Ta'amei Haminhagim* 291–294.

•

criminals immediately prior to their execution in order to lesson their suffering. Therefore, we alert those present that the function of this drink is intended as a celebration of life and not as a preparation for death, God forbid.[242]

Returning to our topic, one of the more primary procedures concerning Kiddush is that it must be recited in the place where one intends to eat the Shabbat meal.[243] Therefore, immediately following the Kiddush, one should be sure to start the meal by washing the hands and eating bread or, at the very least, to eat some cake or similar foods in order to attach a snack to the Kiddush. Even drinking an additional amount of wine would suffice for this purpose.[244]

One should put aside the finest delicacies for the Shabbat day meal.[245] Whenever reciting the blessing over bread on Shabbat, it must always be recited over two whole loaves.[246] Don't forget that there is an important requirement to eat at least three meals on Shabbat.[247]

Just as Shabbat is inaugurated with Kiddush, it is escorted out with Havdala.[248] Once Shabbat has ended, it is forbidden to eat before reciting Havdala. Unlike before Kiddush, however, it is permitted to drink water before Havdala if necessary.[249] Included in the Havdala is a blessing over spices, as well as one for fire. The sweet smell of spices on a Saturday night is intended to lift up our spirits as the additional soul that we received at the start of Shabbat now departs from us. The blessing over fire is recited to recall the creation of fire, which took place on a Saturday night.[250] The candle used for Havdala should have more than one wick. The cup, contents, and

---

242   For more on this issue see Shabbat 67b, Eruvin 65a, Sanhedrin 43a, *Shulchan Aruch Harav* 174, *Kaf Hachaim* 174:55, and *Hayom Yom* (Chabad) to 29 Adar.
243   Pesachim 100b; OC 273.
244   *Mishna Berura* 273:22.
245   Pesachim 105a; OC 271:3; *Mishna Berura* 7; *Shulchan Aruch Harav* 271:8.
246   OC 274:1.
247   OC 291:1.
248   OC 296:1.
249   OC 299:1.
250   OC 298:1; *Mishna Berura* 1.

beverage requirements of Havdala are the same as those regarding Kiddush.

Although one is not obligated to eat a meal after Havdala as one is obligated to do after Kiddush, eating a meal Saturday night, known as the *melave malka*, is a great mitzva.[251] Not only is it a mitzva, but food eaten at the Saturday night meal is said to strengthen the "luz" bone. The luz bone is a tiny bone fragment which never decomposes, and from where the reconstruction of the body will take place at the time of resurrection. Finally, be sure to take a shower Saturday nights – it provides supernatural healing powers![252]

THE MELACHA OF GOZEZ
(SHEARING)

While this book is not intended to be a study on the melachot of Shabbat, it would be remiss to entirely omit any discussion at all. Therefore, let's take a look at one of the easier melachot to master – gozez. In case you may have become nervous while studying melachot of Shabbat in the past, just sit back and relax. With its very simple principles, combined with some very practical applications, gozez will be clear to you in no time!

Among the components of the Mishkan (the portable Sanctuary used while wandering the desert) was included an external cloth covering made out of specially dyed wool. As you can imagine, it was certainly necessary to invest in some heavy duty clippers for such a job. Gozez is the melacha that refers to *all forms of cutting, shearing, and detaching a substance from its source of growth.*[253]

---

251   OC 300:1; *Shulchan Aruch Harav* 300:3.
252   Rashi, Shabbat 119b.
253   This discussion is based entirely on the chapter on Gozez from *The 39 Melachos* by Rabbi Dovid Ribiat (Jerusalem: Feldheim, 2001). Accordingly, no individual references for the halachic rulings are cited.

You may not even realize it, but you likely engage in gozez many times a day! Do you often snack on your fingernails? Biting them when nervous, perhaps? What about going for a haircut or tweezing eyebrows? These are all popular forms of gozez. Even cutting a single hair off your head on Shabbat violates the melacha of gozez.

From the biblical perspective, one only violates gozez when removing a substance from its source of growth in *the normal manner in which it is usually performed.* Other *irregular* forms of removing a substance from its source of growth remain prohibited, but are categorized as *issurei d'rabbanan,* rabbinically prohibited activities.

So, for example, having a haircut at your local salon on Shabbat would be a biblically forbidden activity as that is the normal way of having a haircut. On the other hand, should you choose to give yourself a haircut by pulling out each and every hair on your head (a very unconventional method of hair removal), you would have "only" violated gozez on the rabbinical level.

Although this is no longer an issue today, in the Talmudic era, gazing into a mirror was forbidden on Shabbat. This was because mirrors were constructed in such a way as to provide sharp edges intended for cutting off loose or unwanted hairs. It is, of course, perfectly permissible to make use of mirrors on Shabbat in our times.

One of the more practical applications of gozez has to do with brushing one's hair on Shabbat. Since it is likely for hair to be pulled out while using a hairbrush, several regulations were enacted in order to minimize this concern.

Three conditions must be met in order to permit brushing one's hair on Shabbat:
1. The bristles on the brush must be of the soft and very flexible variety
2. The brushing must be performed gently
3. The brush must be designated solely for Shabbat use

Another issue likely to arise at some point or another in the care of children is the permissibility of removing lice on Shabbat. While all-out combing of the lice remains forbidden due to the inevitability of removing some hair while combing, examining hairs one by one and removing the lice by hand remains permitted, although incredibly tedious.

Similarly, removing a band-aid type bandage from a wound is also likely to pull out some hairs from the area it covers. Therefore, it is preferable that these bandages not be removed on Shabbat. In case of need, however, authorities recommend asking a non-Jew to remove the bandage, or to somehow loosen its hold on the body, making its removal much easier. In a case of great need and when all else fails, it may be directly removed in the normal manner.

A woman who is scheduled to visit the mikva on a Friday night may find herself especially occupied with questions of gozez in the event that she forgot to cut her nails or comb her hair before the onset of Shabbat. In such a situation, authorities offer several solutions, as will be explained.

Due to the importance of ensuring a proper immersion, it is permitted to ask a non-Jew to cut one's fingernails prior to immersion in the event that it was not done before Shabbat. If a non-Jew is nowhere to be found, women are advised to perform an especially thorough cleaning of their nails with special emphasis on dirt that may be hiding beneath the nail. Combing the hair poses more complex halachic issues, and is a little trickier. One is advised to seek rabbinical counsel when stuck in such a situation.

As can be seen, gozez is one of those melachot whose rather easy principles will often allow for many confident and self-directed halachic applications. Of course, when in doubt, be sure to contact your local orthodox rabbi.

BRUSHING TEETH

The permissibility of brushing one's teeth on Shabbat is an issue with a number of halachic concerns. While brushing one's teeth on Shabbat in the normal manner as it is done during the week is prohibited by the majority of halachic authorities, there are, however, many interesting issues that arise which are worth exploring.

The most frequently cited objection to brushing one's teeth on Shabbat relates to the use of toothpaste. Unfortunately for Colgate, the act of manipulating or otherwise changing the form of pastes and thick creams into smoother substances poses a concern for the prohibited activities of *mimachek* (smoothing) as well as *molid* (creating); many authorities forbid the use of toothpastes on Shabbat for this reason.[254] Lenient considerations have been forwarded, arguing that nobody ever brushes their teeth with the intention of changing the shape of the toothpaste! One's intention and interest in brushing is simply to arrive at clean teeth, and then to immediately rinse away any toothpaste residue.[255] No benefit is intended or derived from any smoothing or shape changing that the toothpaste may undergo while being swept around one's mouth. Thinner, more watery toothpastes are available in Israel which may be similar to mouthwash and perhaps permitted to be used even with a toothbrush on Shabbat.

The use of a toothbrush on Shabbat at all is in itself an issue of much discussion. Some authorities argue that the use of a toothbrush violates the prohibition on squeezing, as during the course of the brushing, water is continually squeezed out from between the bristles.[256] Other authorities contest this, arguing that since one has no intention of squeezing anything in the course of toothbrushing, this concern can be dismissed.[257] Additionally, it is argued that a toothbrush can be compared to a scrubber on the end

---

254　*Igrot Moshe*, OC 1:112, *Tzitz Eliezer* 7:30:8.
255　*Yabia Omer* 4:27–30; the permissibility of Ashkenazim following this ruling is highly questionable.
256　*Igrot Moshe*, OC 1:112; and others.
257　*Seridei Aish*, OC 30.

of a handle which is permitted to be used on Shabbat for washing dishes.[258] Rabbi Shlomo Zalman Auerbach concurred that the use of a wet toothbrush poses no halachic concerns.[259] A toothbrush one uses while dry would of course pose no concern either.[260]

Another frequently cited opposition to toothbrushing on Shabbat has to do with issues of *hachana* (preparation) for post-Shabbat activities. Some authorities claim that the act of rinsing off and drying a toothbrush after use is, in effect, preparing it for its next use, likely after Shabbat.[261] Nevertheless, everyday effortless activities that are a part of one's normal routine are not considered to be a violation of hachana by many prominent authorities.[262] Similarly, returning food to a refrigerator after use is permissible even if the next time one may use those foods again will be after Shabbat. Washing off a toothbrush in preparation for its next use is surely a routine and effortless act. Indeed, leaving an unwashed toothbrush lying around is very unappealing.[263]

Another issue of considerable halachic concern is that some people experience bleeding from their gums while brushing. Knowingly causing oneself to bleed on Shabbat is forbidden. Those who frequently brush their teeth and are certain their gums won't bleed need not be concerned with this issue. Those who think that bleeding is likely should not use a toothbrush on Shabbat.[264]

Those of Sephardic background may opt to rely on Rabbi Ovadia Yosef, who finds grounds to allow brushing teeth in the normal manner on Shabbat provided one has a toothbrush specifically designated for Shabbat use and that one preferably does not rinse it off after use.[265]

---

258   OC 320:17 cited in Lebowitz (below).
259   Cited in Lebowitz (below).
260   *Igrot Moshe* 1:112.
261   Ibid.
262   I.e., placing food back in the refrigerator notwithstanding that the food's next use will be after Shabbat. *Shemirat Shabbat K'hilchata* 28:81.
263   From Rabbi Herschel Shachter and *Yalkut Yosef* 326, note 27, cited in Lebowitz (below).
264   *Minchat Yitzchak* 3:50.
265   *Yabia Omer* 4:27.

As can be seen from the above discussion, it is very difficult to brush one's teeth on Shabbat in the normal manner and still comply with the majority of halachic authorities. Personal hygiene and everyone's individual standards of such activities make this issue one of the more sensitive issues relating to Shabbat observance. This is particularly true for people who would fall under the category of *istinis* – those who are a little more finicky with issues in hygiene and comfort.[266]

Moreover, people who become newly observant often have difficulties in quickly abandoning all their past habits. This is especially true regarding hygiene of the mouth – an issue society at large is very mindful of. While it may seem ideal from a halachic perspective to rely on mouthwash for oral care on Shabbat, can there be any alternative for the istinis and others who may have difficulty altering their oral hygiene practices on Shabbat?

Although before having prepared this chapter I had never seen any lenient considerations that allow for brushing one's teeth in the normal manner (according to Ashkenazi practice), I recently happened upon an article on the issue by Rabbi Aryeh Lebowitz.[267] The author, a student of Rabbi Herschel Schachter and a graduate of Yeshiva University, argues the view of his rebbe, along with the view of Rabbi Joseph B. Soloveitchik, that routine brushing of one's teeth should be permissible on Shabbat, and it seems, there is no shortcoming whatsoever in those who choose to do so. These authorities find ample grounds to dismiss the halachic concerns that arise with brushing teeth on Shabbat.[268]

Being that this is a sensitive issue and personal choice, those who would choose to follow one of the less widespread opinions should be sure to discuss the issues with their rabbi.

---

266   For application of istinis see Sukka 29a; Berachot 16b; Rashbam, Bava Batra 145b; OC 613:4.
267   Aryeh Lebowitz, "Brushing Teeth on Shabbos." Available at http://www.bknw. org/library/articles/shabbos/Brushing%20Teeth.pdf.
268   Rabbi Lebowitz also brought to my attention a sefer entitled *Mishmeres Chaim* (Siman 9) by the late Rabbi Chaim Regensburg of Chicago, who also ruled that tooth brushing on Shabbat in the normal manner is permissible.

MUKTZA

The issue of what we may and may not handle on Shabbat is certainly one of urgent practicality. Unfortunately, due to a lack of knowledge in this area, many people inadvertently spoil their Shabbat observance by touching things they really shouldn't. The subject of muktza often scares people away due to its many details and regulations. In reality, however, the opposite should be true. By simply acquainting oneself with several fundamental principles, one will quickly gain a competency in this area and then simply "plug in" these principles to one's individual circumstances. Muktza is a rabbinical enactment that was established to ensure that one does not come to inadvertently violate Shabbat,[269] especially the prohibition on carrying,[270] as well to ensure a more enhanced Shabbat environment.[271]

Make no mistake, it is only forbidden to *move* muktza, but when there is a purpose in merely *touching* it, it is permissible.[272] When a muktza object must be moved in order to prevent a loss, or in order to gain access to a permitted object or space, then it may be moved in a backhanded manner, known as *kilachar yad* (i.e., kicking it, using one's elbow, etc.) or by other indirect methods known as *min hatzad* (i.e., moving a shirt that may contain money in its pockets).[273] This latter method of moving muktza is only permissible where shaking the muktza object away from the desired article is not possible or there is no other backhanded manner of removing the muktza from a needed object.

Although there are others, the three primary categories of muktza are:
- *Muktza machmat gufo*
- *Muktza machmat chisaron kis*
- *Kli shemelachto l'issur*

---

269   Rambam, *Hilchot Shabbat* 25:13.
270   Ra'avad on Rambam, *Hilchot Shabbat* 25:13.
271   Rambam 25:15.
272   OC 308:42.
273   *Mishna Berura* 308:13.

Muktza machmat gufo refers to objects that have absolutely no Shabbat-related uses (e.g., a rock, a brick). Any and all routine movement of such objects is completely forbidden, as there are simply no imaginable uses for them on Shabbat. Of course, if prior to Shabbat one had designated a brick to serve as a paperweight or the like, then it would not be muktza.

Muktza machmat chisaron kis refers to objects of high value (e.g., cameras, store inventory). Movement of these objects is restricted (i.e., they may be moved but only in an unusual manner, such as with one's elbow, in a case of need) due to their fragility and the apprehensiveness one has of ruining them.

Kli shemelachto l'issur refers to objects whose standard usages violate the laws of Shabbat (e.g., a pen, flashlight, or electronic toy). Although routine movement of these latter items is generally forbidden, there are some notable exceptions. All items falling under kli shemelachto l'issur may conceivably be moved or even used on Shabbat if they are needed for a permitted purpose or in the event that one needs the place they occupy. For example, should one desire to eat a walnut and no nutcracker is available, one would be permitted to use a hammer, otherwise forbidden to be handled on Shabbat, for this specific purpose. Alternatively, if a hammer or other kli shemelachto l'issur object is occupying the place where one desires to eat, it may be moved. In both examples cited, the hammer may even be moved in its normal manner. There is no need to kick it or move it in some other backhanded method, as is required when moving other forms of muktza.

Another category of muktza worth exploring is that of *bosis*.[274] A bosis is an object upon which a muktza object has been placed (i.e., a table supporting a radio, computer, or the like) and which itself therefore becomes muktza as well. If, however, a muktza item remains on an object because it was forgotten, accidentally placed, or placed by someone else without your explicit instructions, the supporting object does not become muktza.

Other less common areas of muktza include *machmat mitzva* (e.g., a lulav on Shabbat Sukkot), *machmat mi'us* (repulsive items),

---

274   OC 309:4.

and *nolad* (an item that only came into existence this Shabbat, e.g., a newly laid egg). They, too, are treated like any other form of muktza and may not be moved in an ordinary manner. Repulsive items, however, such as a dead rat or leftovers remaining on a dinner plate, may be removed in the most direct and efficient method possible.[275]

Although the material above is but a highly abridged review of an exhaustive subject, committing the basic principles to memory will enhance our Shabbat observance tremendously.

AMIRA L'AKUM

It is likely no exaggeration to suggest that *amira l'akum*, instructing a non-Jew to do work for us on Shabbat, may be the most improperly applied concept in Shabbat observance. This is especially so regarding the mistaken belief that it is permissible for a non-Jew to do melacha for a Jew so long as it is not directly requested.

Although it is biblically permitted, the rabbis forbade making use of Gentiles to do otherwise forbidden chores on Shabbat.[276] The need for such a prohibition was in order to safeguard Shabbat observance. There was concern that if we were able to accomplish all otherwise forbidden activities via a non-Jew, then the entire sanctity of Shabbat would fall apart, likely to lead to outright Shabbat violation.[277] There is also the Talmudic concept of "one's agent is as oneself,"[278] meaning that one may be responsible for violations that a non-Jew commits on one's behalf.

There are two components to the prohibition of making use of non-Jews on Shabbat. Firstly is the *amira*, which refers to directly requesting a forbidden act to be performed, and secondly, the *hana'a*, which refers to *directly* or *substantially* benefiting from such

---

275   OC 308:34.
276   Most of this chapter derives from the Rambam, *Hilchot Shabbat* 6, and OC 276 and 307, with *Mishna Berura*.
277   Rambam, *Hilchot Shabbat* 6:1.
278   Kiddushin 42b.

an act (e.g., having a non-Jew cook up a meal, etc). *Indirect* benefit
is sometimes permissible, such as in the case where a non-Jew
realized that an open light in a bedroom was preventing someone
from falling asleep. This form of benefit is considered to be indirect
for although sleeping with a light on may be difficult, it is still
possible. Merely enhancing a circumstance is deemed indirect,
while creating one (e.g., the example of a newly cooked meal) is a
direct, substantial benefit and would be forbidden. So too, if a room
is dark but still useable, say, to read, and a non-Jew comes along and
turns on a light, making reading easier, it would be permitted to
remain in the room and enjoy the additional, indirect benefit.

Amira l'akum, and benefiting from it, does include some
permitted situations as well. For example, in the event that a non-
Jew, while acting solely for his own benefit, turns on a light in
a completely dark room, a Jew would thereafter be permitted to
use the room as well.[279] Similarly, if a non-Jew sees that his Jewish
neighbor has left his car lights on before Shabbat began, he would
be permitted to turn them off for his Jewish friend.[280]

Hinting to a Gentile that a certain act is needed may be
permissible as well. Again, if an act that does not produce a direct
substantial benefit is needed, such as in the situation where a light is
disturbing one's sleep, one may "hint" to the Gentile that sleeping
with a light on is difficult, thereby indirectly asking for the non-
Jew to rectify the situation. Direct hints are always forbidden. An
interesting topic that is subject to halachic dispute surrounds the
concept of asking one non-Jew to in turn ask a second non-Jew to
perform a forbidden act on one's behalf. This form of amira l'akum
would be permissible according to some authorities, but forbidden
according to most others.[281]

Notwithstanding all the above, there are, in fact, situations where
directly asking a non-Jew to do a melacha would be permitted. This
is true in situations of severe illness (although please note that in the

---

279   Note: the Gentile must not be aware that a Jew desires the light. Additionally,
      the Gentile may even be asked to leave the light on when he is finished.
280   To review: the Gentile was not directly asked and the benefit is indirect (saving
      his friend the trouble of recharging the battery after Shabbat).
281   *Mishna Berura* 307:24.

case of suspected or actual life-threatening illness, a Jew is himself not only allowed but required to perform any actions necessary for the saving of life and limb) or when needed for many people to accomplish a mitzva (e.g., to have a non-Jew turn on a light in the synagogue).[282]

The presentation here is but a highly abridged summary of the laws of amira l'akum and one should consult a competent halachic authority for further information and practical guidance.

ERUVIN (TZURAT HAPETACH)

Throughout the years, I have been privileged to be involved in the planning, construction, and supervision of several community eruvin. The eruv, of course, is the symbolic enclosure declared upon a neighborhood or even an entire city which then allows the residents to carry objects outdoors on Shabbat. Carrying outdoors (i.e., taking something from the private domain of one's home into a public domain, thereby moving it from one type of domain into another) is ordinarily forbidden, but the eruv turns its entire perimeter into one large private domain, thereby permitting most forms of carrying. In this discussion, we will bypass some of the more introductory issues on eruv construction and proceed right to some of the challenges facing the construction of today's city-wide eruv. While it is certainly an exhaustive subject, below are some of the challenges often faced, and the approaches that the authorities take to deal with them.

The most common and usually simplistic form of eruv construction is that of *tzurat hapetach* (symbolic doorframes). The tzurat hapetach method generally utilizes and designates preexisting electrical or telephone poles along with their overhead cables for the eruv boundary. This design of having two horizontal elements (the poles) along with a vertical element overhead (the wire) is meant to

---

282   Amira l'akum for an individual need may be permitted when dealing with a rabbinically forbidden act, not a biblical one.

give the impression of a door frame, and, by extension, the image of an entire neighborhood converted into one large home. The first issue that must be dealt with in eruv construction is the feasibility of enclosing an area with the tzurat hapetach method.[283]

The challenge with the tzurat hapetach method is that this method can only be used to enclose a *karmelit*,[284] and not a true *reshut harabim*.[285] There is much debate as to how an area is classified as either a karmelit or reshut harabim. A literal reading of the definition of a reshut harabim would put any public area of at least sixteen amot (twenty-four to thirty-two feet) wide under this category. That being said, however, the generally accepted practice is that any area that does not have 600,000 people passing through it each day can be considered a karmelit regardless of its size, and therefore an eruv may be created using tzurat hapetach.[286] An area that is deemed a true reshut harabim would require at least a majority of actual walls, not to mention the possible requirement of actual doors, in order to permit carrying on Shabbat.[287]

Those who subscribe to the authorities who do not recognize the presence of 600,000 people as an additional factor in determining an area a public domain would not be permitted to carry in a tzurat hapetach eruv, as almost every city in the world would then be deemed a reshut harabim because their streets are more than sixteen amot (twenty-four feet) wide.[288]

Another challenge regarding the use of tzurat hapetach is the situation where the telephone or electric cables are not positioned directly on the top of the poles, but rather secured to their sides. This phenomenon is known as *tzurat hapetach min hatzad* – the door frame is on the side, which the Talmud clearly rejects as invalid.[289] While there have been authorities in the past who have sanctioned

---

283 Eruvin 11b.
284 A karmelit is an area where according to Torah law carrying is permitted. The rabbis however prohibited carrying in a karmelit lest one come to carry in a true public domain.
285 A public domain. OC 345:7. See Shabbat 6a for discussion on the four domains.
286 Rashi, Eruvin 6a.
287 Ibid.; OC 364:2; *Mishna Berura* and *Biur Halacha* 364.
288 OC 345:7; Rambam, *Hilchot Shabbat* 14:1.
289 Eruvin 5a.

the use of these wires even when they run along the side of utility poles, this practice is far from normative.[290] To satisfy the majority view, it is necessary to place a *lechi*, a post or other attachable marker[291] of at least ten tefachim[292] high upon the poles in those places where the wire or wires are joined to the side of the pole.

Then, of course, even when the municipal wires cooperate and are indeed on top of the pole, there is always the concern for sagging wires. Ideally, the wires of an eruv should be somewhat straight and stiff, not sagging, just as a real doorframe would be constructed. Nevertheless, with the exception of extreme sagging, common custom is to be lenient and not disqualify even moderately sagging wires.[293]

Even where a tzurat hapetach design successfully encloses an entire area as required, there may remain additional problems in the legitimacy of the eruv. For example, if an eruv surrounds an area that includes a *karfeif* (useless land), the eruv may be invalid.[294] Indeed, any area over 100 x 50 cubits that is not intended for human habitation and enjoyment, or is otherwise inaccessible territory, will disqualify an eruv. This includes cemeteries, large fields, lakes, and the like. Of course, negligible amounts of such space can be disregarded. Even where such large spaces exist, eruvin almost always rely on the Chacham Tzvi, who dismisses most of the issues regarding a karfeif, rendering them negligible within the greater context of the benefits of an eruv.[295]

The next time you're out and about your neighborhood, perhaps examine the wires and poles and consider their possible status within the context of eruv construction.

---

290   *Chavalim Bane'emim* 3:14 as relied upon for the original Toronto eruv.
291   Some allow tape, aluminum foil, or even paint; see OC 362:11; *Mishna Berura* 363:26.
292   The precise measurement of ten tefachim is unclear, with varying opinions ranging between thirty and forty inches.
293   *Aruch Hashulchan* 362:37.
294   OC 358:9.
295   *Chacham Tzvi* 59; interestingly the Chacham Tzvi is not too enthusiastic about this leniency.

KORBAN PESACH

With the imminent arrival of Mashiach and the infinite responsibilities and mitzva opportunities that it will bring, it is imperative upon us to prepare ourselves to celebrate Pesach in its original and ideal form – with the eating of the Korban Pesach, the authentic Pesach sacrificial offering. The many fine details of this mitzva make it quite a complicated topic; let's get started with a review of some of its laws right here. Actually, the laws and procedures that make up the preparation of the Korban Pesach comprise no fewer than eleven of the 613 mitzvot.

The Korban Pesach is a mitzva equally binding on both men and women. Non-Jews are actually forbidden to eat of this sacrificial offering,[296] as well as Jewish males who may not be circumcised for whatever reason.[297]These strict requirements may be to emphasize the unique bond between God and the Jewish people, as well as the covenants He made with us. Those who are exempt from Korban Pesach include minors, those who don't own any real estate, and those who are unable to physically consume the offering,[298] among others.

The Korban Pesach offering must be either a goat or a lamb,[299] between eight days and one year old. The recipe regarding the preparation of the animal is an ancient yet simple secret. A wooden spit is thrust into the entire body of the animal, and it is then roasted upon an open fire.[300] It is imperative to ensure that every part of the animal gets roasted and that none of it remains raw.[301] After the preparation of the meat, the Korban Pesach is eaten together by predesignated groups of people after dark. Those who wish to dine on the offering with others may do so, and although groups are not limited in size, it must be assured that the entire animal will be consumed and that all participants in the offering consume at least

---

296   Rambam, *Hilchot Korban Pesach* 9:7.
297   Ibid. 9:8.
298   Ibid. 2:3.
299   Shemot 12:5.
300   Rambam, *Hilchot Korban Pesach* 8:10.
301   Shemot 12:9.

an olive-sized portion of meat. This is an important detail, as the entire offering must be completely consumed – an appetite beyond the scope of a single person. (An interesting aside is that in ancient times, when families got together to eat the Korban Pesach and enjoy the seder together, no mechitza was ever required to separate the men and women.[302] See "The Mechitza" above.)

The actual partaking of the animal is also a very ritualized procedure. Although in general it is deemed proper manners to take one's food from a serving dish and place it onto one's personal plate, with regard to the Korban Pesach, the meat is to be taken directly from the animal and placed directly into one's mouth – no dishes to wash![303] No desserts may be consumed on Pesach night[304] – the meat of the Korban Pesach must be the last food past your lips in order to ensure that its taste lingers with you into the night. The mitzva of eating matza and maror on Pesach night was originally intended to be in conjunction with the Korban Pesach. Indeed, in our day and age when we eat the maror on Pesach, we are no longer fulfilling a biblical mitzva; the consumption of it is only rabbinically mandated today.[305] The eating of matza in our era, however, does remain biblically required.[306]

In the event that for legitimate reasons someone missed the opportunity of offering or eating the Korban Pesach, there is a second chance.[307] Pesach Sheini – the fourteenth day of the month of Iyar – is known as the "Second Pesach," and is the day allotted for those who didn't offer the Korban Pesach in its proper time to do so now. There are many beautiful Chassidic explanations as to the significance of this concept, many of which highlight the idea that it's never too late to accomplish missed goals in life.

The above discussion represents but a sampling of the details on the importance and centrality of the Korban Pesach within Torah

---

302 Pesachim 64a; compare weddings, bar mitzvas today.
303 Rambam, *Hilchot Korban Pesach* 10:11.
304 *Hilchot Chametz u'Matza* 8:9.
305 Rambam, *Hilchot Korban Pesach* 8:2.
306 Shemot 12:18.
307 Rambam, *Hilchot Korban Pesach* 5:1; legitimate reasons include being impure, far away, or some other unforeseen mishap.

observance. The entire holiday of Pesach is actually none other than a national celebration of our freedom, and the ratification of the Jewish people as a nation serving God. May we soon merit to greet the Mashiach and to observe this special holiday in all its details.

SHABBAT EREV PESACH

In certain years the arrival of Pesach can make for some very unusual forms of preparation. If you thought preparing for an ordinary Pesach was a challenge, in years when Erev Pesach falls out on Shabbat, the thrill seeker is in for even more excitement. Owing to the restrictions relating to Shabbat, holiday preparations are quite tricky in such a year. For starters, the well-known custom for firstborn males to fast on the day before Pesach[308] is not possible in such a year, as fasting on Shabbat is forbidden. Therefore, the fast is advanced to the Thursday before Pesach.[309] Not to worry, though, as the custom of exempting oneself from this fast by attending a *siyum* (a meal celebrating the conclusion of a particular segment of learning) following morning services at your local synagogue applies in such a year as well.

That's not all. There's the hide and seek factor as well. You know, the ritual where we "hide" ten pieces of bread around the house and then look for them some ten seconds later. This too, normally performed the night before Pesach, is not possible in such a year, as lighting a candle and gathering the chametz is forbidden on Shabbat. Therefore, the search for chametz is performed the Thursday night before Pesach.[310]

Just as the search for chametz is advanced, so is its burning. Bonfires should be alight early Friday morning for burning the spoils of the previous night's search. Nevertheless, there is a

308   OC 470:1.
309   OC 470:2.
310   OC 444:1.

small difference with the burning procedures in such a year. The annulment of chametz that is normally recited at the time of burning is postponed to Shabbat. This is because although the chametz is burned on Friday, consumption of chametz remains permissible until late in the morning of the day before Pesach begins (in this case Shabbat morning), as it would be every year. Therefore, the declaration is to be recited only after we've enjoyed our last bites of bread, shortly before it becomes forbidden.[311]

Preparing for the seder is also not permitted on Shabbat. Arrangements must be made to ensure that most of the preparations for Saturday night's seder have been completed before Shabbat begins! This includes preparing the ritual items for the seder plate, and likely, the bulk of the festive meal as well. As in every year, it is vital to ensure that the actual seder does not commence before dark.[312]

Wait a second – this is becoming confusing. My kitchen is supposed to be "Pesachdik" before Shabbat begins, all superfluous chametz put away or burned, yet I am permitted to eat chametz until Shabbat morning? What's going on?

Yes, even though all Pesach preparations have been made before the commencement of Shabbat, the actual eating of chametz is indeed permissible – although not too practical – right through to Shabbat morning. In fact, we are required to eat a meal that includes bread every Shabbat evening and morning.[313] Nevertheless, we must be sure to eat our Shabbat meal early in the day, and not allow crumbs to get scattered around the house. Among the popular solutions to this dilemma is to use pita bread for this meal, as it leaves the least amount of crumbs behind. Any crumbs that do remain can then be flushed down a toilet. In this way, the requirement of eating bread is accomplished and at the same time the home is left

---

311 OC 444:5.
312 OC 472:1.
313 Those who are particular to eat bread at the third Shabbat meal would do so by dividing their morning meal in two by eating one or two courses of the meal, reciting the Birkat Hamazon, and then rewashing for the "new" meal, being sure to finish all chametz consumption within the allowed time.

crumb free. All food that one intends to eat from Shabbat morning onwards should be prepared and eaten with Pesach utensils.

Although a little trickier, preparation for Erev Pesach which falls out on Shabbat is certainly within reach. It may even enhance your seder night, since a leisurely Shabbat afternoon allows you to enter into the seder night well rested and refreshed, often a challenge when the seder falls out on a weekday. Keep in mind that we get credit for even the preparations we undertake for a mitzva. In a year when all Pesach preparations must be completed before Shabbat, therefore, your merits will actually "rise" significantly.

THE MITZVOT OF THE SEDER

While the singing of "Dayeinu" and "Chad Gadya" (not to be confused with "Mary had a Little Lamb") are important components of any Pesach seder, they are not, however, among those things considered to be actual mitzvot, binding obligations of the evening. Although we should not abandon even the most seemingly insignificant customs of the seder, it is appropriate however to emphasize rituals that are halachically required.

There are five such mitzvot that every Jew must be sure to discharge at the seder. Two of these are biblical in origin, and three are rabbinical in origin.

The first biblical mitzva is simply to relate the story of the exodus from Egyptian captivity as is recorded in the Haggada. This mitzva is based on the verse "And you shall relate it [the story of the exodus] on that day."[314] Even a person who is alone for the seder would still be obligated to recite the Haggada audibly to his or herself. Although it is ideal of course, to read and sing the entire Haggada, one must be sure at the very least to recite the portion of the Haggada that begins with the words "Rabban Gamliel used to say."

---

314   Shemot 13:9.

The second biblical mitzva is to eat matza at the point in the Haggada known as *motzi matza*, as it says in the Torah: "In the evening you shall eat unleavened bread."[315] The minimum amount of matza that one must eat at this point is 1.33 ounces.[316] There are other points in the seder where one will be prompted to eat more matza, but it is at this time that one discharges the actual mitzva.

The first rabbinical mitzva[317] is the obligation to drink four cups of wine at specially ordained points in the Haggada. These four cups of wine represent the four different expressions used by the Torah to portray our redemption.[318] All wine glasses should ideally hold at least 3.3 ounces. While it is preferable to drink the entire cup, it suffices to merely drink a majority of the cup. Using white wine at the seder is acceptable, but red wine is to be preferred.[319]

Eating bitter herbs at the seder is another rabbinical and slightly enigmatic mitzva in terms of what is acceptable to be used as maror.[320] Many people mistakenly use the commercial white or red horseradish that comes in a jar for this purpose. While eating this form of horseradish is truly a grueling and bitter experience, one actually does not fulfill the mitzva at all with these products because a) they are not 100 percent pure horseradish, often including beets and sugar and b) the ingredients in these jarred horseradishes include preservatives and the like.

The mitzva of bitter herbs may only be fulfilled with raw vegetables, nothing processed or preserved. One should ideally use carefully washed, insect-free romaine lettuce, despite its not being particularly bitter, as the Talmud seems to prefer it from among the other acceptable species of maror.[321] Some rabbis were known to use even the sweetish iceberg lettuce for maror.[322] One may, of course,

---

315 Shemot 12:18.
316 Some authorities require a double portion of matza to be eaten. *Kitzur Shulchan Aruch* 119:5.
317 Pesachim 108b.
318 Shemot 6:6.
319 OC 472:11.
320 Pesachim 39a.
321 *Mishna Berura* 473:34.
322 The practice of Rabbi Aharon Kotler, cited in Rabbi Shimon Eider, *Halachos of Pesach* (Jerusalem: Feldheim, 1998).

use the raw horseradish root as well, for a truly bitter experience. Here too, one must eat a minimum of 1.33 ounces of maror when prompted in the Haggada.

The third rabbinical mitzva we must be sure to fulfill during the seder is the singing of the Hallel.[323] In what is a break in common practice, the Hallel is divided up, with some of it being recited before the meal, and the rest after the meal. These special prayers focus on praise and thanksgiving to God for having taken us out of Egypt.

There you have it. Make sure on Pesach to "remember the five and ensure your seder is alive." A seder that is experienced and fulfilled in its traditional way will truly allow us to feel the Talmudic outlook that "every person is obligated to see himself as having personally left Egypt."[324]

WORKING ON CHOL HAMOED

Perhaps the least understood aspect of the Torah-mandated holidays is their *Chol Hamoed* component. Chol Hamoed, translated as "the secular [days] of the festival," refers to the intermediate days between the first and last day(s) of the holiday. It is interesting to note that although there are three pilgrimage festivals (Pesach, Shavuot, and Sukkot), Shavuot does not possess a Chol Hamoed component of its own.

Contrary to popular belief, work is actually forbidden on Chol Hamoed,[325] although not in all forms, for as we will see below, the regulations regarding work on Chol Hamoed are unlike those of Shabbat and festivals. Although strictly speaking, work is indeed forbidden on Chol Hamoed, there are however five specific circumstances in which it is permitted.[326] These five circumstances are:

---

323   Pesachim 116b.
324   Ibid.
325   Chagiga 18a.
326   OC 530.

- *Davar ha'aved*
- *Tzarchei hamoed*
- *Bishvil poel she'ein lo ma l'echol*
- *Tzarchei rabim*
- *Ma'asei hedyot*

Davar ha'aved refers to work needed in order to avert a financial loss. This clause is often cited as a dispensation that allows individuals to work at their jobs as normal, if they would be fired or otherwise lose much-needed income by missing eight days of work.

Tzarchei hamoed refers to work needed for the sake of the festival. For example, shopping for holiday clothes or cooking for any and all holiday meals would be permitted under this category. It would be forbidden, however, to bake a cake on Chol Hamoed with the intention of saving it for after the holiday.

Bishvil poel she'ein lo ma l'echol refers to work needed for sheer survival. Although somewhat related to our first category, it is a direct dispensation for anyone to work in their normal manner in order to provide for the bare necessities of life rather than having to beg for charity.

Tzarchei rabim refers to essential services needed for the public welfare. This includes all forms of communal work, from garbage collection to the distribution of charity.

Ma'asei hedyot refers to simple, unskilled labors. It is this last category that deceptively portrays Chol Hamoed as being just an ordinary day. Yes, all menial and simple activities are permissible throughout Chol Hamoed. While this category would permit turning on a light, basic writing,[327] and driving a car among many of our other routine activities, it does however exclude such skilled labors as an artist taking his palette, a scribe writing a Torah, an astronaut piloting a rocket ship, and all other activities in which specialized skill or expertise is involved.

As can be seen, while Chol Hamoed does provide a welcome and relaxed flavor to our holiday observance, it is not simply an

---

327 Rema, OC 545:1; *Mishna Berura* 5:18, 35. Some are careful to avoid any writing at all on Chol Hamoed out of fear that writing on its own may be a forbidden melacha regardless of whether it is professional writing or otherwise.

ordinary day. The Mishna[328] teaches us that among those who lose their share in the World to Come are those who treat Chol Hamoed disrespectfully, as any other weekday.[329]

One would be well advised to bear in mind that the days of Chol Hamoed are holy in all respects. It reminds us of a fundamental idea in Judaism, namely, that everything we do, regardless of how mundane it may seem, can be used to create a link that binds the holy and the mundane as one in the service of God.

S E F I R A T   H A ' O M E R

O f all the holidays, the holiday of Shavuot is the only one actually lacking a specific date it is to be observed. That's right – while the Torah gives the exact dates for holidays such as Yom Kippur and Pesach, the date for the holiday of Shavuot is mysteriously absent. This is where the *sefirat ha'omer* (literally, counting of the omer [offering]) comes in. From the second day of Pesach onwards, we are instructed by the Torah to count forty-nine days and then, on the fiftieth day, to observe Shavuot. It's quite neat, actually.

This nearly two-month observance of a nightly count conspicuously occupies very little space within rabbinic literature – barely two pages of Talmud,[330] and a short chapter in the Shulchan Aruch.[331] Nevertheless, there's a wealth of meaning, as well as details, in this simple Shavuot countdown.

Let's explore this a little deeper. The Torah instructs us: "You shall count for yourselves [from Pesach]...seven full weeks...and thereafter you shall bring a new offering [and observe the Shavuot holiday]."[332]

The commentators struggle with this verse, grappling with the following questions: Since no ritual offerings are brought to the

328   Avot 3:11.
329   Rashi, Avot 3:11.
330   Menachot 65, 66.
331   OC 489.
332   Vayikra 23:15.

Temple in today's age, is there still a mitzva to count these forty-nine days? Is it a biblical mitzva or rabbinical one? Do we have to count the days that have passed, the weeks that have passed, or both? And finally, my favorite, how does one who passes through the international dateline conduct himself with regard to Shavuot? Those who straddle the dateline could easily get "behind" or "ahead" a day, thereby concluding the forty-nine day count earlier or later than the rest of the community! This could potentially lead to observing Shavuot all alone!

The answers to these questions are far from unanimous. It seems that only the Rambam is of the opinion that the sefirat ha'omer count is required by biblical law today, despite the fact that we lack a functioning Temple in Jerusalem. Most other rabbinical authorities rule that sefirat ha'omer has the status of a rabbinical mitzva, similar to the reading of the Megilla on Purim and the ritual handwashing before eating bread. There's even a third opinion that tries to reconcile this dispute and suggests that the counting of the days is a biblical mitzva, while the counting of the weeks is a rabbinical one.[333]

Finally, on the question concerning one who crosses the international dateline one or more times during the sefira period, thus de-aligning oneself from the rest of the Jewish world, the various approaches are as follows.[334] According to some opinions, if one goes for example from America to Australia during the omer period, one does not count the day that was "lost," and on balance nonetheless observes Shavuot as everyone else. According to others, the fifty-day count is a personal one and a person is to observe the Shavuot holiday when he himself has counted fifty days from Pesach, in spite of the possibility that it may require one to observe Shavuot all alone.

Overseas travelers will be pleased to learn that the prevalent custom is to observe Shavuot on the day that it is observed in the

---

333 Rabbeinu Yerucham.
334 See Rabbi Tzvi Cohen, *Sefirat Ha'omer* (Heb.), p. 205, for all the various opinions on this issue.

place that one finds himself, regardless of a loss or gain in one's personal count due to dateline-related issues.

LAG BA'OMER

The holiday of Lag ba'Omer is, of course, the thirty-third day of the Pesach-to-Shavuot countdown ("Lag" is *lamed gimmel*, which is a way of indicating the number thirty-three in Hebrew). Although the day itself is not inherently holy, it does signal the cessation of the public mourning practices of the omer (i.e., the ban on weddings and live music), which began on Pesach. The reason for this period of mourning is in remembrance of the twenty-four thousand students of Rabbi Akiva who perished during this period. It is recorded that their deaths were a Divine punishment for the disrespect they continually showed one another.[335] According to most accounts, the plague "miraculously" ceased on Lag ba'Omer.

One of the more interesting practices that has evolved for Lag ba'Omer is known as *Hillula d'Rashbi* – observing and celebrating the yahrtzeit of the great Talmudic sage Rabbi Shimon Bar Yochai, known simply as "Rashbi." Among his many accomplishments, it is widely believed that Rashbi authored the Zohar, the primary work on kabbala.[336]

The customs and observances for this day vary. Many have the custom to visit the tomb of Rabbi Shimon Bar Yochai, located in Meron, Israel, every Lag ba'Omer and to pray there. The tomb, in fact, attracts well over 200,000 Jews every year on this day. This gathering is, in reality, one massive celebration, and is held in style, complete with music, singing, and bonfires. Many also observe

---

335   Yevamot 62b.
336   The authorship of the Zohar is the subject of much controversy. Some scholars attribute the Zohar entirely to Rashbi; others argue that it was Rabbi Moses de Leon who wrote it. Yet others suggest that it was started by Rashbi or contains thoughts and teachings of Rashbi, but was compiled and completed by de Leon.

the custom of giving a boy his first haircut (known as *chalaka* or *upshirin*) at the grave of Rashbi on this day.[337]

It is interesting to note that some authorities have opposed the graveyard party discussed above, on the basis of the prohibition to "invent" new holidays and observances.[338] Other authorities seem to agree with this reservation as well, noting that yahrtzeits should be observed as days of mourning, introspection, and fasting, and not as days of merriment.[339] It goes without saying that the custom of burning clothes and other valuables in bonfires in honor of the yahrtzeit is totally unacceptable, and is likely a biblical violation of *ba'al tashchit* (wastefulness).[340]

While some oppose observing Lag ba'Omer, it does have its defenders as well. Many consider creating a holiday out of Lag ba'Omer appropriate because Rashbi was miraculously saved from the Roman government, who pronounced death upon him for his spreading of Torah.[341] Rashbi (and his son) had fled to a cave in the city of Peki'in and hid there for thirteen years, surviving on the fruit of a carob tree and a spring that miraculously appeared.[342] Hence, Lag ba'Omer can be seen as a celebration of escaping death.

Ultimately, Lag ba'Omer is unique, enigmatic, and in a league of its own. We celebrate it as a result of and in combination with all the aforementioned reasons, namely, the cessation of the death of Rabbi Akiva's students, a yahrtzeit, and in appreciation of Rashbi being saved from the Romans. Lag ba'Omer should be seen as a celebration of life and continuity of the Torah.

We'll conclude with one of Rashbi's most famous teachings. In the Mishna,[343] Rabbi Shimon bar Yochai states that "there are three crowns that can be bestowed upon a person: the crown of Torah, the crown of priesthood, and the crown of kingship. The crown of a good name, however, rises above them all."

---

337   A tradition started by the Ari himself.
338   Chatam Sofer, YD 233.
339   *Sho'el u'Meishiv* #39.
340   See also Bava Kama 91b, Shabbat 140b.
341   Compare the nineteenth of Kislev being celebrated in memory of Rabbi Shneur Zalman.
342   Shabbat 33.
343   Avot 4:17.

THE THREE WEEKS

Every year in the summer, a three-week period of mourning over the destruction of the two Holy Temples is observed. This twenty-one day period is known in rabbinic literature as *bein hametzarim*, translated as "between the troubles," because throughout our history, this three-week period has been one of perpetual tragedy and suffering. We not only mourn the destruction of the Temples, we are actually mourning the destruction of Jewish life in the Holy Land, and the subsequent two thousand-year exile that assaulted us with crusades, pogroms, and holocausts.

There are actually four levels of intensity to these mourning practices during the course of the three weeks. The lowest level of mourning is the first thirteen days of this period, which is inaugurated with a day of fasting (known as the fast of the seventeenth of Tammuz). With the arrival of the sad month of Av, the mourning is increased, and is then further intensified during the week in which the ninth day of Av actually falls. Finally, on Tisha b'Av itself, we have a day of fasting focused on nothing but the destruction of the Holy Temples and the subsequent desolation of the Land of Israel.

A variety of customs have emerged over the course of the two thousand-year exile regarding how to observe these three weeks of mourning. For example, weddings are completely banned due to the celebrations that accompany such joyous events, which would not be appropriate during this period.[344] Not to worry, though: birthday parties are permitted (but music should preferably not be played). Even purchasing new items such as clothes and jewelry that make one happy should better be put off until after this period.

Dancing and the playing of musical instruments have always been forbidden during this period,[345] but a musician whose livelihood depends on playing music is permitted to work until Rosh Chodesh Av.[346] In recent years, most authorities have extended this

---

344   OC 551:1, 9; *Aruch Hashulchan* 551:8; *Kitzur Shulchan Aruch* 122:1.
345   *Mishna Berura* 551:16.
346   *Kitzur Shulchan Aruch* 122:1.

prohibition to include the playing of tapes, CDs, and other recorded music.[347] However, if the kids are getting cranky and grouchy, it is permitted to play some kids' music such as Raffi or Uncle Moishy for them. Singing in the shower poses no halachic problems.[348]

From the perspective of personal grooming and appearance, Ashkenazi Jews customarily refrain from haircuts during this three-week period,[349] while the Sephardic community merely refrains from haircuts during the week in which Tisha b'Av falls.[350] Gel, hairsprays, hair brushing and other hair beautification are permissible.[351]

While there are many more issues on the customs relating to this period of mourning that could be discussed, there is a much more important note to end on. As we are all familiar, one of the reasons attributed to the destruction of the Temple and the subsequent exile was the disunity and even hatred that existed among the Jews of the time. During this period, let us consider the words of the Rambam, who tells us that "it is a mitzva for every Jew to love every other Jew like his own self.... A person must be complimentary towards his fellow Jew and be careful with the property of others, the same way he is careful with his own property."[352] There is no doubt that if these words were put into practice, this exile and mourning period would be long gone.

TISHA B'AV – TORAH STUDY

Tisha b'Av is of course the infamous day of Jewish national tragedy and destruction, particularly over the destruction of Israel and the subsequent exile of our nation. Although it's a very sad and depressing day, it is actually known in Torah literature as a

---

347   *Mishna Berura* 551:16.
348   *Yalkut Yosef* p.561.
349   Rema, OC 551:4.
350   OC 551:3.
351   *Mishna Berura* 551:20.
352   *Hilchot De'ot* 6:3.

"holiday."[353] This oddity expresses our confidence that this annual period of mourning is only temporary, soon to end with the arrival of the messianic era and the rebuilding of the Temple. The ninth of Av is also the birthday of the Mashiach.[354]

The ritual behaviors of the day mirror those of Yom Kippur through the observance of the five afflictions: no eating or drinking, no washing, no cosmetic beautification, no wearing of leather shoes, and no marital relations. Additionally, in order to further highlight and be continually reminded of the theme of the day, we ought to curb our personal luxuries whatever they may be, such as making our sleeping conditions less comfortable, and the like.

Another quite intriguing restriction of the day that is worth exploring further is that of the prohibition on studying Torah. That's right – with the exception of certain sad and depressing subjects, Torah study is completely prohibited on Tisha b'Av. Why such a prohibition? For fear that Torah study will cause one to be happy, because "the Torah of Hashem is perfect; it refreshes the soul, it makes people become wise, it makes one's heart happy."[355] So, on a day meant to focus on mourning, it would be inappropriate to pursue any activities that make us happy.

Perhaps you may be thinking to yourself – sure, maybe great scholars feel happiness and are put into good cheer from studying a difficult piece of Talmud, but as for me, the common "Joe," I don't get it. Let's face it, in all probability, most people don't feel such a tangible happiness when studying Torah.

It's quite simple. Torah study is considered a rediscovery of lost knowledge. We are taught that before a child is born, the fetus is taught the entire Torah in the womb by an angel specially appointed for the task.[356] At birth, the child is slapped above his mouth by this angel, and all the Torah that was studied throughout the previous nine months is then forgotten, to be relearned during the child's lifetime. Torah study, then, is none other then reclaiming a lost "object." Surely one is overjoyed when finding long-lost objects!

353 Eicha 1:15.
354 Yerushalmi Berachot 2:4; Eicha Rabba 1:51.
355 Tehillim 19.
356 Nidda 30b.

Another angle can be suggested as well. Knowledge, especially practical knowledge, arouses intellectual enjoyment. Even something minor like discovering a new way of maximizing one's time brings a person some measure of joy. How much more so should the same apply when people rediscover and better appreciate their own heritage! Yes, Torah study qualifies as excitement.

Although the halacha is quite clear that Torah study is prohibited, those who simply will not be able to endure twenty-four hours without opening a Jewish book would enjoy the following story told over in the name of Rabbi Shmuel Shtrashun of Vilna, known as the Rashash. The Rashash was once "caught" studying Torah on Tisha b'Av by some of his students. Sure enough, the students quickly rebuked the rebbe for studying Torah on the day of mourning, thereby violating the halacha, as well as what he had taught them. The rebbe, not to be outdone, quipped back: "Yes my students, you are correct, Torah study is forbidden on this day and I have violated the law. But let me ask you, how could God possibly punish us for studying His Torah?"

May we, too, feel such a love and attachment to Torah study, and may the mourning of Tisha b'Av soon turn to joy. Let us remember that "whoever mourns over Jerusalem will merit to share in the joy of her rebuilding."[357]

ELUL CUSTOMS

Although commanding a distinctive status, the Hebrew month of Elul has effectively no intrinsic holiness of its own. True, the creation of the world began on the twenty-fifth of Elul, but let's face it – most people don't even realize it, let alone acknowledge it in any formal way.[358] It's a month whose entire essence is one of daily preparation for the month that follows, along with all the holidays that the month of Tishrei brings with it. It is also worth

---

357   Ta'anit 30b.
358   Tosafot, Rosh Hashana 8b.

noting that the eighteenth of Elul is the birthday of the two great Chassidic luminaries the Ba'al Shem Tov and Rabbi Shneur Zalman, author of the Tanya.

Among the more prominent customs in the month of Elul is the daily shofar blowing following the morning service,[359] as well as the twice-daily recitation of the psalm "Hashem is my light."[360] This psalm is recited in the morning, and then again in the afternoon or night, depending on one's custom. The objective of all Elul customs, of course, is to arouse us in repentance and preparation for the upcoming days of awe.

It is also a common custom and certainly proper etiquette when writing a letter during the month of Elul to add wishes for a happy new year.[361] Considering that the month is intended to allow us to focus on serving Hashem properly, it is considered particularly meritorious to have one's tefillin and mezuzot examined during this month, as well.[362]

Perhaps the most time-honored of all Elul practices is the recitation of the selichot, the prayers of repentance and forgiveness. Ashkenazi custom is to recite the selichot prayers beginning four to ten days prior to Rosh Hashana (depending on the year), ideally early in the morning.[363] The first recitation of the selichot prayers always begins on a Saturday night, at midnight. Sephardic custom is actually to recite the selichot prayers for the entire month prior to Rosh Hashana.[364]

With the arrival of Erev Rosh Hashana morning, we recite the traditional "annulment of vows" in order to free ourselves of any possible unfulfilled commitments to God which we may have forgotten. Men should have their wives in mind during the

---

359   Rema, OC 581:1.
360   Tehillim 27.
361   *Be'er Heitev* 581:10.
362   *Kitzur Shulchan Aruch* 128:3. A mezuzah must be checked at least twice every seven years, YD 291:1. Tefillin that were purchased from a reliable individual and used regularly need never be checked, although it is a good idea to do so, OC 39:10.
363   Rambam, *Hilchot Teshuva* 3:4.
364   OC 581:1.

annulment of vows ceremony in order that it include them as well.[365]

A visit to the cemetery prior to Rosh Hashana is another revered and hallowed custom that many adhere to.[366] It is believed that prayers for a new year recited at the graves of holy people have much influence before God, as the merits of the departed are seen as serving as an advocate for the petitioner.[367] We must remember that we are not to address the dead in our prayers, but rather to beseech God to bestow upon us a sweet new year in the merits of those who are buried before us.[368] Some have the custom not to eat, but only to drink, prior to visiting a cemetery.[369] A special blessing is to be recited upon entering a cemetery if thirty days have passed since one last saw a grave.[370] When leaving a cemetery the hands must be ritually washed three times.[371] Be sure to take into account that it is strongly discouraged, even dangerous, to visit the same grave twice in one day.[372]

Finally, Erev Rosh Hashana itself should be used in preparation for what can be compared to a courtroom hearing – one in which we are confident that we will leave having received only the most favorable verdicts. Under the circumstances, personal grooming is in order, such as cutting one's hair and nails,[373] as well as preparing one's finest clothes for the holiday.[374] Some also immerse in a mikva in preparation for the holy day.[375]

There are various customs of how we are to greet each other over Rosh Hashana. Some wish their fellow Jew a *ketiva v'chatima tova* (a favorable inscription and sealing),[376] others add additional

---

365 YD 234:56.
366 *Kitzur Shulchan Aruch* 128:13.
367 Ibid.
368 Ibid.
369 *Sefer Haminhagim* (Chabad).
370 OC 224:12.
371 OC 4:18.
372 *Rabbi Yehuda Hachassid* 12.
373 OC 581:4.
374 *Shaarei Teshuva*, OC 581:4.
375 Rema, *Rabbi Yehuda Hachassid* 12.
376 OC 582:6.

blessings, while many suffice with *shana tova* (happy new year). So may it be.

O M E N S   A N D   S Y M B O L I S M

Rosh Hashana is unique in that it is a holiday especially abundant in traditions and customs. Yet, upon deeper examination, one will find that from the Torah's perspective, only one activity is actually required of us on Rosh Hashana, and that is the blowing of the shofar. Hence, it seems that the ceremonies, nuances, and emphases of the day are much more heavily drawn from the realm of symbolism rather than obligation.

Whether it's an apple in honey[377] for a sweet year, "throwing" away our sins through Tashlich, or the placing of a fish head on the table so that we may become "like the head and not like the tail," we express our aspirations to God with these indirect hints. According to most authorities, one should be sure to eat a piece of the fruit (e.g., the apple dipped in honey) before reciting the *yehi ratzon* (may it be [His] will) prayer, as it may constitute a forbidden interruption between the blessing and the eating.[378] Others actually encourage us to recite the yehi ratzon prior to eating, considering it an essential component of the preliminary blessing as well as the ultimate reason for eating it at all.[379]

What is it about symbolism, particularly the eating of symbolic foods, that has found such a prominent place on the most hallowed of days? The Talmud[380] teaches that "omens are significant [and have influence]...on the entire year," and hence eating sweet things such as the apple dipped in honey holds much promise in our efforts to sweeten God's verdict for us in the coming year. It was specifically the apple that evolved as the primary symbolic food of

---

377   Have you ever wondered why honey, a by-product of a non-kosher insect, is kosher? See *Tzitz Eliezer* 11:54, *Igrot Moshe*, OC 1:63
378   OC 583; *Magen Avraham, Mishna Berura* 3.
379   *Sefer Haminhagim Chabad.*
380   Keritot 9a.

Rosh Hashana because an apple orchard represents "a field blessed by God"[381] and is also symbolic of paradise.[382] Furthermore, the apple symbolizes the mutual love that exists between God and the Jewish people, as it is written: "Beneath the apple tree I aroused your love." [383]

While the emphasis on symbolic foods reigns supreme, there is a minority opinion that actually suggests that we should not be eating symbolic foods on Rosh Hashana in an effort to influence God.[384] Indeed, some claim this practice borders on witchcraft – something clearly forbidden by the Torah.[385] It is suggested that in order to pacify these authorities, we should keep in mind while eating the symbolic foods that it is God who is in control of all that befalls us, not our diet. Besides the symbolic foods, one would be well advised to focus on the theme of the day: "prayer, charity, and repentance ward off evil decrees."

Nevertheless, eating symbolic foods is a well-accepted and mainstream Jewish practice, even legislated in the Shulchan Aruch,[386] which ought to be meticulously observed by all. In fact, the idea of eating symbolic foods extends even to eating foods whose name resembles any form of good fortune in any language.[387] As the joke goes, perhaps we should consider eating a raisin and celery on Rosh Hashana in the hope that God blesses us with a "raise in salary" (get it?).

Not only do we eat traditional foods in order to arouse Divine fortune for a good year, but there are also foods we should avoid for the same reason. For example, many people prefer not to eat nuts on Rosh Hashana, as the numerical value of the Hebrew word for "nut" (*egoz*) is the same as that of "sin."[388]

For those of you who are not concerned with violating the prohibition on witchcraft as mentioned above, here are some

---

381   Tur and others, Bereishit 27:27.
382   Zohar, Bereishit 27:27; compare *Chakal Tapuchin Kadishin*.
383   Shir Hashirim 8:5.
384   Maharsha, cited at http://www.chaburas.org/simanim.html.
385   Vayikra 19:26.
386   OC 583.
387   Magen Avraham 583.
388   Rema, OC 583:2.

additional Talmudically prescribed ways for you to discover how your upcoming year will turn out:[389] If you want to know if you will live out the year, simply hang an oil lamp in your house; if all the oil burns within ten days, that's evidence that you'll survive. It's easy to identify whether your business interests will succeed. Simply raise a chicken in your home; if it grows fat, then it's safe to invest. Last but not least, if you want to go on a trip and are wary of security issues, simply stand in a dark house; if you are able to see the shadow of a shadow, then rest assured that you will return safely.

Allow me to conclude by sharing one inspirational thought:[390] Regardless of everything else in your life, whether successes or frustrations, keep in mind that if you're reading this book and you have a spouse, a child, or a home, then God has truly showered you with blessings and you are better off than 65 per cent of the people on this planet. It's truly those "little things" that count.

JUDGMENT DAY

Why on Rosh Hashana? Why is it *davka* (specifically) that the first day of the Hebrew month of Tishrei is the day that God has chosen to judge mankind? What is the inherent significance that this day holds?

The primary reason is that the first day of Tishrei was actually the day on which Adam and Eve were created.[391] Not only was it the day on which they were created,[392] but it was also the day they sinned in the infamous episode in the Garden of Eden, by eating that mysterious forbidden fruit.[393] God decided that since it was a day on which He had judged the entire world (then consisting of only two people who were judged on their disregard for God's

---

389   Horayot 12a.
390   Cited in *Tur*, YD 179.
391   Rosh Hashana 10b.
392   They were born as full-grown adults, Chullin 60a and Midrashim.
393   Sanhedrin 70b; the fruit was likely wheat, figs, grapes, or an etrog.

commandment), He would continue to judge all mankind in perpetuity on that very same day.

Taking this idea one step further, it is important to emphasize that it is not merely the Jewish people whom God judges on Rosh Hashana for the upcoming year. All of humanity is evaluated on this day as well – every single person.[394] Indeed, this idea of a worldwide judgment is actually very appropriate, seeing that Adam and Eve are the parents of all humanity. Rosh Hashana is therefore a day with unique relevance and meaning for the entire world. God examines the actions of both Jews and non-Jews, and makes His judgment for each and every human being.

Another reason that Rosh Hashana is significant is due to its role as the beginning of the Jewish year. Our calendar is based on a lunar system (although also modified within a solar framework), the first ever to be put to use, established by God Himself.[395] Many calendars have come and gone, but the lunar one remains the most organic.[396] Rosh Hashana offers us the opportunity to take a step back and meditate on that first day of creation and the beginning of time.

Yes, Rosh Hashana is the beginning of the year for all humanity, and as we have seen, it is certainly appropriate to wish your non-Jewish friends and associates a happy new year.

We certainly pray for the day that all peoples of the world will be enlightened to the truth of the One Infinite God, as we say in the thrice-daily Aleinu prayer: "On that day, God will be One and his name [recognized as] One." May He bless us, as well as the righteous among the nations, for a sweet, healthy, and prosperous year.

---

394 Rosh Hashana 16a.
395 Shemot 12:2.
396 Muslims also use a lunar calendar, but theirs is uncorrected against the solar calendar and therefore falls out of step with the seasons, whereas the Jewish calendar is fully in tune with both lunar and solar reality, as it aligns the months with the lunar cycle and the years with the solar cycle. See the chapter on Adar I and Adar II for more details.

K A P P A R O T

While kapparot may appear to the onlooker as some sort of bizarre tribal incantation, its origins are quite interesting. As the practice is not mentioned anywhere in the Talmud or early codes, there have actually been authorities throughout the ages who have tried to ban the practice[397] – but to no avail.

Indeed, Ashkenazi practice is to view kapparot as a *minhag vatikin* – a venerated practice that one must not neglect. Indeed, we are even taught to use a separate chicken for each and every family member.[398] It is clear that Rashi himself used to perform kapparot, although not with a chicken – he used flowers.[399]

Some have explained the practice of kapparot as being modeled after the idea of offering a Temple sacrifice.[400] The Rambam explains this idea, suggesting that in the event we are worthy of death due to our many sins, God in His mercy allows us the luxury to substitute an animal for slaughter rather than ourselves. Indeed, while performing the ritual, we should contemplate the fragility of life and our gratitude at having our own extended. The chicken should then be donated to the poor for holiday consumption.[401]

Originally, kapparot was performed anytime from before Rosh Hashana right through until the end of Sukkot. However, over the centuries the custom has evolved to reserve this ritual for Erev Yom Kippur.[402]

The question must be asked: Why do we use a chicken? Why not a larger animal more symbolic of sacrifices and of ourselves? Indeed, some suggest using a ram for kapparot in memory of the near sacrifice of Yitzchak on the altar and to recall the ram that was substituted in his place. Since, however, many people were poor and could not afford such an expensive animal, they made do with a chicken. It should also be noted that the Talmudic term for a

---

397   *Teshuvot Harashba* 395.
398   Rema, OC 605:1.
399   Shabbat 81b.
400   *Mishna Berura* 605:2.
401   *Chayei Adam* 144:4.
402   See OC 605.

chicken is *gever*, which can also translate as a "man," affirming a chicken as entirely fitting for the ritual.[403]

What about pregnant women? Should they use one, two, or even three chickens? Some authorities suggest that a pregnant woman use three chickens – one for herself, a chicken in case the child is a female and a rooster in case it is a male.[404] Another approach found in the codes of law is for a pregnant woman to use two birds – one chicken and one rooster.[405] This way, if the fetus is a female, then the mother and daughter are included together in the chicken. If the fetus is a male, then the rooster will have been of use.

In addition to the chicken option for kapparot, money is another attractive, cleaner, and less expensive option for performing kapparot. Swinging money around one's head while reciting the kapparot formula and then donating the money to charity is a legitimate alternative to kapparot with a chicken. Fish is sometimes used for kapparot as well, often seen as a compromise between chicken and money.

In ancient times, there was considerable opposition towards kapparot for a number of reasons. For starters, the procedure somewhat resembles ancient practices of witchcraft and black magic, which we are required to distance ourselves from.[406] Another reason for the opposition to kapparot was due to the tremendous pressure it places on the *shochtim* (ritual slaughterers). It was argued that it was simply not possible for the shochtim to properly slaughter the vast numbers of chickens and still make it home with enough time to personally prepare for Yom Kippur. Such tremendous pressure could easily lead to improperly slaughtered chickens.[407] In deference to this credible concern, one should consider performing kapparot some time before Yom Kippur if intending to use a live chicken.

While kapparot is a topic that allows for even more depth and study, let us conclude and take with us its primary purpose – namely, to bring a person's heart closer to God during this holy

---

403   Rosh, Yoma 8:23; *Tur* 605.
404   Mordechai, cited at http://www.chaburas.org/kapparot.html.
405   *Kitzur Shulchan Aruch* 131:1.
406   OC 605:1.
407   *Aruch Hashulchan* 605:5.

period. Remember, it's not kapparot that will purge us of our sins, it's our change of behavior – specifically repentance, prayer, and charity – that will.

KOL NIDREI

With the recitation of Kol Nidrei, Yom Kippur is officially inaugurated. All Torah scrolls are removed from the ark and then paraded around the synagogue for all to kiss. The Torahs are then held by prominent members of the congregation for the duration of Kol Nidrei.

Perhaps the most anticipated selection from all the Yom Kippur prayers is that of Kol Nidrei. Preparations for Kol Nidrei are somehow able to arouse an inexplicable sense of reverence and religious responsibility. While many are not otherwise punctual when attending synagogue services, it seems that no one would chance missing the chanting of Kol Nidrei. One will note that it is the only nighttime prayer service of the year where a tallit is worn by adult male worshippers.

The most puzzling part of this, however, is that Kol Nidrei has nothing to do with Yom Kippur, or even with prayer and repentance, for that matter. Kol Nidrei is simply a Talmudic formula for the annulment of vows. Believe it or not, although Kol Nidrei is ancient, there have been numerous attempts to delete it from the Yom Kippur liturgy.[408] It is argued that justification for keeping Kol Nidrei part of the service is to be found in the idea that one should not enter Yom Kippur with religious vows that one may have unwittingly made and left unfulfilled, as it would be unbecoming to approach God in such a state. Additionally, non-fulfillment of vows is considered to be a serious violation of the Torah. With all this emphasis on annulling vows, Kol Nidrei also teaches us the power of speech.

---

408   Tur, OC 619.

Make no mistake, Kol Nidrei does not absolve us from our vows as they relate to personal commitments to our fellow man. Throughout history, Jews were portrayed by their anti-Semitic neighbors as an unreliable and deceiving people owing to the Kol Nidrei prayer as a formula that ostensibly absolved Jews from keeping their word, which is simply not true. Kol Nidrei relates only to religious vows one has made between oneself and God. We are still obligated to fulfill commitments made within the human sphere, and to make proper restitution wherever those commitments cannot, for some legitimate reason, be fulfilled.

Interestingly, Kol Nidrei remains one of the few prayers recited in Aramaic. The reason is likely because Aramaic was the vernacular language in the ancient Jewish communities of Babylonia where the prayer was probably composed. Some scholars argue, however, that the prayer finds its source in Spain and Portugal and that the words "we permit prayer with sinners" may be referring to the Marranos and Conversos (who converted under extreme duress to Catholicism). Yet other scholars have no idea at all where Kol Nidrei came from.

Regardless of the mysterious origins of this haunting prayer, combined with the many unsuccessful attempts to do away with it, we see that somehow Kol Nidrei has embedded itself in the soul of the Jewish people, as can be seen in the following story.

When Reb Leizer of Czenstochow walked out of the gates of Buchenwald, he set out to find his youngest son, whom he had deposited with Gentiles for safekeeping. His first stop, of course, was to scour the monasteries, but that turned up nothing.

Reb Leizer then decided to wander from village to village with an organ, and to play his organ in the marketplaces. As more and more children gathered to observe him, he would play Kol Nidrei. He would then observe their faces for any reaction. If he saw recognition of the tune on the faces of the children, he would remind them they were Jews and have them search out their parents and their faith.

According to the story, Reb Leizer never did find his son, but he helped dozens of Jewish children regain their connection with the Jewish people.

SUKKA CONSTRUCTION

The month of Tishrei is simply a mitzva marathon with no time for sinning! Immediately upon the departure of Yom Kippur, we are encouraged to prepare for the next upcoming mitzva, building the sukka, in order to go from one mitzva to another.[409] Although building a sukka is certainly a mitzva, a blessing is not recited before commencing, nor upon completing the construction of the sukka. This is because the mitzva is only considered truly completed when one uses his sukka on the holiday.[410] Women are not obligated to make use of a sukka, but if they choose to, their reward is great.[411]

As the sukka must be directly under the sky without any interposition whatsoever, one must be sure that the sukka is not covered by a tree, a portion of the house or any other separation between the *schach* (sukka roof) and the sky.[412] It is very important to do a preliminary examination of a sukka prior to using it – be sure to look up! For example, if the neighbor's clothes line is directly above your sukka, make sure that there are no clothes hanging above you, which would invalidate your sukka while they hang.[413] Canadians should be sure that there is no snow buildup on top of their sukka, as it too may constitute an invalid separation between the sukka and the sky.[414]

Just as all buildings are subject to legal codes as to their minimum and maximum dimensions, so too regarding a sukka. A sukka over

---

409   Rema, OC 625:1.
410   OC 641:1.
411   OC 640:1.
412   OC 626:1.
413   *Nitei Gavriel* 2:21.
414   *Aruch Hashulchan* 629:2.

thirty feet tall is invalid,[415] as is a sukka shorter than twenty-two inches.[416] There are no maximum width restrictions. The quality and construction of the walls of a sukka are also an important issue. For sukka walls to be valid they must be able to withstand a wind that is common during the season.[417] Although a house with fewer than four sides might appear somewhat odd, a sukka consisting of but two sides plus a slight protrusion representing a third wall remains kosher.[418] Oddly enough, we are instructed to be sure to put up the walls before putting on the roof of the sukka.[419] Sukka construction should not be completed more than thirty days prior to the holiday.[420]

You also wouldn't want to be the subject of accusations of theft or robbery while trying to fulfill the mitzva of sukka. It is forbidden to build a sukka in an area that does not belong to you, or in an area that would otherwise disturb the public.[421] Additionally, don't just mosey on into a neighbor's backyard in order to use their sukka; you should ask permission first! It goes without saying that it is completely forbidden to cut public property such as trees or the like for use as schach for the sukka.[422] Sorry, but in Judaism, the ends don't justify the means.

If you plan on riding animals over the sukkot holiday, be advised that it is permissible to build a sukka on the back of a camel or donkey. One even fulfills the mitzva of sukka while the animal is in motion.[423]

In order for the schach to be a valid covering upon the sukka, it must be from a material that once grew from the earth, and that has not been used as a utensil of any type.[424] It must also be

---

415   OC 633:8.
416   This being the minimum size that can fit most of a person's body. OC 634:1; see *Mishna Berura* 1.
417   OC 630:10.
418   Sukka 6b.
419   OC 635:1.
420   OC 636:1.
421   OC 637:3.
422   OC 637:3.
423   Rambam, Sukka 4:6.
424   OC 629:1.

currently detached from its source of growth.[425] Therefore, branches and leaves still attached to a tree are disqualified from serving as schach. It is certainly prohibited to use plastics and metals for the schach.

The schach should not be too thick – just enough to be deemed a covering while still allowing one to see the stars.[426] Although those who prefer a thicker schach are entitled to lay the covering material more thickly, nevertheless, if the schach is so thick that rain would not penetrate the sukka, then the sukka is invalid.[427] Another qualification for schach to be kosher is that it must provide for more shade in the sukka than sun.[428]

When we sit in the sukka, we should be sure to recall the two themes that the sukka represents: the Clouds of Glory that protected the Jewish people in the desert, and the actual huts the Jews built for living in for forty years.[429] The lesson we are to take from the mitzva of sukka is clear. We should remember at all times that God is always surrounding us and protecting us, and that everything in this world is only temporary; we would be well advised to focus on what's important.

TRAVELING DURING SUKKOT

The intermediate days of Sukkot, known as *Chol Hamoed* (the secular of the festival), are a much anticipated opportunity for enjoying outings and trips with the family. This is especially true in Israel, where Sukkot is a time when to a large extent the country comes to a standstill, as much of the workforce enjoys the seven-day Sukkot period as vacation time.

Traveling during Sukkot will inevitably pose some challenges in our efforts to properly observe the Torah's requirement to "dwell in

---

425 OC 629:13.
426 OC 631:3.
427 *Mishna Berura* 631:6.
428 OC 631:4.
429 Sukka 11b.

sukkot"[430] during the holiday. Some logistics that must be arranged prior to a trip[431] on Sukkot include the feasibility of ensuring that one will be able to eat one's meals in a sukka. Although it is possible to find some support for the practice of not sleeping in a sukka,[432] it remains undisputed, however, that it is forbidden for men to eat a meal outside of a sukka at any time throughout the holiday.[433]

If one needs to embark on a trip, or is otherwise faced with a situation where there may not be a sukka to make use of, what are the procedures that should be followed?

One simple solution is the following: A meal in halachic terminology is defined as an eating session that includes bread. If one were to have, say, fruits, vegetables, and other non-bread-like foods at every eating session throughout the holiday, there would technically never be an obligation to eat in a sukka, because no "meal" is actually being eaten! This is true regardless of how much one eats, or how stuffed one may feel.

Additionally, the Talmud issues dispensations from the requirement to eat in a sukka for the following individuals: those who personally find it a hardship, Israel Defense Forces soldiers, and – believe it or not – travelers.[434]

An interesting aspect of the laws of sukka is that according to some authorities, only those who own a home are obligated to build and use a sukka – the homeless are actually exempt.[435] It may therefore be possible to argue the case that when you travel, you are in effect (temporarily) homeless, and hence by extension, exempt from the sukka obligation![436] Furthermore, there is no obligation to

---

430 Vayikra 23:42.
431 Those needing to travel during Sukkot for pressing matters may be exempt from the sukka entirely. OC 640:8.
432 Due to personal sensitivities; OC 640:4; She'eilat Shlomo 1:191. See also http://www.lchaimweekly.org/lchaim/5752/181.htm for the authentic view of Rabbi Menachem Mendel Schneerson on the matter.
433 There of course exceptions of tzaar and the like which are addressed within this chapter. See also Sukka 25b, 28b.
434 Sukka 26a.
435 I heard in a shiur quite some time ago but I did not find this explicitly written anywhere. It does appear to be a somewhat logical application of: teishvu k'ein taduru.
436 See previous note.

build or eat in a sukka in a place where the non-Jewish atmosphere is such that it makes one very uncomfortable.[437]

Of course, the discussion above dealing with situations where one may not have a sukka are not ideal solutions, nor should one be quick to rely upon them. Indeed, some authorities require even one who is traveling to do everything possible in order to construct and eat in a sukka.[438] Taking this one step further, Rabbi Ovadia Yosef states that all the leniencies written above only apply to one who is traveling for some necessary purpose, such as for pressing business matters or mitzva purposes, but not for mere pleasure trips. He says that for a person to voluntarily place himself in a situation where he has no sukka is not permitted.[439] Rabbi Moshe Feinstein concurs with this view and rules that one should not take trips that would force one to neglect the mitzva of sukka.[440]

Still unsure of how to conduct yourself over Sukkot? Rabbi Ovadia Yosef offers some advice for those who are unsure how to spend their time over the holiday. He writes that a person should refrain from taking day trips altogether and instead spend his time learning Torah. In fact, the Jerusalem Talmud[441] states that in reality, labor was actually forbidden during Chol Hamoed for no other reason than to allow people to dedicate their time to Torah study!

While sitting in a sukka over the holiday, it would be appropriate to reflect for a few moments on how really the entire world is like a sukka – very temporary and unpredictable. May it remind us of where our priorities really should be.

---

437   Levush cited in *Biur Halacha* 640.
438   Ibid.
439   *Yechave Da'at* 3:47.
440   *Igrot Moshe*, OC 3:93.
441   Moed Katan 2:3.

SIMCHAT TORAH

S hemini Atzeret, mistakenly referred to as "the last day(s) of Sukkot," along with its partner, Simchat Torah, is actually the climax and conclusion of the month-long festivities that began with Rosh Hashana. Simchat Torah is an especially jubilant time, as it is the day that the annual reading cycle of the Torah is completed and begun anew. Indeed, once the end of the Torah has been read and completed, we immediately begin reading from the beginning, to undermine any claims by the "accusing angels" that we have concluded our obligations to Torah study and are now about to permanently abandon it.[442] Simchat Torah also brings with it a plethora of joyful customs, many of which are unique to individual synagogues or cities. In Israel, Shemini Atzeret and Simchat Torah comprise a one-day holiday. In the Diaspora (which is, nowadays, a self-imposed exile) it is of course two days, with the Torah completion festivities taking place primarily on the second day.

Indeed, every custom of Simchat Torah, regardless of how goofy it may seem (e.g., pouring water over the one leading the Mussaf service when he says *morid hageshem* [the One Who makes the rain fall]), is considered holy and may not be disregarded.[443] Even these seemingly silly practices all stem from a pure desire of trying to show one's happiness at having completed the Torah reading cycle.[444] The idea of making a party upon completing the reading of the Torah cycle actually originates with former Jerusalem resident King Solomon.[445]

Many commentaries pose the following question: why is Simchat Torah celebrated when it is? It seems so much more logical to coordinate Simchat Torah with, say, Shavuot (the day the Torah was actually given) or even Rosh Hashana, thereby inaugurating the new year with a new cycle of Torah reading. The answer, it is

---

442   *Ta'amei Haminhagim* 829. Similarly, the Rav is reported to have said that Adon Olam, a prayer which is to be found at the beginning of the siddur, is recited again at the end of the service (at least on Shabbat) for the same reason.

443   *Mishna Berura* 669:6.

444   Tur, *Beit Yosef* 669.

445   Ibid.

suggested, is that we are trying to confuse the Satan, who will be caught off guard when seeing such devotion to the Torah even after Rosh Hashana and our annual evaluation has come and gone.[446]

One of the more visible practices of Simchat Torah is certainly the *hakafot* (dancing with the Torah while circling the bima), which symbolizes our desire to get close to Hashem through Torah study. It is also a continuation of the Sukkot-long practice of circling the bima during the Hoshana prayers as was done in the Holy Temple. Some also suggest that it is to remind us of the battle of Jericho, when the Jews circled the city seven times with the Ark.[447]

Another prominent and beautiful custom of Simchat Torah is the continual repetition of the Torah reading in order to allow every congregant the opportunity of receiving an aliya on this special day.[448] Even children under bar mitzva are awarded an aliya, as well.[449]

You'll notice that the Torah is read even at night on Simchat Torah – a practice otherwise forbidden. Some suggest that the reason for doing so is that once the Torahs have already been removed from the ark for the purpose of dancing, it would not be respectful to put them away without having read from them first.[450]

One final custom worth mentioning is the absence of *Birkat Kohanim* (the priestly blessing), normally bestowed by the kohanim of the congregation on holidays during the Mussaf service.[451] Due to the fear of congregants becoming intoxicated because of the Simchat Torah festivities, the Birkat Kohanim is omitted or otherwise recited much earlier in the service, before the drinking would have begun.[452]

Remember, the Torah is your heritage – your gift. Simchat Torah we dance with the Torah scrolls closed to show that the Torah belongs to all Jews – not only the scholars.

---

446   *Sefer Ta'amei Haminhagim.*
447   *Sefer Otzar Minhagim.*
448   OC 669.
449   Rema, OC 669.
450   Cited at http://chaburas.org/simchatora.html.
451   Birkat Kohanim is done every day in most of Israel. See Rema, OC 128:44 and *Aruch Hashulchan*, OC 128:64 for more on this issue.
452   *Mishna Berura* 669:17.

ELECTRIC MENORAS [453]

Chanuka is quite unique among the holidays in that there is an obligation of *pirsumei nisa* (publicizing the holiday and its miracles to the world).[454] Although one may completely discharge the obligation of pirsumei nisa with the daily candle lighting in the front window, it is actually a mitzva without limit. It is in fulfillment of pirsumei nisa that organizations such as Chabad place large menoras in public places and organize large public outdoor lighting ceremonies complete with dignitaries, entertainment, and of course, food.

In modern times, it is now possible to fulfill the mitzva of Chanuka "lights," not with fire, but rather with light bulbs and electricity instead of candles or oil. Before discussing these possibilities further, it is proper to note in advance that the overwhelming majority of halachic authorities actually prohibit the use of an electric menora in place of the traditional oil or candle-based menoras for one's personal lighting. Let's examine the issues while highlighting both sides of the debate.

Among the reasons for the opposition to an electric menora is that it does not appear faithful to the blessing recited when lighting Chanuka candles. The blessing includes the words *l'hadlik ner shel Chanuka* (to kindle the Chanuka light). It is argued that when lighting an electric appliance, there is no real "kindling" actually taking place.[455] Some authorities do counter this reservation by citing the well-known Shabbat prohibition against switching lights on or off. Turning a light on during Shabbat is prohibited because it resembles the act of lighting a fire. Furthermore, the Talmud

---

453　Based on an article by Rabbi Howard Jachter and Rabbi Michael Broyde in *The Journal of Halacha and Contemporary Society* 21 (spring 1991), cited at http://chaburas.org/chanuka15.html.

454　There are other holidays with a pirsumei nisa component as well: the reading of the Megilla on Purim and the drinking of four cups of wine at the seder; see the Maggid Mishna to Hilchot Chanuka 4:12. Shaking a lulav on Sukkot is also considered to be a mitzva with a pirsumei nisa component as well; see Chochmat Shlomo OC 625:1.

455　Cited in the name of Rabbi Tzvi Pesach Frank.

doesn't mention a requirement that the Chanuka menora include "fire," but merely "light."

Another argument in opposition to the use of electric menoras is the requirement for the menora to have the required minimum amount of fuel (e.g., wax or oil) present *at the time of lighting.* It is argued that the concept of home electricity is such that the electricity itself is viewed as not actually being present, but rather as a process of continual generation and instantly "delivered" from the electric company.[456] On the other hand, the chances of a power outage during the required thirty minutes that the Chanuka candles must burn is so remote that it can be considered as if the electricity is actually present.

Further opposition to the use of an electric menora includes the requirement that the Chanuka lights be composed of single, independent flames, and that they may not have a torch-like appearance.[457] According to some authorities,[458] incandescent bulbs contain an arc-shaped, sometime two-ply filament which may have the halachic status of a torch, and not a single flame as required. Others dismiss this claim with the fact that although the filament may be two-ply, nevertheless, light bulbs appear as a single unit of light to the observer. Furthermore, unlike the primary characteristic of a torch, light bulbs don't flicker.

Believe it or not, one of the most hotly contested issues in all of halacha, in terms of the number of opinions that exist on a single issue, is none other than the proper time that the Chanuka menora should be lit. According to the Talmud,[459] the Chanuka candles should be lit daily at sunset. Although this may appear simple and straightforward, it is actually not. There is a ferocious debate, which extends to many other areas of halacha, as to what is to be considered halachic sunset. According to the Rambam,[460] this means at the beginning of sunset, which is when the sphere of the sun recedes below the horizon, while according to the *Shulchan*

---

456   Attributed to Rabbi Shlomo Zalman Auerbach, *zt"l.*
457   Compare the requirement upon the candle used to search for chametz.
458   *Tzitz Eliezer* 1:20.
459   Shabbat 21b.
460   *Hilchot Chanuka* 4:5.

Aruch,[461] it means at the end of the sunset period, when it is nearly completely dark. There are also at least seven additional opinions asserting alternative points between the "beginning" and "end" of the sunset period as the proper time for menorah lighting. The *Aruch Hashulchan*, however, dismisses all opinions and writes that one should only light after dark.[462]

Make no mistake, although the use of an electric menora for one's own personal lighting is to be discouraged, it is certainly a very meritorious practice to place an electric menora in addition to the traditional menora in the window. This way the mitzva of pirsumei nisa is extended for much longer by passersby seeing the still "burning" electric menora and being reminded of the miracles of Chanuka.

THE SHAMASH

It is so commonplace to light a preliminary candle to be used as the candle that lights the others on the menora each night of Chanuka that many don't even realize that it is not actually a halachic requirement.[463] This superfluous candle is affectionately known as the *shamash* (servant). Being that the shamash is not actually a part of the mitzva component of the Chanuka candles, it is generally placed separate from the rest of the lights (higher or lower or otherwise distinguished from them, as we shall soon see in detail). What is this shamash all about?

The Talmud teaches that the ideal place for one to light the Chanuka candles is actually outdoors.[464] Indeed, this was the common practice for centuries. It was sadly noticed, however, that as times changed and anti-Semitism increased, the Chanuka candles, and the homes displaying them, were subject to frequent

461   OC 672:1.
462   OC 672:4.
463   This discussion is based on an article by Rabbi Aaron Ross at http://chaburas.org/chanuka18.html.
464   Shabbat 21.

acts of vandalism. An "executive" decision to change the practice was made by the leading rabbis of the time, and people began lighting the Chanuka menora indoors, a custom that remains with us to this day.[465]

The switch to indoor lighting brought about a halachic complication; among the many specifications comprising the mitzva of Chanuka candles is the requirement that the Chanuka candles not be used for any mundane purpose whatsoever. They are to serve no function other than to recall the great miracle of the original Chanuka oil having lasted eight days. There was concern that in a dark room one might come, for example, to use the Chanuka candles for making reading easier or even for such mundane tasks as counting money or lighting a cigarette. An additional candle was therefore added so that in the event that light would be needed for a mundane purpose, one would be able to make use of the shamash. This arrangement allows us to ensure the exclusivity of the actual Chanuka candles.

In Babylon, the Chanuka lighting had always been conducted indoors due to the climate, and hence the practice of using a shamash may actually pre-date the Talmud. Indeed, it is proper for a person living in a place with a favorable climate in December (e.g., Australia), and no fear of Gentiles ruining the candles, to light outdoors rather than to use the living room window. This is the practice among many in Israel.

In an unconventional approach, the Tur actually advocates using two shamash candles.[466] One due to the concerns raised above (i.e., to avoid mundane uses), and one to actually light the Chanuka candles. Believe it or not, it is the authentic custom of the Jews of Aleppo, Syria, to use two extra candles each night of Chanuka to accommodate this opinion.

There are various approaches of how to differentiate the shamash from the actual Chanuka candles. The Maharil would use a wax candle as his shamash, while using oil for the actual Chanuka lights. Another approach is that of the Orchot Chaim, who says

---

465   Rambam, *Hilchot Chanuka* 4:8.
466   OC 673.

that the shamash should be placed lower than the other candles. The Maharil writes, however, that the shamash should be higher than the other candles. Finally, the Mordechai suggests making the Shamash bigger than the other candles so that its light will be the brightest.[467]

Although it is clear that the actual Chanuka candles possess much sanctity, is there any inherent holiness to the shamash? While we would think not, especially considering that it may be used for mundane purposes, the Be'er Heitev notes that even if one uses the shamash, he should not use it for any demeaning purposes.[468] This teaches us that even the shamash is not just "any" light source, and by extension, we should realize that anything that was even indirectly used in conjunction with a mitzva (e.g., the wooden boards of the sukka walls) should be permanently treated with reverence.[469]

EATING DURING CHANUKA

An always welcomed requirement of most holidays is the mitzva to eat or otherwise be surrounded by food. That's right – as we can quickly recall, most holidays boast a precept requiring us to hold elaborate eating marathons in order to properly observe the holiday. Indeed, one need look no further than Shabbat, with its requirement to eat at least three meals over the course of the day! Halachic literature discusses these meal-related requirements in much detail, such as how many courses the meals must include, what they must consist of, the status of meat, fish, and poultry, and other gastronomical issues. Pesach seder, Rosh Hashana eve, Purim seuda, and the list goes on and on…

---

467   All cited in Rabbi Dr. Daniel Sperber, *Minhagei Yisrael: Origins and History*, 8 vol. (Jerusalem: Mossad Harav Kook, 1998–2007). .
468   OC 673:7.
469   Megilla 26b.

Chanuka, however, remains shrouded in mystery and uncertainty in this area. Is there an actual requirement to feast over this holiday?[470] Is it similar to its cousin, Purim, in which there is indeed a requirement to feast? Can it be that eating potato latkes is a mitzva? What about the oil-drenched, jelly-filled *sufganiyot* donuts?

Turning first to the *Shulchan Aruch*, we find it written that while it may be a widespread custom to hold elaborate meals, and to snack on the famous Chanuka icons, such gastronomic experiences are merely optional, not required, nor even necessarily recommended.[471] The Rema, however, notes that there are indeed authorities who consider elaborate meals in honor of the holiday an element of a mitzva. This opinion takes into consideration that Chanuka also commemorates the rededication of the altar in the Temple, an event worthy of a celebratory meal in its own right. According to these authorities, gathering together for a meal complete with songs and praise is certainly commendable.

The Mordechai and the Tur argue that while feasting may be meritorious, it simply cannot be placed in the realm of *mitzvot* (obligations). They write that on Purim there is a mitzva to feast, because Purim commemorates the physical and national annihilation that Haman was plotting. Hence, physical pleasures are appropriate and even required on Purim. The Greeks, however, had no interest in physically annihilating the Jews; their goal was merely to convert them out of their faith. Chanuka therefore commemorates a spiritual near-holocaust, not a physical one. Hence, all rituals on Chanuka focus on spirituality, not on physical or material matters.

That notwithstanding, there are those who still insist that there is an obligation to have at least a minimum number of festive meals over the Chanuka holiday. This was particularly apparent for the Sephardic authorities, who note that the Rambam's usage of the

---

470   This chapter based on an article by Rabbi Aaron Ross cited at http://chaburas. org/chanuka9.html.
471   OC 670:2.

word *simcha* regarding Chanuka celebrations seems to allude to the idea of holding elaborate holiday meals on Chanuka.

While the major halachic authorities remain unimpressed with attempts to force any eating requirements onto Chanuka, we can suggest, however, an interpretation from an external source. The section of the *Shulchan Aruch* that deals with our daily routines concludes with the following advice: "A festive disposition is always a good thing."[472] There can be no doubt, similar to those authorities quoted above, that all celebrations, meals, gifts, greetings, and rituals that are done out of love for God, Torah, and Chanuka are certainly worthwhile and beloved before Him.

ADAR I AND ADAR II

Glancing at your Jewish calendars may sometimes be cause for confusion. That's because in some years the Hebrew month of Adar seems to extend a lot longer than just thirty days. And wait – why isn't Purim mentioned in such Adars? That's right – unlike a secular leap year which brings with it merely one additional day, a Jewish leap year brings with it an additional month, a second Adar.

This additional month, which surfaces seven times within a nineteen-year cycle, is an essential Torah-mandated appendage, primarily intended to ensure that Pesach will never fall out in the winter. The Torah tells us that Pesach must be observed "in the spring."[473] With the lunar calendar being "behind" the solar calendar by eleven days each year, sooner or later Chanuka would fall out in July and Pesach in December – an unacceptable arrangement.[474]

This additional month of Adar does make for some legitimate confusion. For starters, which Adar is the real one, the first or the

---

472   Rema, OC 697:1.
473   Shemot 13:4.
474   This is the case with Muslim holidays such as Ramadan – arriving earlier every year.

second? This Adar ambiguity is especially evident with regard to the observance of yahrtzeits, bar mitzvas, and perhaps most importantly, Purim.

Conveniently, with regard to Purim, the Mishna is very clear in ruling that the Megilla reading and other related mitzvot of Purim must be observed in the second Adar, making the first Adar appear to be the supplementary one.[475] Nevertheless, the first Adar is viewed with some sanctity, as well. For example, according to many authorities, the halachic requirement to be joyful in the month of Adar applies in the first Adar as well.[476] An interesting complication of a double Adar is that in many instances, if two people enter into a "year-long" agreement, and it is then discovered that there's an additional Adar that year, then the agreement may be binding for thirteen months![477]

The laws of mourning are somewhat different from the example above. The laws of mourning are actually a unit classified as "twelve months" and not "one year." As odd as this may sound, in a year containing a second Adar, mourning restrictions will nevertheless cease after twelve months, even though an entire calendar year may not have passed.[478]

The laws as they apply to yahrtzeits are yet distinctive as well, with no definitive opinion on how to conduct oneself. Some authorities rule that all Adar yahrtzeits are to be observed in the second Adar,[479] while others rule that they are to be observed in the first Adar.[480] There is, of course, an additional opinion which rules that a yahrtzeit is to be observed in both Adars![481]

With regard to a bar mitzva boy, the practice is by and large as follows: if there were two Adars in both the year that the boy was

---

475   Megilla 6b.
476   Rabbi J.B. Soloveitchik, cited in Rabbi Aharon Ziegler, *Halakhic Positions of Rabbi Joseph B. Soloveitchik* (Northvale, NJ: Jason Aronson, 1998); see also *Sha'arei Halacha u'Minhag* (Chabad) and OC 1:286, among others.
477   Erchin 31a.
478   YD 391:2.
479   OC 568:7.
480   Rema, OC 568:7.
481   OC 568:7; Vilna Gaon, *Magen Avraham*. See *Mishna Berura* 568:42; see *Sefer Chassidim* 712 for an alternative approach.

born, and then again in the year of the bar mitzva, then everything is straightforward. If, however, the boy was born in a year that had one Adar, and in the year of his bar mitzva there are two Adars, then the bar mitzva is to take place in the second Adar.[482] Here's something intriguing: it is actually conceivable for a boy who is younger to become bar mitzva before one who is older! For example, a boy born on the tenth of Adar II will become bar mitzva before a boy born on the eighteenth of Adar I, if in their bar mitzva year there's only one Adar!

This is only a small sampling of the mathematical entertainment that the month of Adar has to offer. Regardless of which authorities you choose to follow for your observances, remember – there is no disagreement that being joyful at any opportunity is a tremendous mitzva.[483]

THE FAST OF ESTHER

The Fast of Esther is perhaps the least understood among the fast days, in terms of what it represents and why we truly fast.[484] Contrary to popular belief, the fast we observe today prior to Purim was not the authentic fast as observed by Esther. In fact, Queen Esther's original fast was actually a three-day abstention that coincided with the start of Pesach.[485] That's right – Esther had

---

482 OC 55:9.

483 *Likutei Moharan* 2:82.

484 "When a man fasts and he offers his heart and his will, he brings a perfect sacrifice, for it pleases the Holy One, blessed be He, that he should offer him his fat, his blood, and his body, and bring to Him the fire and the fragrance of his mouth. These diminish through fasting, and are like the fat, blood, and flesh of a sacrifice. The heat and odor of a fasting man's breath stand for the fire of the altar and the fragrance of the sacrifice." *Zohar Chadash, Midrash Ruth*, 79d–80a, *Sefer Chassidim* 171.

485 The record holder for the longest fast is Adam, who fasted for 130 years; see Eruvin 18b.

no Pesach seder that year.[486] Curiously, the Fast of Esther is not mentioned anywhere in the Talmud.[487]

There are a number of opinions as to what the status of today's Fast of Esther really is. According to one school of thought, we observe the fast in order to recall the fast that Queen Esther undertook on behalf of the Jewish people, notwithstanding that we observe it on a different day than she did.[488] According to this opinion, the observance of this fast has the status of a rabbinical commandment.

Others are of the opinion that no, since the fast is not even observed on its original day, it doesn't earn the status of a rabbinical commandment, and rather, it's merely a custom. According to this school of thought, the fast is intended to commemorate the preparations Esther made in advance of her meeting with King Achashverosh, where she was to plead that he save the Jewish people from Haman's plot.[489]

Yet an alternative approach, one which would appear to be more timely and meaningful, is to teach us that when under attack, we are to join together and turn to God for our salvation through fasting and prayer. One will notice that the Fast of Esther takes place on the thirteenth of Adar, which was the day before the Jews were permitted to take revenge upon their enemies. Everyone fasted and prayed for success in the battle that was to be launched the next day. Indeed, throughout history, we find that the Jewish people often fasted before going to war.

Unlike other communal fast days, the Fast of Esther has both a mournful flavor as well as a festive one. It is mournful in that it recalls the near annihilation of the Jewish people at the hands of Haman and Co., yet at the same time, it is joyful in that it expresses our confidence that God will continue to save us from our enemies in the future, as He did in the days of Purim.

What if one is unable to fast due to illness, weakness, or the like? According to the Rema, the fast is actually not an obligation, but

---

486   Megilla 16.
487   *Maggid Mishna*; Rambam, *Hilchot Ta'anit* 5:5.
488   Rambam, *Hilchot Ta'anit* 5:5.
489   *Beit Yosef* 686.

rather a custom.[490] Accordingly, he allows those pregnant, nursing, or otherwise ill to forego the fast. It goes without saying that those who do eat on a fast day should eat only the minimum and not indulge in delicacies.

It is interesting to note that Purim is one of the holidays that will continue to be observed in the messianic era. Whether this includes the Fast of Esther or not is a matter of dispute. We'll just have to wait and see.

MATANOT LA'EVYONIM

A well-known mitzva related to the holiday of Purim is the mitzva of *matanot la'evyonim* (giving gifts to the poor). Although a seemingly simple directive, the way in which we are to perform this mitzva is subject to some debate. As will be seen, this is a result of the various interpretations offered on the verse which instructs us in this mitzva: "the days when the Jews had rest from their enemies, and the month which was turned from sorrow to gladness, and from mourning into a good day – they should make them days of feasting and gladness, and of sending portions one to another, and gifts to the poor (*matanot la'evyonim*)."[491]

One will readily notice that both the words *matanot* and *la'evyonim* are written in the plural, which could lead to the assumption that we are required to give multiple gifts to a number of people. Can it be that issuing a generous check to an organization that helps poor people would not be adequate for the mitzva, as it would be only "one" gift? Surely it would be unreasonable to require those who choose to issue a check for matanot la'evyonim to supplement it with an additional gift in order to "pluralize" it.

No less an authority than Rashi[492] declares that the mitzva is to give at least two poor people gifts on Purim, but that only one gift

---

490   OC 686.
491   Esther 9:22.
492   Megilla 7a.

per person is required. The fact that the word "gifts" is written in plural is of no consequence, merely a figure of speech. The Rambam supports this interpretation and rules that only one charitable gift per person is mandated.[493] This gift can be of any form – clothes, money, or even food. It would be remiss not to point out that there are those who adopt a more literalist approach and insist on two separate gifts to each poor person.[494] Everyone agrees, however, that the mitzva of matanot la'evyonim does require a minimum of two poor people.

Another interesting question discussed by the poskim concerns the giving of matanot la'evyonim to a poor couple, husband and wife. Is it considered charity to two separate individuals or to one? Some authorities rule that it is to be considered as having given two different people charity and that the mitzva is thereby discharged.[495] Others disagree and argue that since they live together and likely share each other's incomes, they are to be considered as one unit.[496]

Not all gifts were created equal. There is a minimum value that the matanot la'evyonim gifts must be worth. Indeed, it is crucial that the gifts be worth at least twenty-five cents, as anything less is considered insignificant from the perspective of halacha. Besides, we are encouraged to distribute handsome gifts in honor of the holiday in order to ensure the recipient a feeling of dignity. Some suggest that the financial value of matanot la'evyonim be at least the amount needed for the individual to purchase a meal for the holiday.[497]

Halachic authorities encourage us to follow this latter view, at least for the minimum two people we are obligated to assist.[498] All agree that it is better for one to increase in gifts to the poor, rather than in sending *mishlo'ach manot* (gifts of food) to friends.[499]

---

493   *Hilchot Megilla* 2:16.
494   *Kitzur Shulchan Aruch* 142:1.
495   *Kaf Hachaim* 696:10.
496   *Aruch Hashulchan* 694:2.
497   *Sha'arei Teshuva* 694:1.
498   *Kaf Hachaim* 694.
499   Rambam, *Hilchot Megilla* 2:17.

Make no mistake, the mitzva of matanot la'evyonim is equally incumbent on both men and women.[500] Indeed, this is true regarding all the mitzvot of Purim – women must fulfill them just like men, as they too were saved from Haman's decree!

It is important to be aware that the mitzvot of matanot la'evyonim as well as mishlo'ach manot must be done on Purim day. One does not fulfill the obligation if they are given on Purim night.[501] Nevertheless, if you send your matanot la'evyonim or mishlo'ach manot by mail and they arrive at the recipient on Purim day, the mitzva is fulfilled.[502]

One final note. Although we are only obligated to assist two poor people on Purim, there is the beloved adage of *kol haposhet yado notnim lo* (whoever stretches out his hand we give to him)[503] – on Purim we should endeavor to give charity to absolutely anyone who requests it.

MISHLO'ACH MANOT

Purim is certainly one of the most joyous and festive days on the Jewish calendar. And why not? A good party is certainly a suitable means of commemorating having been saved from total extermination. But that's not the only obligation of the day. The mitzvot of Purim include hearing the Megilla reading twice, sending gifts of food to friends, dispensing charity to the poor, partaking in a Purim feast, and lastly, indulging in a little more alcohol than normal.

Although a thorough review of all the mitzvot of Purim is beyond the scope of this discussion, let's take a deeper look at the mitzva of *mishlo'ach manot* – the obligation to send gifts of food to friends. The requirement of sending two gifts of food to at least

---

500   *Mishna Berura* 694:1.
501   *Magen Avraham* 695:13.
502   *Kaf Hachaim* 694.
503   OC 694:3.

one friend is derived from the Megilla, the book of Esther, as it is written: "to make them [Purim] days...of sending portions of food to one another."[504]

Several reasons are offered as to the hidden purpose of observing this mitzva. For one, it helps to ensure that everyone will have food to eat for the holiday.[505] Another reason offered is that it nurtures friendship and unity among Jews.[506] This is especially true regarding packages received from long lost friends! Because of this, mishlo'ach manot may not be sent anonymously.[507]

The mitzva of mishlo'ach manot is incumbent upon men and women alike,[508] and parents should prepare supplementary mishlo'ach manot parcels for their children to distribute.[509]

Although Purim is a twenty-four-hour holiday, one may only fulfill the mitzva of mishlo'ach manot during the daylight hours.[510] Indeed, one should endeavor to send[511] mishlo'ach manot as early in the day as possible, for if the recipient is already drunk and thus unaware of having received the package, one would not have properly performed the mitzva.[512]

To properly fulfill the mitzva of mishlo'ach manot, one is obligated to send at least two gifts of food to at least one person,[513] or one type of food and one type of drink,[514] or even two types of drink.[515] Some foods, such as pizza for example, although consisting of at least two different types of food (cheese and bread), are only considered to be one food for the purpose of mishlo'ach manot.[516]

---

504   Esther 9:22.
505   *Terumat Hadeshen* 111.
506   Chatam Sofer, OC 196.
507   *Ktav Sofer* 141.
508   Rema, OC 695:4.
509   *Pri Megadim, Eishel Avraham* 695:14.
510   OC 695:4.
511   While the sender of the mishlo'ach manot packages can deliver it himself, some prefer the custom of using a messenger for the deliveries. *Mishna Berura* 695:18, *Tzitz Eliezer* 9:33.
512   *Nitei Gavriel* 26:16.
513   Rema, OC 695:4.
514   *Mishna Berura* 695:20.
515   *Aruch Hashulchan* 695:4.
516   *Be'er Heitev* 695:7.

Additionally, all mishlo'ach manot foods should ideally be ready-to-eat, with no further preparation required to consume them.[517] Although it would seem from the Talmud[518] that the minimum quantity of mishlo'ach manot food would be that of an entire meal, rabbinical authorities have ruled that any "honorable" amount is sufficient.[519] Some even sanction gifts of food the size of an olive, or even smaller if need be.[520] If you're wealthy, though, you mustn't be stingy with what you send on Purim.

While the issue is somewhat debated, it seems that one cannot fulfill the mitzva of mishlo'ach manot by sending cigarettes, Torah-related materials (food for the soul!), or even money with which the recipient can buy food.[521] There is a minority opinion that allows for women to send clothes to other women as mishlo'ach manot.[522]

Although Purim is certainly a day for festivity, we must be careful not to lose our dignity. The Talmudic sage Rabba got a little carried away one Purim and accidentally murdered his best friend, Zeira. Not to worry, though. He later recited some blessing and resurrected him. Needless to say, Zeira never went over to Rabba's house on Purim again.[523]

PURIM MESHULASH

The Purim of 2005/5767 was the rare occurrence of a *Purim Meshulash* – a three-day Purim. The holiday of Purim as observed by most of the Jewish world is always on Adar 14, which, after the establishment and finalization of the Jewish calendar, can never fall on Shabbat. It's just one of those things. The sages established the Jewish calendar in this way, fearing that if Purim fell out on

---

517   *Magen Avraham* 695:11.
518   Megilla 7b.
519   *Pri Megadim, Mishbetzot Zahav* 695:4.
520   *Nitei Gavriel* 27:5.
521   *Nitei Gavriel* 28:1.
522   *Nitei Gavriel* 28:2.
523   Megilla 7b.

Shabbat, it might lead to a Megilla being carried in a place with no eruv, causing widespread violation of Shabbat.[524]

In a regular year, however, Jews who live in cities that in ancient times had a wall surrounding them observe Purim one day later – on the fifteenth of Adar. That's right – Jews who live in Tel Aviv celebrate Purim the day before those who live in Jerusalem. The fifteenth of Adar, however, can fall on Shabbat, as it did for example in 2005.

The procedure in such a situation is that Jerusalemites and others who live in cities that had a wall surrounding them in the days of Joshua read the Megilla a day earlier than their usual date. With this adjustment the entire Jewish world is reading the Megilla on the exact same day, as well as performing the mitzva of matanot la'evyonim – distributing gifts to the poor. The Purim meal for those who live in walled cities, however, is delayed until Sunday, along with the mitzva of mishlo'ach manot – sending gifts of food to friends. Considering that Purim is split into two, with some of the mitzvot being observed on Friday and some on Sunday, Shabbat is seen as a bridge of sorts between this two-part observance, thus making it into a Purim Meshulash, a triple (three-day-long) Purim.

This concept of walled cities is worth exploring further. The principles, definitions, and applications of a "walled city" are a fascinating topic. Sure, while the old city of Jerusalem had a wall around it in ancient times, what is to be done in our day, when Jerusalem and its modern-day neighborhoods extend many kilometers away from the original old city? Furthermore, how do we know which cities were truly walled in ancient times?

To answer the second question first: indeed, in a case of doubt as to whether or not a city was surrounded by a wall in ancient times, Purim is to be observed twice. Such a situation exists with such cities as Jaffa, Acre, Gaza, Lod, Tiberias, Shechem, Hebron, Tzfat, and even Haifa. Some communities in these cities observe two days of Purim every year to ensure that they get the right day![525]

---

524   Megilla 4b; compare the case of a shofar on Shabbat Rosh Hashana.
525   OC 688.

As for the newer neighborhoods in and around ancient Jerusalem – yes, they conduct themselves as if they, too, were surrounded by a wall in ancient times and observe Purim on the fifteenth of Adar. This is due to a Talmudic principle[526] which states that any city that is "close to" or "can be seen" from a city that had a wall around it in ancient times is to be considered as a borough of that city for the purposes of Purim.

"Close to" is considered by many authorities to be any uninterrupted stretch of residential neighborhoods no matter how far away from the site of the original wall. Therefore, since neighborhoods around Jerusalem such as Neve Ya'akov, Ein Kerem, Ramot, and Har Nof are part of an uninterrupted chain of residential areas eventually leading right to the old city of Jerusalem and the Western Wall, they too gain the halachic status of ancient Jerusalem, although they are many miles away from the site of the original walled city.

PURIM AND CHANUKA

Purim and Chanuka, two holidays observed somewhat close to one another, are often compared and contrasted to each other. They are, in fact, somewhat related – cousins, perhaps.[527] For starters, both are post-biblical, rabbinically established holidays. There is also the common denominator of the need to publicize the miracles that occurred to our nation on these days in ancient times. Even the Rambam in his *Mishna Torah* groups the laws of these two holidays together into a single unit.

Nevertheless, there are several differences between these two holidays that are worth highlighting, and, more importantly, pondering. The most obvious difference is that Purim has a text,

---

526 Megilla 3b.
527 Based in part by an article by Rabbi Aaron Ross, based on an article by Rabbi Nathaniel Helfgot in Yeshivat Har Etzion's *Israel Koschitzky Virtual Beit Midrash* (available at http://www.vbm-torah.org/chanuka/chanuka.htm), cited at: http://www.chaburas.org/chanuka10.html.

a scroll of its own, while Chanuka does not.[528] Purim, therefore, is more deeply rooted within Scripture, and may even border on a higher status, with some commentators actually considering it to be somewhat of a biblical holiday, and not purely a rabbinical one. Chanuka, on the other hand, is completely rabbinical in nature and flavor.

Here is something to think about: We know that it is prohibited to add new holidays to the Jewish calendar. This should be especially true of Chanuka, considering that the only scriptural text that records the miracles of Chanuka was never even accepted into our canon. Where, then, is the precedent or authority to add Chanuka, or any new holiday for that matter, to our list of observances?

The answer, it is suggested, is that Chanuka and Purim are counted as completely rabbinical holidays, and their accompanying mitzvot are rabbinical ones as well. The rabbis were permitted to add additional holidays and mitzvot, which do not pose any threat to the Divinely issued 613 mitzvot of the Torah. Indeed, there is no restriction on rabbis adding mitzvot. We see this, for example, with the institution of Shabbat candles, the ritual hand washing, and several other practices.

Here are some points for you to think about on your own. Several answers have been suggested to these queries, but whatever you can come up with would be a welcome Torah interpretation as well.

- Think about it: Notice how, before Chanuka, it is forbidden to fast, while before Purim, it is a mitzva to fast.
- Think about it: When a close relative has died, it's forbidden to eat meat or drink wine prior to the burial. Interestingly, the law is that such a person, who has suffered the death of an immediate relative, may even consume meat as part of the Purim feast![529] While normally

---

528   While there does exist a two-volume "Book of Maccabees," it is considered to be part of the "Apocrypha" – the "hidden books" which were never accepted into the Jewish canon. Among the reasons for its rejection are a) Apocryphal books were never viewed or even suggested as having been Divinely inspired; b) many parts of the Apocrypha are clearly legendary, fictitious, and contain historical errors; c) these books often suggest unacceptable ideas or practices. Nevertheless, they do contain valuable information on life during those periods.

529   OC 696.

meat and wine are forbidden to one whose close relative has not yet been buried, Purim is an exception. Commentators explain the reason for this oddity by stating that "the prohibition upon an individual cannot override the Torah-mandated obligation of the community to have a feast on Purim." What? Torah mandated? We see from here that Purim is awarded a somewhat biblical status!

- Think about it: A topic that is always of interest is that of the woman's role in the holiday. The Talmud rules that women are obligated to hear the reading of the Purim Megilla, since they also took part in and were beneficiaries of the miracles.[530] The Behag rules that women may not read the Megilla on behalf of men, since he is of the opinion that their obligation is to *hear* the Megilla, but not necessarily to *read* it. It seems, then, that the obligations of the two genders are on different levels, a factor which may obstruct women's ability to fulfill this mitzva on behalf of men.

- By contrast, there is virtually no debate regarding the lighting of Chanuka candles, which women may light on behalf of men when needed. The Be'er Heitev actually writes that women may fulfill the mitzva of lighting the menora on behalf of men, "unlike the reading of the Megilla." Since Chanuka is entirely a rabbinical holiday, it was established that both men and women would be on equal standing in terms of their obligations.

---

530   Megilla 4a.

WOMEN AND FAMILY

KOL ISHA

The prohibition upon men with regard to listening to a woman sing is known in halachic parlance as *kol isha* (literally, "the voice of a woman"). This concept is based on the Talmud, which lists a woman's voice as being an intimate part of herself and, by extension, sexually arousing.[531] Although there are sources that advocate extending the prohibition of kol isha to include even a woman's speaking voice,[532] halacha limits its concerns of kol isha to women and song only.[533] Although there are a number of circumstances that allow the restrictions of kol isha to be waived or compromised, matters concerning kol isha should be approached with reverence along with all other rabbinical enactments.[534]

While there have been authorities who have suggested that the prohibition on listening to a woman sing applies only when one is in the midst of reciting the Shema[535] or other prayers, normative halacha applies the concept of kol isha at all times.[536]

Although, as mentioned, there are many variables as to how and when the prohibitions of kol isha are to be applied, there are two specific cases that frequently arise and will be dealt with here: kol isha in relation to singing in unison with other women, such as at the Shabbat table, and kol isha as it applies to listening to the radio and other recorded music.

Although no observant individual should join a co-ed choir, singing along with, or sitting in the presence of women singing would be within acceptable boundaries at occasions such as the Shabbat table when it is customary to sing. At issue is whether women should participate in the singing of "Shalom Aleichem" and other Shabbat songs in the presence of men other than their husbands (or brothers, fathers, sons, and grandsons).

---

531   Berachot 24a.
532   Kiddushin 70a.
533   Rema, OC 75:3.
534   *Yabia Omer* 1:6.
535   Ritva, *Shita Mekubetzet*; Berachot 24a.
536   EH (Even Ha'ezer) 21:2.

Many authorities justify the practice of women participating in such singing, citing the Talmudic principle of "two voices cannot be heard simultaneously";[537] when singing in a group, no individual woman's voice would be distinguishable from the others. Furthermore, in such a situation it is unlikely that a woman's voice will be arousing, which was the primary concern for the legislation of kol isha in the first place.[538]

Another reason for leniency is that we don't find anywhere that women are disqualified from chanting religious texts based on kol isha considerations. Today's practice of not allowing women to read from the Torah is not based on any kol isha considerations whatsoever, but rather on *kavod hatzibbur*, issues relating to the dignity of a congregation.[539] Based on these considerations, many authorities allow for the singing of zemirot and other religious songs in groups consisting of numerous men and women together.

The other common occurrence of kol isha-related issues has to do with listening to the radio. Whether by choice or due to external factors, one may find oneself listening to music on the radio that may include female vocalists. Some authorities permit one to listen to a woman singing if one does not know what the singer looks like.[540] Other authorities relax the prohibition of kol isha if one is careful and does not intend to focus on the woman's voice.[541]

These rulings are especially relevant for those who would otherwise choose not to listen to the radio in their home or car, but find themselves in a situation that is beyond their control, such as when in a taxi or bus and the driver is playing music that includes a woman's voice.[542] It would be remiss not to mention that many poskim prohibit listening to a woman's voice even when it is not known who is singing or what she looks like.[543]

---

537   Megilla 21b.
538   *Seridei Aish* 2:8.
539   Megilla 23a.
540   Maharam Shik, EH 53.
541   *Tzitz Eliezer* 5:2.
542   See *Yabia Omer*, OC 1:6 for an extensive review of this and other kol isha-related issues.
543   *Chelkat Yakov* 1:163.

Although there are certainly legitimate and lenient considerations within the issue of kol isha when full compliance is not possible, make no mistake, kol isha is an important part of Torah-observant Judaism, and one who is careful in this area while making sure not to embarrass or hurt anyone in the process will surely merit many blessings.

M I K V A

A mikva is perhaps the most significant and certainly the most vital accessory for wholesome Jewish living. The construction of a mikva is so essential that it takes precedence even over the construction of a synagogue.[544] Its primary usages are for the immersion of married women following their menstrual cycle, the immersion of new dishes, and to finalize conversions. While there is no occasion in our day and age that a man is truly required by Torah law to immerse himself in a mikva, a number of customs have evolved throughout the years in which men have voluntarily taken upon themselves to do so. Among these occasions are immersions prior to Shabbat and holidays. Some even immerse daily.

The Torah teaches us that the secret to ritual purity lies in immersing in a specially constructed mikva or other naturally flowing spring or ocean.[545] Although a mikva must contain a minimum of forty se'ah of rainwater, a naturally flowing body of water actually has no minimum quantity requirements.[546] The exact modern-day equivalent of the forty-se'ah measurement is subject to much dispute. Accordingly, mikvaot are constructed to err on the side of caution and usually contain no less than one thousand liters of water. Rivers should be avoided for mikva use when possible.[547]

---

544   *Igrot Moshe*, CM (*Choshen Mishpat*) 1:42
545   Vayikra 11:36.
546   Mikvaot 1:7, 8; *Aruch Hashulchan* 201:9.
547   YD 201:2.

Do you know how a kosher mikva is constructed? Have you ever wondered how the waters of a mikva can stay clean and fresh in places where rainwater is scarce? I'm going to share a little secret with you: For those who have immersed in a mikva in the past, guess what – the body of water you immersed in was none other than 100 percent pure tap water! That's because halacha declares any body of water that leads to or that has even been touched by kosher mivka waters to assume the status of "kosher water" in its own right, as will be explained. There are three primary methods of mikva construction in which this is accomplished and they are: *hashaka, zeria,* and *bor al gabay bor.*

Hashaka (literally, "kissing") refers to the method of mikva construction in which the tap water-filled immersion pool sits side by side with the tank containing the true mikva water. A small opening in the common wall between them transforms the tap water pool into a kosher mikva in its own right, by virtue of the two waters mingling through the hole.[548]

Zeria (literally, "seeding") refers to the method whereby the necessary amount of kosher rainwater is allowed to accumulate in its specially constructed reservoir. Afterwards, large quantities of tap water are then added to this reservoir, allowing for the waters to overflow and fill the actual immersion pool. The overflowing tap water that enters the immersion pool is now itself deemed as kosher water since it first mingled with the authentic kosher waters.[549]

Bor al gabay bor (literally, "a tank on top of a tank") is the method of mikva construction devised by the fifth Rebbe of Chabad, and is the preferred method of construction in Chabad-supervised mikvas. In this method of construction, the kosher rainwater is stored in a tank that sits below the actual immersion pool. A specially placed hole in the floor allows the bottom and top waters to touch, thereby transforming the upper waters into a kosher mikva as well, similar to hashaka. This method is viewed as having several advantages, too numerous to discuss here.

---

548   Mikvaot 6:7.
549   Mikvaot 6:8.

Although one may never rely on the use of a swimming pool or the like for the purposes of a mikva, it may in fact have some validity from an academic perspective.[550]

As one can see, the centrality of a mikva in Jewish life cannot be underestimated. We are also taught that God Himself is the mikva of the entire Jewish people – purifying them when their hearts are turned towards Him.[551]

INTIMACY

Judaism views love and intimacy between a husband and wife as part and parcel of both the service of God and spiritual growth. Jewish law even contains a legal and ethical code for proper sexual relations, known as the laws of *nidda*. Engaging in procreation is of course a mitzva of the Torah[552] which actually provides for God Himself to join in the marital union.[553]

The Torah's laws of family purity are fundamental in ensuring not only a halachic marriage, but a healthy one as well. While a complete review of these laws is not possible within the scope of this discussion, an abridged version of the laws and philosophies (not to be relied upon without rabbinic consultation) is discussed below.

Upon a woman's sighting of menstrual blood, husband and wife are to separate from all physical contact until the flow has completely ceased, followed by an additional seven-day preparatory period. Following this approximately twelve-day interval, women then immerse themselves in a spiritual spa – a mikva. Following proper immersion in a mikva, sexual relations may be resumed by

---

550   There are ways to derive from the Mishna and halachic texts a "loophole" which could possibly permit the use of a swimming pool for a mikva; nevertheless, we do not rule this way and no one may ever do so. Rambam, *Hilchot Mikvaot* 4:9.
551   Yoma 85b.
552   Bereishit 1:28.
553   Kiddushin 30a.

husband and wife. These laws provide many undeniable benefits to a marriage.

In Judaism, sexual relations are not considered shameful, sinful, or obscene. Likewise, contrary to the misconception of many individuals, sexual activity is not exclusively intended for the sole purpose of procreation. Related to this idea is the fact that although strictly regulated within halacha, birth control is permitted in principle,[554] so long as a couple is committed to fulfilling the mitzva to "be fruitful and multiply."[555] In Judaism, sexual desire is no different than hunger or thirst, which is to be satisfied in the proper times, places, and manners. When mutually satisfying relations take place between a husband and wife, it transforms the act into an exceptional mitzva. Actually, one should not even initiate intercourse until an intense desire has been achieved through preliminary affections.[556]

Believe it or not, engaging in sexual relations is a Torah-mandated obligation, primarily upon a husband to ensure that he pleases his wife,[557] especially when requested.[558] In fact, sexual relations may only be conducted with the wife's permission.[559] Forcing one's wife into relations is a serious transgression,[560] as is depriving her of sexual relations for the sake of a trip[561] or even for a mitzva. Be advised that according to halacha, sexual relations must be engaged in while unclothed.[562] Indeed, if your partner insists on engaging in intercourse only when dressed, then you are entitled to a divorce.[563] Ideally, sex should take place at night and in the dark,[564] but if need be, it is permissible during the day, in a darkened room, as well.

---

554   *Bnei Banim* 1:31, 2:38, 39. This issue is discussed by virtually all contemporary halachic authorities – *Igrot Moshe, Teshuvot v'Hanhagot, Tzitz Eliezer*, etc.
555   Yevamot 61b. One has fulfilled this mitzva after producing a boy and a girl or two boys.
556   Shabbat 140b.
557   Nedarim 15b.
558   Nedarim 20b.
559   Chagiga 5b; see *Sefer Chassidim* 516.
560   Eruvin 100.
561   Gittin 6b.
562   Ketubot 48a.
563   EH 76:13.
564   Nidda 17.

One may not engage in sexual relations when drunk[565] or angry.[566] Contrary to popular misconception, halacha allows all forms of pleasurable contact during intimacy.[567]

There is no denying that we all seek a rewarding and fulfilling "love life." The problem, unfortunately, is that many people look for the recipes in all the wrong places. The Torah contains the answers for all we seek in life. We need look no further than our own tradition for the key to a harmonious marital life.

WOMEN'S HAIR COVERING

The well-known stamp of an observant married Jewish woman is that her hair is always covered in public. The explanation of this requirement is that a married woman's hair is considered to be an intimate part of her body, to be reserved only for her husband.[568] While there seems to be some basis[569] for the *Fiddler on the Roof* folklore of even unmarried girls covering their hair, this is certainly not the practice today. There are some authorities[570] as well who try to regulate the covering of a woman's hair by making it dependent on her virginal status, but that too is not normative practice.

The source for the practice of a married woman to cover her hair is from the Talmud,[571] which discusses a category of practices that fall under what is known as *Da'at Moshe* and *Da'at Yehudit*, which can be loosely translated as "Torah law" and "Jewish custom," respectively.

Within the discussion of what is to be considered Da'at Moshe, the example of a woman going out with her hair uncovered in

---

565   Pesachim 110.
566   Nedarim 20b: Tosafot, Yevamot 34b.
567   Nedarim 20b; Tosafot, Yevamot 34b, Kalla 1:9, Rambam, *Hilchot Issurei Biah* 21:9; *Sefer Chassidim* 509.
568   Berachot 24a; *Sefer Chassidim* 110.
569   Tur, EH 21.
570   *Be'er Heitev*, EH 21.
571   Ketubot 72a.

public as being forbidden is cited. The scriptural source for this rule is the "Sota" – the woman suspected of adultery who is forced to "uncover her hair" as part of the inquiry process regarding her possible infidelity.[572] Commentators explain that when the Torah tells us to uncover the Sota's hair, we can deduce from this that the norm was for a married woman's hair to be covered.

It seems from the Talmud that strictly speaking, any head covering would be permitted, even one that would leave some hair exposed.[573] Nevertheless, the concept of Da'at Yehudit, normative Jewish custom, requires a more significant hair covering to be worn. Although this level of observance of the practice is far from a requirement, the Talmud favorably discusses a woman named Kimchit who never, ever allowed her hair to be uncovered, even within her own home.[574]

How much hair, therefore, is a woman actually required to cover? According to some authorities,[575] the Talmud means to teach us that the requirement is to ensure that a woman does not go in public *rosha parua* – with her hair completely unattended and exposed. It can therefore be suggested that it may be permissible to allow the exposure of some hair from beneath a head covering, or otherwise to display a limited amount of hair. The Rema himself seems to tolerate this position as well.[576] According to this view, the exposure of up to a *tefach* (fist length) of hair would be permitted. Clearly this opinion is not unanimous, as the *Shulchan Aruch* itself recommends divorcing a woman whose hair is covered with a cloth that allows for even a little bit of hair to be exposed.[577]

What a woman should use to cover her hair is worthy of an essay on its own. Historically, women were encouraged to wear kerchiefs and the like as their hair covering, to the exclusion of everything else.[578] In modern times, wigs have become very popular among

---

572 Bamidbar 5:18.
573 The type of head covering cited is called a *kalta*, which most commentators explain as a hair covering in which some hair would be exposed.
574 Yoma 47a.
575 *Igrot Moshe*, EH 1:58.
576 OC 75:2.
577 EH 115.
578 *Tzemach Tzedek*, Berachot 7.

women due to their realistic look. There are some rabbis nowadays who advocate the wearing of wigs to the exclusion of everything else, citing their tight fit and ability to cover the entire head.[579] Nevertheless, there are a significant number of authorities who oppose the wearing of today's modern wigs.[580] They argue that wigs look identical to real hair, and even result in a woman appearing even more attractive, which is contrary to the spirit of the law. The uproar on the issue of wigs originating from India is beyond the scope of this discussion.

Women who are divorced and widowed are generally expected to continue to cover their hair as well, although there are authorities who allow such women to revert to uncovered hair under very pressing circumstances.[581]

There is no better way to end off a study on such a subject than with the words of Rebbetzin Feige Twerski: "The Almighty, in His great wisdom, has provided us with the laws of *tzniut* [modesty] …the de-emphasis of the outer self that enables the essential self to emerge."[582] When a woman is certain to keep her hair covered, she awakens a certain modesty within herself. Make no mistake, even a married woman must always make herself attractive, but not attracting, saving the latter exclusively for her husband.

CHILDBIRTH

With the impending arrival of a new child to a family, excitement continues to build, especially in the final weeks

---

579   Rema, OC 75:2; *Igrot Moshe*, EH 2:12; this was the view of the late Rabbi Menachem Mendel Schneerson.

580   Over seventy modern-day poskim prohibit the exclusive use of wigs; see *Yabia Omer*, EH 5:5.

581   *Igrot Moshe*, EH 1:57.

582   Cited at http://www.aish.com/family/rebbitzen/On_Hair_Covering.asp. See the article for further philosophical ideas and repercussions of this issue.

leading to delivery.[583] While pregnancy is generally a nine-month (or forty-week) enterprise, things just don't always go as we'd expect. Babies sometimes come late, and sometimes they even come early, however halacha is opposed to inducing a birth, except under very extenuating circumstances.[584] Among the reasons that inducing childbirth is frowned upon is that it causes a soul to enter this world at a time possibly not destined for it to arrive. We are taught that all people are born under some sort of personal *mazal*, and an early delivery could possibly interfere with this Divine intention.[585] Indeed, it is taught in kabalistic works that predetermining birth may cause the child to die at a younger age, God forbid.[586]

It is also possible that inducing a birth may be based on a miscalculated time of conception and hence the baby could be born prematurely with possible health risks. The opposition to inducing is also based on the Mishna, which teaches that one enters this world "against his will." [587] To arbitrarily decide the appropriate time for birth on one's own seems to contradict this venerated rabbinical teaching. It goes without saying that in a situation of the mother's or baby's health being at risk, no matter how slightly, inducing upon a doctor's recommendation is a mitzva and an obligation.

As with all elective surgery, an induced delivery, whether through medication or caesarian section, should ideally never be scheduled on a Thursday or Friday, as according to halacha one should never deliberately put oneself in a situation that may cause an unpleasant Shabbat.[588]

While it is a mitzva to do all that is necessary for a woman in childbirth even on Shabbat, care must be taken to do so minimally and respectfully when requested tasks involve Shabbat violations.[589]

---

583   This chapter based on several articles and rulings by Rabbi Doniel Neustadt, among them http://www.torah.org/advanced/weekly-halacha/5757/tazria.html, and http://www.torah.org/advanced/weekly-halacha/5761/tazriah.html.
584   The Chazon Ish ruled that once a baby is two weeks overdue, inducing is permitted.
585   Rokeach, Kohelet 3:11.
586   Arizal, quoted in *Sefer Hakaneh*.
587   Avot 4:24.
588   *Mishna Berura* 248:4.
589   *Mishna Berura* 330:1.

It goes without saying that all lifesaving measures can be performed on Shabbat or yom tov. If one anticipates a Shabbat delivery, all preparations for Shabbat should be made beforehand including the packing of items one will be taking along to the hospital. Some authorities recommend praying that one's wife not give birth on Shabbat, in order not to "lose" a Shabbat, nor have to face issues of Shabbat desecration.[590] In fact, there were authorities in the past who suggested banning intercourse on certain nights of the week so as not to incur a Shabbat delivery![591]

Being driven to the hospital on Shabbat by a Jew is permissible, but it must be done in a way that minimizes Shabbat transgression, and maximizes the holiness of the day. For example, one should be sure to use the shortest possible route to the hospital, and the interior light in the car should be put in the "off" mode. If there is a need to phone a taxi, doctor, or the like, some authorities recommend that the receiver of the phone be lifted off its cradle and the number dialed in an unusual manner, and the conversation should be as minimal as possible.[592]

On a side note, while it is halachically permissible for the father to be present in the delivery room during delivery, most authorities prohibit the father from observing the actual birthing process.[593]

A short, special blessing known as Hatov v'Hameitiv should be recited promptly after the birth of a son,[594] and when a girl is born, the blessing Shehecheyanu should be recited.[595] It is also recommended that mothers begin to nurse their babies with the left breast, on the side where the heart is.[596]

Of course, everything written here is intended to merely present the various issues involved. For actual halachic guidance, be sure to contact your rabbi. May all children arrive with only blessings and success!

---

590 *Sefer Chassidim* 793.
591 Nidda 38a.
592 Forbidden Shabbat activities that are performed in an irregular manner are far less severe than when performed in their normal manner.
593 See *Bnei Banim* 1:32 for a comprehensive discussion on this issue.
594 OC 223:1.
595 *Mishna Berura* 223:2.
596 *Rabbi Yehuda Hachassid* 55.

A D O P T I O N

For a variety of reasons, couples and families often decide to adopt a child. This unique circumstance of raising a child not biologically related to the family often presents some interesting halachic issues, as well as challenges. Below is a presentation of some of the more routine issues facing those who would choose this option.

Make no mistake, adoption is a highly regarded decision which was exercised by even the greatest figures of the Tanach.[597] For starters, adoption is a great mitzva lauded by the Talmud.[598] Couples who have not had children naturally and decide to adopt are considered to have equal merits and to have fulfilled the requirement to procreate, as all other parents.[599] For the purposes of all of a parent's practical, familial, and social responsibilities, adopted children are considered as biological ones.[600] That's right – adoptive parents are obligated to feed their children just like all others.[601] At the same time, the child is fully enjoined to treat his adoptive parents as other children treat their biological ones, particularly with regard to the mitzva of honoring one's mother and father. It is worth noting that, for a variety of reasons, adopted children should be told at an early age that they are adopted.[602]

One of the considerations when preparing for adoption is whether to prefer a child who is biologically Jewish, or to adopt a child born from a non-Jewish woman. While adopting a Jewish child may often be preferred to some, securing definitive information on the genealogy of the child is often difficult and indeterminate, which could lead to a number of challenges when the time comes to find a spouse. On the other hand, when adopting a non-Jewish baby who is converted shortly after birth, one must bear in mind that

---

597   For example, Mordechai adopted Esther, Michal the wife of King David adopted children. See Sanhedrin 19b.
598   Megilla 13a.
599   *Chochmat Shlomo*, EH 1:1.
600   Rashi, Bereishit 37:10. See CM 42, regarding inheritance.
601   Ketubot 65b.
602   *Teshuvot v'Hanhagot* 2:674.

at maturity, the child may legally abandon Judaism and disqualify the earlier conversion if he or she so desires.[603]

Some of the more difficult halachic issues to deal with in adoption are those of physical contact between the children as they grow up, and with the parent of the opposite sex. Although ordinarily hugging and kissing between members of the opposite sex is forbidden, some authorities allow parents to do so with their adoptive children who were adopted when they were infants.[604] This is because the relationship that develops from such an early age is identical to one that is developed with biological offspring, with no fear of ulterior motives from the parent. Other authorities insist, however, that all regulations such as the prohibition of being alone with the opposite sex, as well as touching, apply to adopted children.[605]

It is interesting to note that there is some debate as to which names should be used on halachic documents, such as a *get* (divorce decree) or *ketuba* (marriage contract) – those of the biological parents or the adopted ones. Some authorities suggest using the adoptive parents' names, but specifying in the document that, indeed, they are adoptive parents.[606] Others are a little more hesitant to completely ignore the child's biological origins, and require the name of the biological parents to be used on all documents.[607] With regard to calling adoptive sons to the Torah, there is more room to consider calling them as "son of" the adoptive father.[608]

End of life issues with regard to adoptive parents are essentially treated the same, in terms of the adopted child's responsibilities.[609] For example, children are to sit shiva and recite kaddish on the passing of their adoptive parents. In reality, however, it would be remiss not to point out that according to many eminent authorities

---

603 Ibid.
604 *Igrot Moshe*, EH 4:64; *Tzitz Eliezer* 1:42.
605 *Shevet Halevi* 5:205.
606 *Igrot Moshe*, EH 4:26; i.e., "Ploni son of Ploni who raised him as his own."
607 *Tzitz Eliezer* 4:22.
608 *Lev Arieh* 1:55, cited in *Minchat Shmuel* by Rabbi Shmuel Khoshkerman (Atlanta: privately printed, 5759 [1998]).
609 *Teshuvot Harama* 118, *Sdei Chemed Aveilut* 156, cited in Khoshkerman, *Minchat Shmuel*.

there is actually no punishment for not doing so, if the child so chooses.[610]

In conclusion, adoption should not be viewed as any different or less meaningful than all other family ties. As with all important decisions in life, a competent orthodox rabbi should always be consulted.

DIVORCE

While marriage is intended to be a once-in-a-lifetime arrangement, unfortunately it isn't always the case. Just as there are stringent requirements on how to formalize a marriage within Jewish law, there are also very exact ways of dissolving one. The objective of it all is to ensure that a woman receives the divorce document from her husband known as a *get*. The get is vital, as without it, a woman is forbidden to remarry.

Sometimes, though, a husband will postpone or otherwise withhold this document from his wife for a variety of motives, thereby imprisoning her in a nonexistent marriage. A complicated question emerging from such behavior is whether or not it is permissible to compel a husband into issuing his wife the get. Sometimes the answer is yes, and even with the use of force, as will be discussed below.[611]

The Mishna[612] teaches us that several types of husbands are obligated to divorce their wives, and that the divorce may even be forced upon them. Among these categories are: one with bad skin afflictions, one with bad breath, and one who gathers manure for a living. A woman whose husband falls into one of these categories is entitled to divorce him at her leisure.

---

610   *Mishne Halachot* 10:153, cited in Khoshkerman, *Minchat Shmuel.*
611   Based in part on "Coercing a Husband to Give a Get" in *Gray Matter: Discourses in Contemporary Halachah* by Rabbi Chaim Jachter with Ezra Fraser (New York: Noble Book Press, 2001), p. 3.
612   Ketubot 77a.

There is, however, another category of husbands for which there is no clear consensus whether a divorce may be forcefully imposed.[613] Rabbinical authorities are divided over whether the *beit din* (religious court) can impose a divorce on a severely strained marriage. On the one hand, there is the Rambam, who maintains that a man can be forced into divorcing his wife if she so desires for absolutely any reason.[614] Other authorities are a lot more hesitant to allow women this dispensation of forced or coerced divorces for fear of ulterior, unbecoming motives.[615] Normative halacha seems to accept this latter view.[616]

There is, however, an additional dimension that allows for imposing a divorce on a rebellious husband, such as one who refuses to support or cohabit with his wife.[617] Modern-day authorities permit forcing such husbands to issue a get.[618] The remaining and forever unsolvable issue is determining who is a "rebellious" husband, other than the example just cited. Does it include an adulterous husband? A thief? What about a husband who abandons Judaism? Furthermore, even when coercion is deemed permissible, it may almost never involve non-Jews in any way,[619] or the divorce could be invalid.

To properly appreciate why rabbis are so hesitant to ever exercise their authority to impose a divorce, it is vital to understand that a woman who remarries after receiving a get that is halachically invalid for any reason is deemed an adulteress, although that is certainly not her intention. Furthermore, any children born after an invalid divorce would be considered *mamzerim* (illegitimate children), a status that is permanent and irrevocable and that strongly affects the child's future marriage prospects and the status of his or her own future children as well.

---

613 Ketubot 70b.
614 *Hilchot Ishut* 14:8.
615 Tosafot, Ketubot 63b.
616 EH 77:2.
617 EH 154:3.
618 *Igrot Moshe*, EH 1:137.
619 I.e., non-Jewish courts, etc.; Gittin 88b.

The emotional and psychological turmoil for women in this situation is unimaginable. The evil that such uncooperative husbands exhibit is indescribable. Sadly, there is no consensus on how these cases can be solved. In light of this, there are authorities in the orthodox rabbinate who have devised a prenuptial agreement of sorts, which combines Jewish and secular law in a way that simply precludes such horrible situations from ever arising. Young couples would be well advised to research this option prior to walking to their wedding canopy.

MARRIAGE

Getting married is a tremendous mitzva, and is, in fact, a biblically mandated obligation.[620] Parents are encouraged to take an active role in all aspects of preparing their children for marriage, as well.[621] As is known, planning a wedding is often a heavy financial burden that many families cannot properly afford. Financially assisting a needy bride and groom with their wedding expenses is considered to be so great a mitzva that a special award awaits in the World to Come for those who do so.[622] This mitzva, known as *hachnassat kalla* (providing for a bride), is best done anonymously.[623] If need be, one may even sell a Torah scroll in order to provide for the wedding needs of a bride and groom.[624] The mitzva of marriage is one of the few dispensations that permit one to leave the Land of Israel.[625]

Our sages have suggested that the ideal age for a man to marry is eighteen years old, but not earlier than thirteen. Not being married by twenty is considered to be very inauspicious.[626] It seems that

---

620   EH 1:1.
621   Kiddushin 29a.
622   Peah 1:1.
623   Sukka 49b.
624   EH 1:2.
625   Avoda Zara 13a.
626   Kiddushin 29b.

women don't have any age guidelines regarding a preferred age to marry – simply whenever they feel ready.[627] Younger sisters should not marry before the older ones in the family.[628] Never marry a woman without checking out her brothers first – your kids may turn out like them![629] And please, do not marry a woman whom you intend to divorce shortly after the wedding.[630]

A man should not marry a woman whose first name is the same as that of his mother.[631] The distinguished rank of the kohanim amongst the Jewish people places upon them numerous restrictions regarding whom they can and cannot marry. For instance, kohanim are prohibited from marrying converts and divorcees, among others.[632]

While going on a blind date may be fun, going on a blind marriage is forbidden. A couple is required to have met face-to-face at least once before getting married.[633] Children need not obey their parents who may oppose their choice of a spouse.[634] One is halachically required to offer a financial reward to the *shadchan*, the individual responsible for having introduced a couple to one another.[635]

Although in theory, a wedding performed on Shabbat would be valid *ex post facto*, common practice is to ensure that weddings are never held on Shabbat for a number of reasons. For one, considering that the finalization of a marriage requires the signing of certain documents, there is a fear that if weddings were conducted on Shabbat, one could inadvertently come to violate the prohibition of writing.[636] Additionally, weddings were forbidden due to their resemblance to a business transaction, which is certainly forbidden to conduct on Shabbat, as technically, a man actually "acquires"

627 Kiddushin 41a.
628 Bereishit 29:26.
629 Bava Batra 110a.
630 Yevamot 37b.
631 *Rabbi Yehuda Hachassid* 23.
632 EH 6:1.
633 EH 21:3.
634 Rema, YD 242.
635 Rema;CM 185.
636 Beitza 37a.

his wife.[637] Similarly, weddings should not be performed on Fridays, lest the festivities lead into, and by extension violate, the sanctity of Shabbat.[638]

It is customary for a groom and bride to fast on their wedding day until after the ceremony has taken place, or until nightfall, whichever comes first.[639] This is because one's wedding day is viewed as a mini Yom Kippur when all of one's sins are forgiven.[640] Additionally, fasting was instituted as a mechanism to ensure that no one would be drunk under the chuppa. If a wedding takes place during certain holidays or other days of significance on the Jewish calendar, the fasting is often waived.[641]

The wedding ceremony as conducted under the chuppa actually consists of two components, the *kiddushin* and *nisuin*. The kiddushin is essentially the formal designation of the bride to the groom, which can be seen as a "halachic engagement" of sorts. In ancient times, the kiddushin was performed as much as a year before the wedding was to take place.[642] Common custom is to perform this ceremony with a gold ring, although any item of value would be acceptable, as well.[643] The concept of a bride giving a ring to the groom under the chuppa as well, often referred to as a "double ring ceremony," is to be strongly discouraged for a variety of reasons.[644]

While there is so much more that can be discussed on this topic, allow me to conclude with wishing you only the greatest peace and success in your marriage. Remember not to get discouraged over an occasional argument with your spouse. Our sages teach us that "there is no marriage without some quarrel."[645]

---

637   EH 4:5.
638   Rambam, *Hilchot Ishut* 10:14.
639   Rema, EH 61:1.
640   Yevamot 63b.
641   OC 573:1.
642   Ketubot 7b.
643   EH 27:1; Kiddushin 2a.
644   *Igrot Moshe*, EH 3:18.
645   Shabbat 129b.

INTERMARRIAGE

Although readers of this work surely do not need convincing on the ills of intermarriage, nevertheless a review of the relevant sources is always therapeutic and strengthening in our commitment to Torah values. It goes without saying that only through fierce resistance to intermarriage can the continuity of the Jewish people truly be assured.

The disapproval of intermarriage is actually one of the oldest Torah-based practices. Indeed, beginning with Avraham, the Jewish nation has been warned to be extremely exclusive about who they do and don't marry. If one examines the extensive preparations that all three Jewish patriarchs – Avraham, Yitzchak, and Yakov – undertook in preparation for the marriage of their children, one will see quite easily how particular they were about who is to be considered a fitting spouse.

For example, when Avraham began searching for a wife for his son Yitzchak, he delegated the selection and interview process to his servant, Eliezer. When instructing Eliezer where to search for a wife for Yitzchak, he strongly and even obsessively stated his expectation that Eliezer search only from among his [Avraham's] family.[646] This is because the Jewish lifestyle was known to be a more dignified one than that of the Gentiles of the time.[647]

With the giving of the Torah, the opposition to intermarriage eventually evolved from merely being a preferred choice to being halachic legislation, as the Torah itself says: "You shall not intermarry with them [the Gentiles]."[648] Of course, this ruling of the Torah is codified as normative halacha.[649]

There are authorities who argue that the true prohibition on intermarriage actually applies only to marrying Gentiles of the

---

646   Bereishit 24:2–8.
647   See Bereishit 19 (Sedom), 20 (Avimelech), 23 (Efron), to name a few Gentile societies with less dignified lifestyles.
648   Devarim 7:3.
649   Avoda Zara 36b; EH 16:1.

nations that existed during the time of the Tanach.[650] Nevertheless, we do find that Nechemia and Malachi extended and enforced the prohibition as referring to all non-Jews.[651] They also forced all those who had previously intermarried to divorce their wives as a prerequisite for admittance into the Land of Israel upon return from the exile.

In all of the above biblical situations, the underlying idea of the prohibition seems to be ideological. Jews have a unique identity that is connected to their purpose in the world, namely, "to be a light unto the nations." They were chosen to propagate ethical and monotheistic values to the world. Intermarriage would inhibit this mission at best, perhaps even destroy it.

In order to deter possible intermarriage, the sages of the Talmud introduced a series of prohibitions not found in the Torah. They did this based on a biblical dispensation awarded to rabbis to create prohibitions that would help strengthen the observance of the Torah's commandments.[652] All of their innovations were accepted as normative and practical Jewish law for all time. These preventative decrees include not eating bread baked solely by a Gentile,[653] not drinking wine prepared by a Gentile,[654] not eating food cooked solely by a Gentile,[655] and sexual intimacy with Gentiles.[656]

The Talmud states that a child born of a Gentile father and a Jewish mother is Jewish.[657] To support this position, the rabbis of the Talmud cite the verse "He [the non-Jewish idolater who is the father of the child] will wean your son away from Me."[658] With this verse, the rabbis teach us that the words "your son" clearly refers to the child of a Jewish mother, and we must therefore conclude

---

650 I.e., the Hittites, the Girgishites, the Amorites, the Canaanites, the Perizzites, the Hivvites and the Jebusites.
651 Nehemiah 10:31; Malachi 2:8–14.
652 Devarim 17:11.
653 YD 112.
654 Avoda Zara 36b; YD 123.
655 YD 113.
656 Bamidbar 25:6–8, Sanhedrin 82a.
657 Yevamot 45.
658 Devarim 7:4.

that at all times and in all cases a child is Jewish if he or she is the offspring of a Jewish woman.[659]

A second reason advanced in support of the view that it is the mother's lineage that counts in determining the Jewishness of a child is that at the moment of birth one is always sure who the biological mother of a baby is, but one cannot be truly positive of the identity of the child's father. Jewish law therefore determined that if a child's mother is Jewish, the child is Jewish, and that Jewishness is passed down to all future generations until the end of time regardless of the father's status.[660]

Many people are not even sure why or where it states that intermarriage is forbidden. Others are embarrassed to discuss the issue for fear of being called racist.[661] We should never forget that our choice of who we marry is based on nothing less than Torah law.

---

659   Kiddushin 68; see also Vayikra 24:11, Melachim I 7:13.
660   See EH 4:5, 19.
661   Make no mistake, opposition to intermarriage is not racist, as anyone can convert regardless of race.

INTERPERSONAL ISSUES

USING FIRST NAMES

Have you ever thought about whether or not it is proper or even permissible for students to address their teachers or for children to address their parents by their first names? According to the Talmud, not only is it forbidden to do so, but the prohibition remains in place even after their passing.[662] It goes without saying that cursing one's parents is forbidden regardless of whether they are living or deceased. As the Rambam explains, even though a parent may not hear or suffer in any way from a child's curse, the parent's dignity is nevertheless being compromised, and it is therefore forbidden.[663] Indeed, during the first year of mourning for a parent, one should accustom oneself to say "that is what my father (or mother) and teacher said" and "let me be an atonement for him (or her)." After the first year, a child is to add the words "may his (or her) memory be a blessing" each time the parent's name is mentioned.[664]

Returning to the question of addressing teachers by their first names, so severe is this act of seemingly innocent informality that the Talmud declares that one who does so is to be considered an *apikores* – one who has deliberately distanced himself from Jewish norms.[665] Gehazi was punished only because he referred to his teacher, Elisha, by his first name.[666] If, however, a title prefaces the teacher's name, it is permissible.[667] That is why the common Israeli practice of addressing a teacher by first name, preceded by "Morah" or "Moreh" (i.e., "Morah Shira"), is halachically acceptable. The Mishna teaches us that one should fear one's teacher just as one would fear heaven.[668] In the Talmudic era, the title "rabbi" was

---

662 Kiddushin 31b. When being called to the Torah one must refer to his father as "Reb" or "Avi Mori." Whenever referring to one's mother, one can use the title "Ha'isha," "Imi Morati," or "Marat." YD 240:2.
663 Rambam, *Hilchot Mamrim* 5:1.
664 YD 240:9.
665 Sanhedrin 100a.
666 Melachim II 8:5.
667 YD 242:24.
668 Avot 4:12.

actually used more for signifying a personal relationship, and not so much as an honorific appellation or scholarly title.

Indeed, one will quickly note that many of the Talmudic sages are not even addressed with the title "rabbi." This was due in part to the cessation of the Sanhedrin, and by extension, the classical *semicha*, or rabbinic ordination procedure.[669] In our day and age, however, the term "rabbi" is always used as a title, and, therefore, reverence is in order when referring to one's Torah teachers. In any event, it is always proper manners and good behavior to speak to our teachers, as well as everyone else, with respect.[670] It would be remiss not to point out, however, that rabbis, teachers, and other people in positions of authority are entitled to forgo any formalities owed them, and to be addressed by their first names.[671] Rav Huna, on the other hand, was very particular to be addressed with his rabbinical title.[672]

Honoring parents, in contrast, is a lot more difficult than merely not calling them by their first names.[673] The Talmud teaches that we may not even sit or stand in a parent's customary place.[674] Furthermore, while common practice may appear to be the reverse, we are also obligated to feed, clothe, and assist our parents with all their chores.[675] These latter obligations reflect our responsibilities with respect to our parents in their old age.

As we have seen, showing respect for other human beings, especially parents and teachers, is not a custom, but rather Torah-mandated practice.

The Talmud relates that when Rabbi Eliezer fell ill, his disciples came to visit him.[676] They asked him, "Rabbi, teach us the correct

669   See http://en.wikipedia.org/wiki/Semicha for more information.
670   *Sefer Chassidim* 579.
671   Kiddushin 32b.
672   Pesachim 86b.
673   We must honor our parents with *sever panim yafot* (pleasantness, literally a pleasant facial countenance); YD 240:4. It is also written that in order to properly perform the mitzva one must view one's parents as royalty. *Sefer Chareidim* 1:35, Chayei Adam 67:3.
674   Kiddushin 31b.
675   Ibid.
676   Berachot 28b.

manner of living so that we may merit to enter the World to Come." Among his responses was: "Make sure to show respect for others!" If you're looking for an easy ticket to heaven, chances are that just being nice to the guy next to you will do the trick.

LENDING MONEY

The prohibition on lending money to another Jew with interest, as well as the mitzva to offer interest-free loans, appears twice in the Torah. Lending money is actually an extraordinary mitzva, with some commentators suggesting that it is as great or even greater than giving charity.[677] This is likely because receiving a loan is far less embarrassing than asking for personal handouts or charity.[678]

An additional benefit to a loan over charity is that a loan may further assist one in becoming financially independent by investing the interest-free money or otherwise putting it to profitable use. Indeed, the Rambam teaches that the greatest form of charity is to help someone become financially independent.[679] Nevertheless, a creditor is certainly entitled to demand a collateral or some other form of guarantee before issuing a loan.

Considering the severe prohibition against taking interest from another Jew,[680] how is it possible, say, for banks in Israel to operate if dealing in interest-generating transactions isn't permitted? Is it not a reality that even observant Jews engage in interest-generating ventures? Could it be that mortgages are interest free in Israel?

Although taking interest is indeed prohibited, there is a procedure in which interest-generating transactions may be performed under a pretext of a "mutually beneficial business transaction." When two parties embark on an interest-generating venture, a special

---

677 Rambam, *Matanot Aniyim* 10:7; see *Sefer Chassidim* 1034.
678 *Sefer Hamitzvot* 197.
679 *Hilchot Matanot Aniyim* 10:1, 7–4; this is the idea of "give a man fish and you've fed him for a day; teach him how to fish and you've fed him for a lifetime."
680 Note: the prohibition against dealing with interest lies on the creditor as well as the borrower. See also *Sefer Chassidim* 1076.

document, known as a *heter iska*, is signed by all parties involved. The heter iska is an innovation instituted by the rabbis in order to ensure that business ventures don't violate the Torah prohibitions on interest; it allows any interest monies to appear as mutually profitable investments. The many exhaustive details on interest and the heter iska are far beyond the scope of this discussion. One must never proceed with interest-related exchanges without first seeking competent rabbinical guidance.

Judaism includes other similar legitimate legal fictions, such as the selling of the chametz before Pesach, the Shabbat eruv in order to permit carrying, and the *prozbul* – the dispensation to collect loans during and after the sabbatical year, an activity otherwise forbidden.[681]

The mitzva of lending interest-free money to a fellow Jew is a positive commandment, even a requirement of the Torah.[682] This mitzva applies regardless of the financial status of the recipient or the purpose of the loan. It is considered meritorious to delay requests for the repayment of a personal loan for as long as one's financial position allows. Nevertheless, one may not begin to demand repayment of a loan until at least thirty days have passed, unless it was agreed to at the time of the loan.[683]

With regard to priorities in issuing loans, relatives always take precedence. Of course, those who are legitimately poor will take precedence over a relative who does have some financial stability, albeit with difficulty. Furthermore, with all things being equal, those immersed in Torah-related occupations take precedence. With the exception of the poor of your own city, there are authorities who rule that the poor of the Land of Israel take precedence over the poor in the rest of the Diaspora.[684] Under most circumstances, it is considered better to lend several small amounts of money to different people rather than one large amount to a single individual.[685]

681 I would include "mezonot bread" in this category as well!
682 *Sefer Hachinuch* 66.
683 Makkot 3b.
684 YD 251:3.
685 CM 97.

The world we live in actually runs on a single economy – acts of kindness. This point is well brought home by God's declaration "I have decreed that the world is built through kindness."[686] Helping others in need in any capacity, particularly the financial, is considered to be partnering with God in the functioning of the world.

CHARITY

Rav Yochanan says: Separate a tenth of your

earnings so that you will become wealthy![687]

One of the first biblically mandated forms of charitable donations relates to our agricultural profits. The Torah teaches us that one who harvests a field should leave a portion of the field untouched so that the poor may come and take of it.[688] Similarly, should one accidentally drop individual stalks when gathering produce, they must not be picked up, but rather left for the poor to come and gather.[689]

Of course, the Torah also instructs us to care for the poor in terms of our financial resources, as well. Not only is it required to give money to the poor,[690] but even offering a loan is considered an important form of charity.[691] The Torah teaches us that being charitable is one of the signs that a person is a true descendant of Avraham our forefather.[692]

---

686 Tehillim 89:3.
687 Ta'anit 9a.
688 Vayikra 23:22.
689 Vayikra 19:9.
690 Vayikra 25:35.
691 Devarim 15.
692 Bereishit 18:8.

It was actually our forefather Avraham who introduced the well-known custom of tithing one's income, known as *ma'aser*, namely, giving ten percent of one's net income to charity.[693] This theme of tithing our resources continues in several other places throughout the Torah, as well. Indeed it is only with regard to charity that one is permitted to tease and test God, as it were. That's right – you may "threaten" God that you're giving charity "on condition" that you become wealthy.[694] We are taught that God ensures high dividends for those who give charity with noble motives.[695]

There is a difference of opinion amongst the halachic authorities as to whether this idea of donating 10 percent of one's income to charity is truly an obligation per se. Some authorities insist that donating ten percent of one's income is actually a biblical requirement,[696] while others limit it to a rabbinically instituted requirement. Yet other authorities assert that the concept of donating ten percent is not a requirement at all, but rather a recommended and meritorious custom. This latter ruling is actually the majority view. Be advised, however, that donating more than twenty percent of your income to charity is actually forbidden[697] unless you're really wealthy.[698]

Regardless of how much one gives, donating to charity is a mitzva required of everyone. Of course, should one be so poor as to not even earn enough money to cover bare essentials for proper sustenance, then such a person would be exempt from making charitable donations.[699] People often forget or don't realize that it is more important to pay off outstanding debts and loans to others before dispensing charity, no matter how noble the cause![700]

No doubt you've often wondered to yourself: which causes are worthy of receiving monies earmarked for charitable purposes? This is an exhaustive topic; a general rule is that supporting actual poor

---

693   Bereishit 14.
694   YD 247:4; *Sefer Chassidim* 144.
695   *Sefer Chassidim* 321.
696   Discussed in *Aruch Hashulchan* 249:5.
697   Ketubot 50a.
698   Chachmat Adam, *Hilchot Tzedaka* 144:10.
699   *Aruch Hashulchan* 251:5.
700   *Sefer Chassidim* 454.

individuals is seen as the ideal use of ma'aser money, although other mitzva-related projects and institutions are legitimate as well. In the event that one has amassed an amount of money intended for charity, but does not desire to distribute it at this time, the money may be put aside in a special fund to be used at a later date.[701]

Who are the poor people we should support? As with lending money, when supporting poor people with charitable gifts, we are taught to support the poor of our community first,[702] but prior to supporting the poor of other communities, the poor of Eretz Yisrael come first.[703]

As can be seen, issues surrounding charity and charitable donations are ones that Judaism takes seriously. May we be found worthy of never needing to be dependent on charity, but rather blessed with the ability to give it handsomely!

WAITING YOUR TURN

No doubt that at one time or another you were standing patiently in some line, and all of a sudden out of nowhere, somebody "butted" into the line. Perhaps complete chutzpa, perhaps someone trying to assist a friend in quickly completing his business. In Israel this upsetting occurrence is commonplace. Frightening screaming matches often break out over the issue. What does halacha have to say about this?[704]

Although it may be hard to believe it, butting into a public line is actually a full Torah prohibition just like any other! More precisely, it falls into the category of theft. Time is money, and butting in front of someone is a theft of his time. It is also a second violation

---

701   *Igrot Moshe* 1:144.
702   Shach, YD 251:6.
703   YD 251:3.
704   Based on an article by Rabbi Aron Tendler, which was based on an article by Rabbi Tzvi Shpitz available at http://www.torah.org/advanced/business-halacha/5757/vol1no04.html.

of the Torah prohibition of "taking advantage of another person."[705] Those who "butt in" are halachically required to reimburse those people in line for their time.

Halacha is so tough on this rude behavior that it is absolutely forbidden for you to tend to your friend's business for him even when it's your turn in line. Say, for example, you're waiting in line at the bank to conduct a routine bill payment, when all of a sudden, a friend walks up to you and asks you to do the same for him. This would be strictly prohibited, as he is required to wait in line just like everyone else! If your intention when arriving at the bank was to do so, however, then it would be perfectly acceptable. These rulings and their parameters are discussed in the *Shulchan Aruch*.[706]

Where do these laws come from, you ask? The Talmud actually introduces these halachic regulations in the context of procedures in a beit din, a rabbinic court. It says there that rabbis must receive congregants and inquiries on a first-come-first-served basis. [707]

Another interesting source for these rules is from a passage in the Talmud, which deals with marine traffic.[708] Say that there are two boats that arrive at the same time to pass through a narrow canal – who goes first? How is a compromise to be found? The answer is that one boat is to proceed first, while compensating the other one for the time it lost while waiting for its turn. You see, no boat truly had the right of way over the other – therefore, the one who chooses to pay for the time saved is entitled to go ahead. Can you imagine what could have possibly happened if one boat was actually in line first with the second boat butting in?

It is quite interesting to see how sometimes obsolete rulings and scenarios can be transplanted to modern-day situations, and actually, quite logically. The Torah and Talmud are teaching us that time truly is worth money. Your spot in line is worth cash!

Now, in the ideal world, the one who pushed ahead of you in line at the grocery store would be willing to pay you the appropriate Torah-mandated damages. The question is, what's your time worth?

---

705 Vayikra 25:15.
706 CM 272:14.
707 Sanhedrin 8a.
708 Sanhedrin 32b.

Although this may not sound too attractive, halacha defines all cases with respect to time reimbursements to be based on the salary of a simple unskilled laborer, and in this specific case – half of it. Say the minimum wage is $10 per hour and you were kept waiting one more hour than necessary – you would only be entitled to $5.

With proper practice of laws such as these one will truly highlight the rabbinic teaching that "Someone who strives for piety should study the laws of damages against one's fellow."[709]

RETURNING LOST OBJECTS

The famous schoolyard saying of "finders keepers, losers weepers" is a concept completely foreign to Judaism. To happen upon a lost object puts an enormous responsibility on one's shoulders, and the laws of how to proceed in such a situation are incredibly complex. The category of halacha that concerns itself with the return of lost objects is known as *hashavat aveida*. So essential is returning lost objects to their rightful owners and taking care of our neighbors' property, that this area of halacha occupies more space within rabbinic literature than tefillin, tzitzit, prayer, and even marriage and divorce. Those who ignore their responsibilities with regard to lost objects violate up to three Torah commandments.[710] The obligations of hashavat aveida apply equally to men and women.[711]

When finding a lost object, one should actually look upon the occurrence as a gift from God, giving one the opportunity to perform this very rewarding mitzva. To begin with, one who finds an object that appears to be lost is obligated to strive to see that it returns to its original owner. This is assuming, of course, that the object has some minimal value, say, of at least five cents. An item

---

709   Bava Kama 30a.
710   Bamidbar 22:3; *Sefer Chassidim* 104.
711   Kiddushin 34a.

virtually worthless (i.e., a toothpick) need not be returned.[712] So too, an item that appears to be intentionally abandoned, such as an old couch or refrigerator at the curb, also need not be returned.[713]

The mitzva of returning lost objects only applies as long as the rightful owner of the item has a realistic hope that the item stands a chance of being returned.[714] If, however, it is reasonable to assume that the owner has abandoned hope of ever recovering the item – say, a person lost a one-hundred-dollar bill in Penn station – then the Torah does not obligate the finder to return it. Accordingly, the finder of such objects may keep them.[715] Nevertheless, it is commendable and very meritorious to go beyond the letter of the law, and attempt to find the owner, especially if the item has identifying markings.[716]

The concept of identifying markings is an interesting topic in its own right. Jewish law offers five very clear definitions as to what is considered to be an identifying marking. These are: an object with an uncommon shape, an object found in an exceptional location, distinctive packaging, an uncommon quantity, and lastly, unique weight.[717] Money (currency as well as coins) is considered to be unidentifiable from the perspective of Jewish law.[718] This is true even if one has memorized the serial numbers on one's paper currency.

Losing an object is truly a frustration, and sometimes even a fearful experience. For those more esoterically inclined, it is taught that donating to charity while saying the words *"Eloka d'Meir aneini* (May the God of Meir answer me)"* repeatedly will encourage the guardian angels of lost objects to quickly reunite you with your lost item.[719] While many attribute this mystical formula to the sage

---

712   I.e., worth a "peruta" or less. See CM 262:1.
713   Bava Metzia 23a.
714   See *Igrot Moshe*, CM 74.
715   Bava Metzia 21b, 26b.
716   CM 259:5.
717   CM 262.
718   CM 262:13.
719   Based on Avoda Zara 18.

Rabbi Meir, the "Meir" in the words *Eloka d'Meir aneini* actually refers to God Himself.[720]

Although observing routine rituals such as prayer, Shabbat, and kashrut is important for our spiritual growth, our sages teach us that the true secret to achieving piety and saintliness is to familiarize oneself with the laws above, and to show concern for other people's property.[721]

HANDICAPS AND BLEMISHES

While the Torah puts every Jew on equal standing and values each one exactly the same, there do exist situations in which handicaps and other imperfections disqualify a person from various capacities. This does not make the disabled person inferior, of course. "Equal but different" is a recurring concept within Torah values.[722]

For example, while one from kohanic lineage is always regarded as a kohen, he is, however, disqualified from most Temple-related duties should he possess certain physical imperfections.[723] The reason for this is that the kohen, who acts on behalf of the entire nation and even represents them before God, should be perfect in every way, both physically and spiritually. We are even instructed to find ways to honor the kohanim and to uphold their dignity, as is befitting their status.[724] Nevertheless, there are some types of duties that even blemished kohanim are permitted to perform, such as preparing the wood for the altar fire and several other custodial

---

720   Maharsha, Avoda Zara 18.
721   Bava Kama 30a.
722   It is worth citing that "every place that the Torah mentions the holiness of the people of Israel, women are also included on an equal basis." *Igrot Moshe*, OC 4:49.
723   Megilla 24b.
724   Gittin 59b; OC 135:3. There are three primary areas in which a kohen is to be honored: to be called to the Torah first, to lead certain prayers and blessings, and to be the first to take his food at a meal. See however *Magen Avraham* 201:4.

procedures. During the Temple era, each kohen actually underwent a daily "blemish-check" by the Great Temple Court.[725]

The basis for excluding those with certain blemishes is from the Torah itself, as it is written: "He who has a blemish shall not approach to make offerings to God."[726] The definition as to what is deemed a blemish is very specific, with the Rambam enumerating no fewer than 140 disqualifying physical blemishes.[727] So serious is this prohibition that a kohen who knowingly served in the Temple while physically imperfect was liable to thirty-nine lashings. It goes without saying that any offerings or services he performed were completely invalid, and that new ones were required.

Only external blemishes disqualify a kohen, and not internal ones, such as the lack of a kidney or appendix. This even includes external blemishes that aren't seen. For example, if the circumcision of a kohen was not cosmetically appealing, it must be repaired even though it may have been properly performed.[728] Even temporary blemishes such as a wart prevent the kohen from performing his duties until the problem goes away.[729] A kohen who arrived to work dirty was sent straight to the showers, and even given some cologne to use. He would also be given breath fresheners if needed.[730]

Another area where Jewish law addresses physical handicaps is regarding those who are deaf and blind. The first mention of such individuals in the Torah is from a sympathetic perspective: "You shall not curse the deaf nor place a stumbling block before the blind, and you shall fear your God; I am the Lord."[731] The status of one who is deaf is discussed at length in the Talmud and codes of law. Although this is now known to be utterly foolish, in ancient times it was believed that those who were deaf were mentally incompetent as well.[732]

---

725   *Sefer Hachinuch* 276.
726   Vayikra 21:17.
727   Rambam, *Hilchot Biat Hamikdash* 7, 8.
728   Shabbat 136a.
729   Eruvin 103a.
730   Rambam, *Hilchot Biat Hamikdash* 7:13.
731   Vayikra 19:14.
732   Chagiga 2b.

Deaf people could not serve as witnesses in a Jewish court,[733] and they were often not held liable for injuries that they themselves caused.[734] The deaf were also banned from real estate transactions,[735] and were limited in ritual responsibilities, including being disqualified from blowing the shofar on Rosh Hashana[736] or serving as a ritual slaughterer.[737] There were even additional limitations that were placed on those who were both deaf and mute.[738]

Make no mistake, all modern-day halachic authorities consider those who are deaf but otherwise fully functional to be legally equal to all other Jews and obligated in all ritual duties.[739] Indeed, in all congregations, those who are deaf but can otherwise function normally are counted for a minyan and invited for aliyot to the Torah just like all other congregants.

Let us pray to soon see the promised day when all sickness and suffering will be healed, "the eyes of the blind shall be opened and the ears of the deaf shall be unstopped,"[740] with the arrival of Mashiach.

LIFESPANS

We all know that when wishing people long life, we traditionally wish them a life of 120 years. Have you ever explored the source of this idea?

Our first encounter with the concept of defining a lifespan to be 120 years is found early on in the Torah, as it is written: "And God says My spirit shall not always contend on account of man since he is but flesh, his days shall be 120 years."[741] This verse,

---

733   CM 35:11.
734   CM 424:8.
735   CM 235:17.
736   OC 589:2.
737   Chullin 2.
738   Chagiga 2b.
739   *Shut Rav Azriel* 2:58.
740   Yeshayahu 35.
741   Bereishit 6:3.

which appears almost immediately after the creation of man, is an obvious association of 120 years as being the ideal human lifespan. Some interpretations suggest that this may be because 120 years is the amount of time needed for a person to properly prepare to meet the Creator.[742] Indeed, God allowed Noah 120 years to complete the construction of the ark, in order to allow the rest of the world the opportunity to properly repent and perhaps avert the flood.

Notwithstanding the aforementioned, the prominence and focus of the "120 years" adage likely emerged due to its association with Moses, the most revered and cherished Jewish leader of all time, who lived to be 120. Before he died, Moses said, "I am one hundred twenty years old this day, I can no longer go out and come in."[743] Many commentators explain that "I can no longer go out" refers to a Divine decree that life must end by 120 years of age.[744]

According to tradition four people lived to be precisely 120: Moses, Hillel, Rabbi Yochanan Ben Zakkai, and Rabbi Akiva.[745] There were some individual exceptions to this rule, but their explanations are beyond the scope of this discussion. Here are some tips for a better chance of living to a ripe old age: never use a synagogue as a shortcut, be the first one to the synagogue every day, don't call anyone by a nickname, never miss Kiddush on Friday night, and never stare at evil people.[746] Ladies – lighting your Shabbat candles with olive oil will increase your odds for a long life even more.[747]

Although living to 120 years old is certainly a commendable goal, we do see that it is not an absolute ideal, and that shorter lifespans are also considered dignified accomplishments. Among the exceptional lifespans was Rabbi Yehoshua Ben Karcha, who lived to 140. It is noted that Rabbi Yehoshua Ben Karcha had blessed Rabbi Yehuda Hanassi (author of the Mishna) that he merit to attain "half of my age,"[748] thus affirming seventy years as a legitimate lifespan.

---

742   Sforno, Sanhedrin 108.
743   Devarim 31:2.
744   Rashi and Sforno, among others.
745   Tosafot, Bechorot 58a.
746   Megilla 27b, 28a.
747   *Sefer Chassidim* 272.
748   Megilla 28a.

Moses himself seems to certify seventy years as a complete lifespan as well when he says, "The days of our years are seventy years, and with might, eighty years."[749]

Once we do leave this world, is there ever a return? Although not unanimously, it is generally accepted that reincarnation is, in fact, a Jewish concept.[750] It is implemented by God in the event that a soul has not completed its mission in this world, allowing the soul to return to finish that task.[751] Other authorities reject the idea of reincarnation outright, citing it as an example of pagan influence on Judaism.[752]

Regardless of whether the ideal lifespan is seventy, eighty, or 120 years old, what is certain is that this world is no more than a vestibule and a preparatory period for the eternal World to Come.[753] And one day soon, may we merit the fulfillment of the prophecy that "those who sleep in the dust will awaken and sing joyful praises"[754] with the resurrection of the dead. Amen.

---

749 Tehillim 90:10.
750 Iyov 33:29; all writings of the Arizal; Ramban, Bereishit 28:8; and many others.
751 Zohar I 186b.
752 Rabbi Yosef Albo in *Sefer Ha'ikarim* 4:29, and Rabbi Saadia Gaon in *Emunot v'Deot* 6:8.
753 Avot 4:21.
754 Yeshayahu 26:19.

INDIVIDUAL
CHOICES

BIRTHDAYS

"Most people cherish the day on which they were

born and make a party on that day."[755]

Judaism teaches that a birthday is not just another day. The Torah even offers some insights and party tips on how a birthday is to be observed.[756] Everyone should be sure to know the date of his or her Hebrew birthday.

The Jewish nation as a whole celebrates its birthday every year – Pesach! This holiday of liberation and redemption has often been referred to as the birthday of the Jewish nation. Indeed, no less a personage than the prophet Ezekiel recommends that we observe Pesach as a national birthday party.[757] Rashi even suggests that we should each imagine that we're newborn babies every year at Pesach.[758] It is interesting to note that the date on which the world was actually created remains unresolved, and hence, we don't know when to celebrate its true birthday.[759]

While birthday parties include delicious cake, and rightfully so, we should perhaps discourage the practice of lighting candles on a birthday cake, as it is actually an evil pagan custom, according to Philochorus, the Greek historian. It was even believed that birthday candles have the power to make dreams come true, hence the custom of making a wish before blowing out the candles.[760] It is also worth bearing in mind that blowing out candles at any time is to be discouraged, due to the close symbolic connection between a candle and a soul.[761]

---

755   Midrash Sechel Tov, Bereishit 40:20.
756   Bereishit 40:20.
757   Based on Yechezkel 16:4.
758   Ibid.
759   Rosh Hashana 10b.
760   Cited in Rabbi Avrohom Blumenkrantz, *The Laws of Pesach*, 2001.
761   Mishlei 20:27.

The day of one's birth offers that individual the mystical benefits and powers of what is known in kabbala as "ascending fortune." It is therefore considered worthwhile to seek a blessing from one celebrating his or her Hebrew birthday. Such blessings are said to have a good chance of being fulfilled. On one's birthday it is appropriate to focus on one's individuality and reflect on one's personal interpretations of the Talmudic teaching that "the world was created for me."[762]

The acceptance of good resolutions in honor of one's birthday contributes to the Jewish nation as a whole, and brings us closer to the messianic era. The power of change on one's birthday has the potential of bringing redemption on that very day.[763]

It goes without saying that the twelfth birthday for girls and the thirteenth birthday for boys has special significance. The Zohar explains that in terms of joy, the day one is bar or bat mitzva is comparable to the day of one's wedding.[764]

Just as the birthday of our people is celebrated each year with rites and rituals, so too, the birthday of every individual Jew should be appropriately observed. In recent years, rabbinical authorities, most notably the late Lubavitcher Rebbe, have compiled a number of customs to be observed in honor of one's birthday, which include to endeavor to be called to the Torah on the Shabbat before one's birthday (when the birthday occurs on a day that the Torah is read, you should be called to the Torah on that day, too), to dispense extra charity on your birthday, and to throw a party with your family and friends in honor of your birthday. Additionally, in the spirit of the day, it is commendable to pray with greater intensity and concentration (especially with the recitation of psalms), to accept taking on some new act of piety or Torah observance, and to make resolutions for the coming year.

As we can well see, a Jewish birthday is not a day to be wasted, but rather a day to be maximized with Torah study and religious

---

762 Sanhedrin 37a.
763 Based on Tehillim 95:7.
764 Zohar Chadash, Bereishit.

practices. We must also be sure to thank God for our milestone, which some do by reciting the blessing of Shehecheyanu.

SECULAR STUDIES

Upon conclusion of the Flood, and mankind's return to dry land, Noah bestowed blessings (and curses!) upon each of his sons.[765] The blessing he bestowed upon his son Yefet is quite unclear, even mysterious. Noah blesses him: "May God expand Yefet, and may he dwell in the tents of Shem."[766]

Why should Yefet dwell in his brother Shem's tents? What is so special and what kind of blessing is it to have to rely on someone else?

To properly understand this blessing, we must understand what the sons of Noah represent. Yefet was the forerunner of the Greek nation, while Shem was the forerunner of the Jewish nation. This blessing thus prophetically relates to the beauty and intellectual accomplishments of Greek culture. The Talmud explains the meaning of the blessing to be "May the beauty (i.e., intellectual accomplishments) of Yefet reside in the tents of Shem (i.e., serve well for the Jews)."[767]

Noah's blessing served to link his sons Yefet and Shem together, thereby connecting the national cultures of their descendants, the Greeks and the Jews. What is the extent of this relationship, however? We all know from the story of Chanuka that these two civilizations clashed violently during the Second Temple period. How can we justify praying that the Greek culture reside in the tents of Israel?

Intriguingly, the Talmud never explicitly prohibited studying Greek philosophy nor banned having any relationship with

---

765 Based on an article by Rabbi Chanan Morrison adapted from Rav Kook, *Moadei Hare'iya* pp. 182–84. Article available at http://www.geocities.com/m_yericho/ravkook/NOAH65.htm.
766 Bereishit 9:27.
767 Megilla 9b.

Greek culture. In fact, it is actually recommended to study Greek philosophies and other secular knowledge in one's free time, as Rabbi Yishmael instructed his nephew: "Find an hour...and study Greek wisdom."[768]

Although secular culture and wisdom may have beneficial purposes and uses, the timing for such studies must be ripe and responsible, lest it replace the centrality of Jewish studies. For example, our sages teach that "Cursed be the one who teaches his son Greek wisdom."[769] Secular knowledge is fine, but at the right time and for the right audience. One does not study the Talmud before one has been acquainted with the Torah. So too, we ought not study foreign subjects until our own are well established within us. Young students need to first acquire a solid basis in Torah. Only then will they be able to discern the difference between legitimate Torah thought and ideas that derive from foreign sources.

Contrary to popular belief, there are actually many authorities who encourage the study of secular subjects when intended to qualify one for earning a living, or even to just gain a better understanding of the wonders of creation.[770] The Rambam at the beginning of his *Mishna Torah* explicitly says that one should meditate on the wonders of nature, as explained in science, in order to better achieve love of God and fear of heaven. The debate as to what to study and when to study it is also to be found in the *Shulchan Aruch*, with several authorities permitting the study of secular subjects as long as Torah knowledge is one's primary academic pursuit in life.[771]

In a published essay, Rabbi Mordechai Willig addresses a variety of secular subjects one by one, discussing the various views that exist regarding the permissibility of studying each of those subjects.[772] A fascinating point worth highlighting here is that while citing the *Shulchan Aruch* as an authority that bans the study of history,[773]

768   Menachot 99b. While this Gemara can be interpreted as forbidding Greek culture, others suggest that it comes to encourage an emphasis and centrality in Torah study – not necessarily that other studies are forbidden.
769   Bava Kama 82b.
770   Tanya 8; Berachot 35b.
771   Rema, YD 246:4.
772   *Torah Umadda Journal* 1 (1989).
773   OC 307:16.

Rabbi Willig quotes Rabbi Yakov Emden, who writes that it is important that a scholar not appear unlearned or otherwise an ignoramus in the eyes of others. This is a tremendous insight. The possible perception that Jews are incompetent in worldly matters is nothing short of a *chillul Hashem* (desecration of God's name). The Yeshiva University model is probably the best known example of an appropriate balance between religious and secular studies.

Do note, however, that secular wisdom as a philosophy or way of life is illegitimate when it contradicts Torah thought or values. To quote Rabbi Norman Lamm: "We are committed to secular studies, including our willingness to embrace all the risks that this implies, not alone because of vocational or social reasons, but because we consider that it is the will of God that there be a world in which Torah be effective; that all wisdom issues ultimately from the Creator, and therefore it is the Almighty who legitimates ALL knowledge."[774] We have no need to borrow from the content of foreign cultures when our own traditions are so rich, meaningful, and stimulating. We may, however, accept ideas from other peoples that can add to or enhance the beauty of Judaism. Even after all the clashes with Hellenism, the sages still taught us that it is fitting to adopt stylistic enhancements: "May the beauty of Yefet be in the tents of Shem."

It is not an embarrassment for us to utilize what other nations have developed. It was none other than Moshe Rabbeinu who sought counsel with a Midianite priest on establishing an efficient judicial system.[775] King Solomon himself turned to Hiram, the king of Tyre, for his expertise on building the Holy Temple: "For we have not any among us who know how to hew timber like the Zidonians."[776] Enjoy and utilize those ideas to strengthen your Judaism. As the Rambam writes, "Accept the truth from whatever its source."[777]

---

774   Cited at http://israelvisit.co.il/top/ll8.shtml from "Modern Orthodoxy's Identity Crisis," *Jewish Life* (May-June 1969): 7.
775   Or Hachaim, Shemot 18:21.
776   Melachim I 5:20.
777   In the introduction to his commentary on Pirkei Avot.

TAX EVASION

With tax season forever looming above our heads, it is always an appropriate time to discuss the halachic issues involved with tax evasion and other seemingly innocent and insignificant dishonesties. How about not paying taxes altogether? Is there a difference between sales taxes and income taxes? Let's explore some of the pertinent issues.

It's undeniable that there is an undercurrent of almost silent social acceptance that getting away with not paying taxes, or more specifically, not paying the right amount of taxes, is acceptable. No doubt that it is no surprise to learn that Jewish law is opposed to cheating on taxes – a violation of both secular and religious law.[778] As the Talmudic sage Shmuel decreed: "You must follow the laws of the land you live in!"[779] This ruling dictates that any laws of the countries in which Jews live that do not violate Torah law must be meticulously obeyed. Even more than this – such secular laws may even assume the status of Torah laws themselves! It goes without saying that it is forbidden to assist others in breaking secular laws.[780]

The Rambam eloquently clarifies these laws regarding our tax-related responsibilities and states that tax evasion is especially severe in a place "that the currency is stable and accepted throughout the land and that the citizens of the country are governed by and accept upon themselves a single sovereign authority"[781] – referring to countries governed by the rule of law, which likely includes almost every place in the world where Jews reside today. Rabbi Moshe Feinstein writes that tax cheaters require extensive repentance including a commitment never to do so again.[782] And no, tax evasion is not permitted even when the money saved will be dedicated for mitzva purposes.[783] Additionally, some people mistakenly believe

---

778   *Sefer Chassidim* 278.
779   Bava Kama 113a.
780   Vayikra 19:14.
781   Rambam, *Hilchot Gezeila* 5:18.
782   *Igrot Moshe*, CM 1:88.
783   Sukka 30a.

that one is not required to pay taxes in Israel.[784] It may however be permitted to avoid paying taxes in a country where Jews suffer from state-sponsored persecution. A full treatment of all these laws however, is beyond the scope of this discussion.

Purchasing items from a Jewish merchant who forgoes reporting sales tax is also a serious issue dealt with at length in the Talmud.[785] In such a case, both the customer and the merchant would be guilty of violating one or more Torah prohibitions. The late Rabbi Joseph B. Soloveitchik is known to have stated that patronizing a Jewish merchant who cheats on his taxes is forbidden.

The Jewish people are supposed to behave and set an example as "a kingdom of priests and a holy nation."[786] Dealing dishonestly is in the severe category of transgressions referred to as an "abomination."[787] It was due to none other than dishonest behavior that in the era of Noah, God decided to send a flood and destroy the world.[788]

When a Jew gets caught in dishonest dealings, a true desecration of our people, religion, and nation ensues. Causing such a disgrace is a severe Torah prohibition in its own right.[789] For those who believe that it is permitted to steal from non-Jews,[790] get this: theft from a Gentile may actually be worse than theft from a Jew due to the terrible humiliation it places upon all Jews. [791] Furthermore, Rabbi Gamliel specifically stated: "Don't steal from Gentiles!"[792] Not only are we forbidden to steal from others from a financial perspective, but we also may not steal from an intellectual perspective either, such as knowingly offering bad advice or otherwise acting deceptive or phony.[793]

---

784 Ran, Nedarim 28a; compare CM 369:6.
785 Bava Metzia 75b.
786 Shemot 19.
787 Devarim 25:16.
788 Rashi, Bereishit 6:11.
789 Vayikra 22:32.
790 CM 359:1.
791 Tosefta, Bava Kama 10:8; *Sefer Chassidim* 358, 1074.
792 Yerushalmi Bava Kama 4:3; *Sefer Chassidim* 358.
793 Tosafot, Chullin 94a, Gittin 62.

We are commanded as Jews, let alone as upright citizens, to keep to the highest levels of business ethics. In fact, the Talmud teaches that when we reach the heavenly court at the end of days, we'll be asked, "Did you conduct business honestly?"[794] Let's work on ourselves to ensure that we will be able to proudly respond with the right answer.

GAMBLING

Although many casinos today are large and beautiful edifices of multimedia entertainment, with hardly a scent of the gaming imagery of old, there are however numerous issues that every Jew should be aware of in order to make educated decisions about patronizing casinos and engaging in other gambling-related activities.

The Mishna in two separate places states that one who gambles is disqualified from serving as a witness in ritual matters.[795] Although this may appear trivial and insignificant, it is actually considered to be a drastic penalty. Such a status would disqualify someone from even being able to certify or be relied upon to say such-and-such food is kosher!

There is a difference of opinion as to what constitutes halachically problematic gambling and at what point someone is to be considered a gambler and disqualified as a witness. According to Rabbi Yehuda, gamblers are only ostracized when they rely on gambling as their sole source of income.[796] If, however, they do engage in a trade or some kind of stable profession, it would be considered tolerable to

---

794   Shabbat 31a.
795   Rosh Hashana 22a; Sanhedrin 24b. Although issues relating to testimony generally apply only to a man, this disqualification would extend to women as well. The Talmudic rule of *Eid echad ne'eman b'issurim* (any single person suffices in matters relating to prohibitions) allows women to serve as witnesses in such matters as kashrut (Chullin 10).
796   In Sanhedrin 24b, as explained by Rashi.

occasionally gamble. Indeed, this position seems to be the halacha as legislated in the Shulchan Aruch.[797]

The Talmud's displeasure with gambling is twofold. Firstly, gambling is not considered to be a dignified or appropriate use of one's time and resources, and furthermore, it is likely to breed unbecoming behavior.[798] An additional, more serious concern as to why gambling is frowned upon is that when two people enter into a wager, each one is confident that he is going to emerge victorious and that the opponent will lose. Since the loser does not truly willingly surrender the wagered money, the winner is considered in the eyes of halacha to actually be committing a form of theft when he collects.[799] A thief is ineligible to serve as a witness or judge.[800] The Rambam takes this form of theft – receiving money from someone who doesn't truly wish to give it – most severely.[801] Other authorities add to the displeasure with gambling, arguing that it leads people to unproductive lifestyles.[802] Indeed, King David wastes no time admonishing those who spend their time in unproductive and meaningless pursuits.[803]

In a casino setting, however, the structure is such that no single individual loses personal income when the dealers or machines lose at the games, and therefore, the concern of theft could perhaps be dismissed. Although there are authorities who prohibit any form of card playing at any time,[804] institutionalized and government-regulated gambling today can be viewed differently than it was in the past. Indeed, casino gambling today is more like a business transaction or entertainment when done with responsible moderation. Some authorities allow any gambling even between individuals, as long as no real skill is involved.[805] In any event, the Rambam seems to allow one to gamble if he currently holds

---

797 CM 34:16.
798 Sanhedrin 24b.
799 *Sefer Chassidim* 400.
800 Sanhedrin 24b.
801 *Hilchot Gezeila* 6:10.
802 The view of Rav Shehset in the Sanhedrin reference.
803 Tehillim 1:1.
804 *Biur Halacha*, OC 670:2.
805 CM 207:13; i.e., playing dreidel.

a steady source of income and his gambling is merely occasional entertainment.[806] Alternatively, it may be suggested that if one would like to engage in casual gambling, it should be in the company of family and close friends and not with complete strangers.[807]

If you're the type who stands in line at the lotto booths, don't panic. Lotteries are slightly different from the issues of gambling discussed above. Indeed, even yeshivot and synagogues are known to hold annual raffles. Many authorities sanction this practice, especially when the prize is a donated object.[808] Common lottery tickets are also permitted by many authorities as a business transaction and entertainment and are not considered problematic gambling.[809] No need to purchase more than one lottery ticket per drawing, though – if God intends for you to win or lose, it'll happen whether you buy one, ten, or fifty lotto tickets![810]

On a more serious note, regardless of the halachic permissibility of the matter, it must be recognized that gambling has been the cause of divorce, suicide, and other evils. As with all addictive substances and behaviors, including those that Judaism may allow, moderation is strongly advised. One should not be afraid to seek professional help if needed.

CAREERS

While a Jewish parent typically wants his or her child to end up something like a doctor or a lawyer, the Talmud has its own approach regarding what is to be deemed a proper and worthy occupation. Choosing a career is not merely an arbitrary decision, and it too is an issue discussed and even regulated by our sages. One thing is for certain: a lifestyle revolving around intentional unemployment is completely unacceptable from the perspective of

---

806   *Hilchot Edut* 10:4.
807   Shabbat 149b.
808   Discussed at length in *Yabia Omer*, CM 7:6.
809   *Yaskil Avdi* 8:5. For an opposing view see *Yabia Omer*, CM 7:6.
810   Mishlei 16:33.

Torah thought.[811] Even the greatest Talmudic sages had "real" jobs. For example, Hillel was a woodchopper,[812] Shammai built houses, and Abba Shaul dug graves for a living.[813] Rashi even managed to master every single Jewish text and still found time to preside over his French winery.[814] In recent times, the much celebrated Chafetz Chaim was a grocer. As a matter of fact, it's quite mind-boggling that so many parents encourage their children to become doctors, as all doctors eventually end up in hell![815]

Before we explore the various pearls of wisdom offered by our sages on this vital issue, it is important to highlight that, ultimately, the Talmud's only prerequisites in choosing a profession are that it be a dignified occupation and that it allow time for spiritual pursuits. Nevertheless, it is far better to hire oneself out to do menial labor than to rely on charity.[816] As a practical matter it is recommended to follow in the professional footsteps of one's parents.[817] One should never, but never, rely on one's wife's earnings for a family's livelihood.[818]

Money earned during the course of one's profession is to be considered as a reward from God,[819] and must be used for noble purposes.[820] The Talmud also tells us how to manage our financial portfolios to ensure maximum returns: diversify![821] We are also taught that engaging in our business pursuits honestly will ensure much-needed Divine assistance in our financial security.[822]

Are you one of those people who looks to bring home the big bucks regardless of the type of work that it may require? The Talmud teaches that the ideal trade to engage in if it's wealth that

---

811   Ketubot 59b.
812   Yoma 35b.
813   Nidda 24b.
814   *Teshuvot Rashi* 382.
815   Kiddushin 82a.
816   Bava Batra 110.
817   Erchin 16b.
818   Pesachim 50b.
819   Ta'anit 9a.
820   Eruvin 68a.
821   Bava Metzia 42a.
822   Nidda 70b.

you seek is to open a brewery.[823] If that doesn't work, raise cattle.[824] If you would like to ensure that you never become wealthy, become a scribe – poverty is assured.[825] Furthermore, if you seek a job that will ensure that you'll never get dirty, become a tailor.[826] A rabbi will never be poor, [827] but may drop dead while on the job.[828] If you seek happiness, become a spice dealer.[829]

There are yet additional professions worthy of consideration, as well. If you're looking for a job that assures you a place in heaven, become a clown.[830] Are you one who strives to emulate God? These days He's working as a matchmaker,[831] so maybe try that as well.

One should of course avoid all professions that encourage dishonesty, immorality, and arrogance. It also appears that becoming a donkey driver, sailor, or even a storekeeper is not recommended.[832] Never forget that your local butcher is to be considered your enemy.[833] A tax collector is really a robber in disguise.[834] A man is advised not to take a job in which he will be constantly surrounded by women.[835] Consequently, jewelers, perfume salesmen, and hairdressers are prone to bad character.[836] A lumberjack will never see a sign of blessing in his work.[837]

There you have a sampling of the Talmud's perspectives as to which professions our children should and should not enter. As mentioned above, whatever profession you do choose to pursue, be sure to always do it honestly and with integrity.

---

823   Pesachim 113a.
824   Chullin 84.
825   Pesachim 50.
826   Berachot 63.
827   Shabbat 151b.
828   *Sefer Chassidim* 70.
829   Bava Batra 16; early aromatherapy, perhaps?
830   Ta'anit 22a.
831   Sota 2a; Bereishit Rabba 68.
832   Kiddushin 82a.
833   Ibid.
834   Sanhedrin 25b.
835   Kiddushin 82a.
836   Ibid.
837   Pesachim 50b.

PETS

It's quite common in many homes to find all sorts of pets, and as with everything else in our lives, halacha has much to say on pet care and related issues. Actually, one would be well advised to be extra careful in this area of Jewish practice, as Moses was chosen leader of the Jewish people due to his great concern for animals.[838]

Indeed, there is no lack of material in the Talmud on this subject, as pets were fairly common during the biblical and Talmudic periods. In fact, the children of the Talmud regularly played with birds[839] and locusts,[840] among other pets. Be advised, however, that it is recommended that one not raise pigeons or doves as pets – it could be fatal.[841]

Today's most common household pet is certainly the dog. Although the halachic authorities are far from unanimous, it is generally accepted that a gentle dog with a soft bark is permitted to be kept as a pet.[842] However, owning a dog or any other pet that instills fear or causes harm, whether through bark or bite, is clearly forbidden.[843] Indeed, there are documented cases of pet dogs that have caused pregnant women to miscarry due to their frightening bark.[844] Nevertheless, it may just be that dogs in biblical times were exceptionally wild and nasty,[845] unlike Snoopy and Marmaduke. It is also worth mentioning that among all the guests in Noah's ark, there were only three that violated God's commandment not to have sexual relations while on the Ark.[846] They were: Noah's son Ham, the dog, and the raven.

---

838 Shemot Rabba 2:2.
839 Bava Batra 20a.
840 Shabbat 90a.
841 *Rabbi Yehuda Hachassid* 8 (Nosafot).
842 Bava Kama 80a; Rambam, *Nezikei Mamon* 5:9, 10.
843 Bava Kama 15b.
844 Ibid. 83a.
845 Tehillim 22:17, 59:17.
846 Rabbi Yochanan said: Had the Torah not been given, we would have learned modesty from the cat, [the prohibition of] theft from the ant, [the prohibition of] forbidden relationships from the dove, and the proper method of conjugal relations from fowl," Eruvin 100b. *Sefer Chassidim* 47.

There are other Torah-related issues that arise in the care of animals, as well. For example, the Talmud requires us to feed our pets prior to feeding ourselves,[847] and this is even legislated halacha.[848] When thirsty, though, it is permissible to grab a drink prior to offering one to your equally thirsty pet.[849]

Believe it or not, pets are also obligated to keep kosher. Actually, that is not entirely true, but it is forbidden to feed them a mixture containing both milk and meat. This is because the Jewish people are forbidden to make use of milk and meat mixtures in any way, even for serving to animals.[850] Pets also may not be fed any chametz on Pesach. In fact, one must "sell" all the chametz dog food to the Gentile, along with the rest of one's household chametz.[851] Rabbi Pinchas Ben Ya'ir's pet donkey would reportedly eat only glatt kosher.[852]

A Jew's pet is actually in some ways considered a Jew as well. Jewish-owned pets must observe Shabbat like the rest of us. For example, one may not allow one's pet to carry something in a public area where there is no eruv.[853] Furthermore, on Shabbat, one must avoid trapping one's pets in any way[854] and even limit any physical contact with them due to their *muktza* status (items that have no Shabbat use are rabinically forbidden to be touched on Shabbat lest one come to absentmindedly use them). Don't be alarmed if your pets suddenly begin to speak to you – it wouldn't be the first time.[855] Last but not least, those who require the use of guide dogs will be pleased to know that they are eligible for membership and seating privileges in any synagogue.[856]

The issues discussed above are but a drop in the sea of halachic and ethical issues involved in pet care. One would be well advised

---

847   Berachot 40a.
848   OC 167:18.
849   Bereishit 24:14; *Kitzur Shulchan Aruch* 42:1.
850   Chullin 115.
851   OC 448:17.
852   Chullin 7a.
853   Shemot 20:10.
854   Shabbat 106b.
855   Bereishit 3:1; Bamidbar 22:28.
856   *Igrot Moshe* 1:45.

to seek sound rabbinic advice prior to assuming the role of pet owner.

COSMETIC SURGERY

With beauty occupying such a prominent role in our materialistic lifestyles, the question of cosmetic surgery often arises as part of the beautifying wardrobe. Beauty has joined forces with modern medicine and has come to the point where one can actually shape and sculpt one's body to conform to one's every desire and taste. Would this be a blasphemous form of "playing God"? Even worse, it may be a form of rejecting God and his plans for our individual bodies. What does Jewish law have to say on cosmetic surgery?

It is well known that any surgery, especially involving general anesthetic, poses significant risks. The first issue that arises when dealing with this question then is obviously the permissibility of purposely causing a wound to one's body, an activity that the Talmud clearly prohibits.[857] Indeed, contact sports like boxing, wrestling, and karate may pose serious halachic concerns as they, too, are activities in which one knows that physical harm is likely to ensue.[858] To hit another person, even when it is clear he won't be wounded, is strictly prohibited by the Torah. Similarly, it is biblically prohibited to expose oneself to any apparent dangers for no valid reason.[859]

Make no mistake, surgical procedures that can save one's life are permissible, even obligatory.[860] Where, however, do all these tucks, lifts, nose jobs, liposuctions, and intimate body enlargements fit within halachic parameters?

---

857 Bava Kama 91.
858 Rambam, *Hilchot Chovel* 5.
859 Devarim 4:9, consider, for example, skydiving.
860 Vayikra 18:5.

Probably the two most prominent contemporary authorities to directly address this issue have been Rabbi Moshe Feinstein and Rabbi Eliezer Waldenberg (the author of the *Tzitz Eliezer*). Rabbi Waldenberg argues extensively against the practice of cosmetic surgery, claiming that a doctor's role should be purely that of a healer of illness, and not that of a beauty consultant.[861] He also mentions well-known cases of cosmetic surgery leading to illness and even death (e.g., silicone implants), as well as the negative side effects of the anesthetics. Rabbi Waldenberg also considers plastic surgery sacrilegious and a prohibited form of attempting to intervene in God's designs and handiwork. Attempting to enhance one's looks is also known to have disastrous effects on one's character.[862]

A more lenient approach to plastic surgery comes from Rabbi Moshe Feinstein. Among the lenient considerations he puts forward is the possible humiliation a person may be continually feeling inside due to his or her appearance. In this sense, cosmetic surgery can be the solution to one's embarrassment, and help with one's self-esteem, which is ultimately a beneficial and praiseworthy purpose.[863]

Some of the more lenient authorities also apply a far-reaching Talmudic principle that even when something may be slightly dangerous, but has nevertheless become a mainstream practice, then it is minimal cause for concern and even permitted.[864]

Another somewhat similar angle that may allow for cosmetic surgery is in a case where a person is suffering extreme psychological and emotional distress over appearance. Mental health is taken quite seriously by halacha, and is considered comparable to other medical conditions for which one should and must seek healing.[865] For example, while normally prohibited, abortion may be permitted for a rape victim, who would have severe mental and emotional distress throughout her life if she were to carry the fetus to term, and

---

861   *Tzitz Eliezer* 11:42.
862   Ta'anit 23b.
863   *Igrot Moshe*, CM 2:66, *Chelkat Yakov* 3:11, *She'arim Metzuyanim b'Halacha* 190:4.
864   Shabbat 129b.
865   Tosafot, Shabbat 128b, 50b.

even more so if she would have to raise the child. A full treatment of this issue is beyond the scope of this discussion.

Cosmetic surgery is an option that may be appropriate for some and not for others. Proper rabbinical counsel is always advised. Nevertheless, if it's the size or shape of your nose that is bothering you, relax – even some of our greatest sages had imposing noses[866] or were otherwise unattractive![867]

VEGETARIANISM

To present a case for the prominence and centrality of meat in Judaism is simply a no-brainer. Whether it's chicken on a Friday night, flanken in the cholent, or a brisket on yom tov, meat is never far from a Jew's table. What we'll examine here is whether or not a vegetarian lifestyle is compatible with Torah-observant Judaism. Although consuming meat is purported to provide for increased intellectual capabilities,[868] it may not be the only way to go.

For starters, there is little doubt that God's initial intention when He created the world was that humankind adopt a vegetarian lifestyle, an ideology promoted in many scriptural verses.[869] In fact, from the very beginning, mankind was forbidden to kill any living creature for the purpose of food. In the Garden of Eden, only herbage and the like were permitted for consumption.[870]

It was only after the episode of Noach and the flood that mankind was granted permission to eat meat, and as some commentators explain, it was only as a concession to human desires and weaknesses.[871] It is fascinating to note that immediately following the permission to eat meat and mankind's indulgence in such, we find that the lifespans of biblical figures decrease drastically. While

---

866   Ta'anit 29a
867   Ta'anit 20b.
868   Bava Kama 72a.
869   Bereishit 1:30, 2:16 and 3:18, to name but a few.
870   Sanhedrin 59b.
871   As explained by Rav Kook and others.

Adam had lived until 930 years old on his vegetarian diet, Avraham by contrast, lived only to 175. The Ramban states unequivocally that this was due to the growing problem of air pollution and change in diet.[872] These words are ever so relevant in the present day, considering, for example, how today's hot dogs and other meats are drenched in sodium nitrites and other cancer-causing agents. It goes without saying that the state of the environment and the levels of air pollution are a eulogy unto themselves.[873] Some authorities teach that in the messianic era, mankind will once again become vegetarian.[874]

It is clear that meat does wield some eminence with its frequent appearances in the Jewish lifecycle. With its prominent role in Jewish life, is it possible to be an observant Jew without meat? Is there life without pastrami? Make no mistake, the *Shulchan Aruch* nowhere insists that meat must be consumed as part of any religious observances such as the Shabbat or yom tov meals. Furthermore, the Talmud actually cautions against the routine consumption of meat[875] and rules that meat should only be consumed by those knowledgeable of all that goes into the process of preparing it.[876] An ignoramus is almost forbidden, as it were, to consume meat. Indeed, some explain that since an ignoramus does not contribute to the world's spiritual advancement, he is not justified in taking an animal's life for his food.

Although many individuals are under the impression that the consumption of meat is mandatory on holidays, and indeed, there are authorities who insist that this is so,[877] the Talmud is rather clear that the requirement for meat to be consumed on festivals no longer applies since the destruction of the Holy Temple.[878] Accordingly, the mitzva of "rejoicing" on yom tov can be fulfilled

---

872   Bereishit 5:4.
873   God said to Adam: "Do you see how good and praiseworthy my works are? All that I have created, I made for you. Don't destroy My world – for if you do, there is no one after you to repair it." Kohelet Rabba 7:13.
874   The position of Rav Kook, among others.
875   Chullin 84a.
876   Pesachim 49b.
877   Rambam, *Hilchot Yom Tov* 6:18.
878   Pesachim 109a.

with wine or other delicacies, should one prefer them.[879] On an unrelated note, consider celebrating the holidays in Iraq – they are supposedly more joyous there.[880]

Although this is far from obligatory, it seems from the Talmud that it is considered ideal to use mezuzot, tefillin, and Torah scrolls made from animals that have died naturally rather than through other means, perhaps even better than from shechita.[881] It is also worth mentioning that one who keeps a home devoid of meat will never come to violate the severe prohibition of mixing milk and meat. Some authorities suggest that those who do choose to eat meat only do so on Shabbat and other days when Tachanun is not recited.[882]

Should one choose to adopt a vegetarian lifestyle, however, some modifications to one's rituals would be needed. To name but one example, the seder plate on Pesach calls for a shank bone, which cannot possibly be prepared in a home lacking meat utensils. In such a situation, one may substitute a beet or mushroom in its place.[883] Although there are no halachic restrictions on eating vegetables, be sure to never eat your greens at night – it'll give you bad breath.[884]

While meat certainly has its place in contemporary Jewish life, it is clear that those who do choose a life of abstinence from meat based on spiritual considerations[885] are well within the parameters of authentic Torah tradition.

---

879   Rambam, *Hilchot Yom Tov* 6:18.
880   Shabbat 145b.
881   Shabbat 108a.
882   *Pele Yoetz*, s.v. "Basar."
883   Pesachim 114b.
884   Shabbat 140b.
885   It goes without saying that those who choose vegetarianism due to the "cruelty" of taking an animal's life (including via shechita) are distant from normative Jewish thought.

APPEARANCE AND ATTIRE

As many of my friends know, I have an adept eye for men's formal fashions. I'm one of those people who notes the clothing that others wear, be it the style, quality, or message conveyed. Yes, I'm even on style guru Harry Rosen's mailing list. The Talmud teaches that dressing well can fool others into believing that you are exceptionally smart or important.[886] So, don't be fooled!

That being said, there is plenty of room for discussion on whether preoccupation with fashion and dress is an act of petty snobbery, or whether it may perhaps have some redeeming religious value. In an attempt to present authentic Jewish tradition through modern language and outlook, let's see what Judaism has to say about this issue.

The Torah teaches us that the purpose of the clothing worn by kohanim was for "honor and glory."[887] By this, the Torah is clearly teaching us that the way we dress displays our sense of standing and purpose as those created in the image of God. This kohanic attitude actually applies to us all, as the entire Jewish people are called a "kingdom of priests and a holy nation."[888] Furthermore, we are to learn from the kohanim the importance of regular bathing and fresh breath.[889]

Indeed, the Torah and the rabbinical literature is replete with references to proper attire and presentation. For starters, the Midrash teaches us that Adam wore only the finest garments.[890] Actually, even God Himself takes appropriate dress very seriously. Indeed, God personally ensured that even while wandering the desert, the Jewish people were well dressed throughout the entire forty years. How so? We are taught that God personally cleaned and pressed the clothing of every Jew each day and even made sure that all garments were perfectly tailored to the wearer.[891] As we can see, He

---

886 Shabbat 145b.
887 Shemot 28:2.
888 Shemot 19:6.
889 Rambam, *Hilchot Biat Hamikdash* 7:13; OC 4:17.
890 Bereishit Rabba 20:12.
891 Rashi, Devarim 8.

provided the ultimate in custom clothing complete with lifetime professional care.

It goes even further – we are taught that God also ensured that the Jews wandering the hot desert never suffered from body odor, as the manna He fed us for forty years was not only a delicious food, but also contained properties that served as an anti-perspirant deodorant.[892]

Wearing nice shoes is also extremely important, as the Talmud teaches: "One should sell even the beams of his house in order to buy shoes for his feet."[893] It is also important to ensure that one's shoes fit well.[894] Never go around barefoot.[895]

A Talmudic maintenance tip for your clothing: never sit on a new mat or other surfaces – it'll ruin your clothes.[896] Similarly, be very careful when holding children – they are known for dirtying one's clothes.[897] Here's a Talmudic tip to ensure your house smells nice: sprinkle your floors with wine.[898]

The importance of proper attire is further emphasized as we prepare for Shabbat. The Jewish people are encouraged to wear especially nice clothes for Shabbat.[899] The Talmud[900] derives the obligation of having special Shabbat perfumes and other finery from Naomi's words to her daughter-in-law Ruth, "Wash yourself, perfume yourself, and put on your fine garments."[901] It is suggested that everyone, young and old, possess a perfume reserved exclusively for Shabbat use.[902]

Rabbis, scholars, and others in leadership roles are cautioned to be even more particular with the way they dress than others. The Talmud teaches, for example, that any Torah scholar who goes out

---

892   Ibn Ezra, Devarim 8.
893   Shabbat 129a.
894   Shabbat 141b.
895   Pesachim 112a; OC 2:6.
896   Pesachim 140b.
897   *Mishna Berura* 262:6; *Sefer Chassidim* 18.
898   Pesachim 20b; Bava Kama 115a.
899   Yeshayahu 58:13.
900   Shabbat 113b.
901   Ruth 3:3.
902   Ibn Ezra, Ruth 3:3.

in public with a stain on his clothes is worthy of death.[903] Although such a death penalty was never implemented, it does give us a sense of the severity and importance in portraying a proper image. Appearing before God in prayer also demands a dignified dress and appearance.[904]

Believe it or not, not only do we have a Jewish approach to clothing, but there are also instructions that teach us how to get dressed! For example, we are taught that in all matters we should give precedence to the right side. For example, we are instructed to put the right arm or foot into clothing and shoes first.[905] When getting dressed, we are cautioned never to wear clothing inside out, nor to put two garments on at once as it can cause you to lose your mind![906] Please note that clothes are not meant to serve as pillows![907] Never rip your clothing in anger.[908]

Dress and appearance certainly have their place in Yiddishkeit.[909] Although being well dressed is nowhere near as important as honesty, charity, and kindness, we must keep in mind that clothes don't just cover a person – they expose a person.

---

903   Shabbat 114a.
904   *Sefer Chassidim* 18.
905   Shabbat 61a.
906   *Mishna Berura*, OC 2.
907   Ibid. 2:2.
908   *Sefer Chassidim* 71.
909   Kohelet 9:8.

ISRAEL

THE LAND OF ISRAEL

B efore discussing the issue of Eretz Yisrael, or anything even
remotely related to the State of Israel and its politics, it is
absolutely essential that we are very clear on what our sole and
legitimate right to the Land of Israel actually is. Our right to the land
is not the result of some Englishman's declaration, not because of a
vote in some international body, nor is it even the result of military
victory. Rather, our sole, legitimate, and eternal right to the Land
of Israel is that God has decreed that the Land of Israel belongs to
the Jewish people.[910] Simply put, God is a religious Zionist and real
estate agent par excellence. So beloved is the land to Him that His
eyes are constantly focused on it and its people every second of
every day.[911] Furthermore, it is important to bear in mind that the
State of Israel as it appears today on a map is but a fraction of the
land that is ours by biblical right. All territory "from the Red Sea
until the Euphrates"[912] belongs to the Jewish people.

It is a well-known teaching that the Torah only began with the
story of creation in order that all mankind realize that the entire
world belongs to God, and He is entitled to give any part of it to
whomever He wishes.[913] In fact, the Land of Israel was created before
anything else in the world.[914]

So connected is the Land of Israel to the Torah and the Jewish
people that all mitzvot were initially given with the intention
that they would be observed in Israel. Some authorities go so far
as to suggest that mitzvot performed outside the Land of Israel
are merely to be considered as practice in preparation for the next
time one will find oneself there![915] Likewise, the Jewish people were
especially programmed to function better inside Israel than in the

---

910   Bereishit 13.
911   Devarim 11:12.
912   Bereishit 15:18.
913   Rashi, Bereishit 1:1.
914   Ta'anit 10.
915   Ramban, Vayikra 18:25.

Diaspora.[916] It is interesting to note that the vast majority of the 613 mitzvot can only be performed in the Land of Israel.

As a sign of affection, it is a common custom to kiss the Land of Israel upon departure and arrival.[917] Additionally, when one is in Israel, one performs a mitzva with every few steps one takes.[918] We are also taught that breathing the air of Israel makes one wiser[919] and that the Torah is better understood when studied there.[920] By actually living in Israel, one is considered to be fulfilling the equivalent of the entire Torah on a daily basis,[921] and all of one's sins are forgiven.[922] It is even taught that God prefers the simple Jews who have made aliya to even the greatest sages who live in the Diaspora.[923]

Did you ever realize that God offers executive portfolio management for those who live in the Land of Israel? Indeed, those who live outside the Land of Israel receive their Divinely ordained blessings and sustenance only via an intermediary agent, while those who live in Israel receive blessings directly from God Himself.[924] Be advised that even a visit to Israel is considered a component of the mitzva of *yishuv Eretz Yisrael* (settling the land).[925] Hopefully on your next visit to Israel you'll come across a great deal on a home and purchase it immediately. So critical is the mitzva of purchasing a home in Israel that even on Shabbat one may instruct a Gentile to do so on one's behalf, including all that is required for it, such as the signing or the transfer of any monies.[926]

No, God does not expect us to immediately pick up and leave our homes in fulfillment of the mitzva of living in Israel (although it is worth noting that one spouse can compel the other to move

---

916   Bamidbar Rabba 23:6.
917   Ketubot 112.
918   Ketubot 111.
919   Bava Batra 158b.
920   Bereishit Rabba 16:7.
921   Sifrei, Re'eh.
922   Sifrei, Ha'azinu.
923   Talmud Yerushalmi Sanhedrin 86.
924   Ta'anit 10a.
925   *Magen Avraham*, OC 248:15.
926   Gittin 8b.

there),[927] but we are expected to recognize that living in Israel is what is best for us and our spiritual fulfillment. Those who still live in the Diaspora should reflect Moses' attitude, "I am a stranger in a strange land."[928]

THE ISRAEL DEFENSE FORCES

Along with the mitzva of making aliya comes the mitzva and obligation of serving in the Israel Defense Forces. Although my desire to move to Israel never came as a surprise to anyone, my excitement at the possibility of serving in the army certainly did, to both my secular friends as well as my more orthodox ones. To this end, I've had to field numerous inquiries by those who erroneously believe that the Israeli army is foreign to orthodox Jews. Make no mistake, my interest in serving in the Israel Defense Forces (IDF) has nothing to do with any political views I may hold, but rather what I see as a fulfillment of Torah law. While ultimately the army rejected my candidacy as a solider outright on a number of occasions, it is still worth exploring the halachic issues associated with such a "mission."

It is well known that members of the ultra-orthodox community in Israel arouse anger and contempt among secular Israelis with their refusal to serve in the army. This is true notwithstanding the creation of "halachic units," complete with glatt-kosher food, no women allowed, and minyan thrice daily. Nevertheless, there are thousands of God-fearing, observant Jews who do indeed join the forces and even excitedly anticipate their induction to the IDF. Why the difference in approach by two different segments of the orthodox community?

Throughout all of Tanach we find that only religiously observant individuals were permitted to serve in the Jewish army.[929] Anyone

---

927   Ketubot 100.
928   Shemot 2:22.
929   Rashi, Bamidbar 31:3.

found to be in poor halachic practice was promptly expelled from the forces. Indeed, even the greatest of our forefathers were intrepid soldiers, as the Talmud says: "Our forefathers were gentle when it came to ritual, but tough when it came to war."[930] Gideon had no patience for soldiers who did not meet his piety standards.[931] Additionally, we find that one of the characteristics of the Messiah is that he will be proficient and triumphant in battle.[932]

Even those from the most sanctified of lineages – the kohanim – were permitted to override the severe prohibition of being in the presence of a dead body in order to fight in the Jewish army.[933] The prophetess Devora[934] gave special praise to the religious soldiers who helped in defeating the Canaanites.[935]

It appears to this writer that the hesder yeshiva arrangement in Israel is a wonderful example of the biblical models above, where yeshiva students combine their studies concurrently with their military obligations. The hesder program was actually conceptualized by our forefather Avraham,[936] then reinstated in 1954 by Rabbi Chaim Yakov Goldvicht in the Kerem b'Yavneh Yeshiva. The non-Zionist (but very pro-Israel) Lubavitcher Rebbe declared all who serve in the army as *tzaddikim* (completely righteous Jews).[937]

On a contemporary note, the war against terror that Israel faces today is known in halacha as a *milchemet mitzva* (an obligatory battle).[938] We are taught that in such a situation, all Jews are obligated to serve in the army, even a bride and groom on their wedding day.[939]

It emerges from the above discussion that serving in the army is not only permissible, but is actually a mitzva of the Torah.[940]

---

930   Mo'ed Katan 16b.
931   Rashi, Shoftim 7:5.
932   *Hilchot Melachim* 11:4.
933   Kiddushin 21b.
934   There were seven female prophets: Sarah, Miriam, Devora, Hanna, Avigail, Hulda and Esther. Megilla 14a.
935   Radak, Shoftim 5:14.
936   Rashi, Bereishit 14:14.
937   Cited at: http://amerisrael.com/article_rebbe.html.
938   *Hilchot Melachim* 5:1.
939   Sota 43.
940   Bamidbar 33:52.

I'll be the first to admit that there are certainly opposing views on the issue of the permissibility of orthodox Jews serving in the Israeli army. However, based on the discussion above, perhaps the orthodox authorities should reckon with a different question, namely: is it halachically permissible for non-orthodox Jews to serve in the Israeli army?

As I once saw on a bumper sticker, I would suggest that the ideal solution would be for every yeshiva boy to join the army, and every soldier to join a yeshiva!

HALLEL ON YOM HA'ATZMAUT

The orthodox community is divided over whether or not the Hallel prayers should be recited in honor of Yom Ha'atzmaut, Israel Independence Day. As is customary, the Hallel is recited on most holidays where miracles were performed for the Jewish people. The question with no simple answer, however, is whether or not the creation of the State of Israel is to be awarded religious standing for the purpose of reciting Hallel. The Talmud teaches us that Hallel must not be excessively or even routinely recited, but rather, it must be reserved for very distinguished occasions.[941] Let's take a deeper look at the issues.

The Talmud teaches us that King Chizkiyahu was severely rebuked by God for not having recited the Hallel upon his miraculous victory over Sancheriv.[942] In fact, we are told that Chizkiyahu could have been confirmed as the Messiah had he done so. It's not only upon military victories such as Chizkiyahu's that Hallel should be recited. The Talmud states that the prophets decreed that Hallel must be recited whenever the Jewish people emerge from disasters and troubles.[943] Emerging from the Holocaust to the absolutely

---

941   Shabbat 118b.
942   Sanhedrin 94a.
943   Pesachim 117a.

miraculous establishment of the State of Israel is surely consistent with this principle.

The halachic codifiers are very clear that even a small community, let alone the entire nation, is permitted to institute an annual holiday on the day a miracle occurred for them.[944] In fact, even the renowned Rabbi Avraham Danzig, the Chayei Adam, describes how he instituted an annual holiday as a token of thanks for a miracle that occurred to his family.[945]

Based on the above, it would appear logical, perhaps even mandatory, that the Hallel prayer be recited on a day like Yom Ha'atzmaut. If that's the case, how do those who oppose the recitation of Hallel on Yom Ha'atzmaut view the issue?

Opponents will counter with the contention that perhaps the creation of the State of Israel was not necessarily a miracle that spiritually benefited the entire Jewish people. They add that hundreds of thousands, if not millions, of non-Jews have immigrated to Israel under the guise of the "Law of Return." Furthermore, many among the orthodox community consider the lack of a functioning Temple in Jerusalem a major blemish in the renewal of Jewish life in the Holy Land. Lastly, another frequently cited objection to the observance of Yom Ha'atzmaut is that it takes place during *sefirat ha'omer*, the annual period of mourning when most forms of celebrations are banned. This is especially true of celebrations that include music and dancing, both of which are mainstays of Yom Ha'atzmaut festivities. There are additional issues on both sides of the debate which are beyond the scope of this discussion.

One thing, however, that is often overlooked by those on both sides of the debate is the teaching of the Mishna, "Do not separate yourself from the community."[946] At least from the perspective of this writer, regardless of which opinion you personally accept upon yourself in practice, to violate the teaching of the Mishna is certainly worse than following either opinion.

---

944   *Mishna Berura* 686:8.
945   Chayei Adam 55:41.
946   Avot 2:5.

Therefore if the congregation you find yourself participating in on Yom Ha'atzmaut doesn't say Hallel, while you yourself customarily do, then simply recite it at the conclusion of services. So too in the reverse: if the congregation does in fact recite Hallel, while you yourself don't personally subscribe to that view, simply say it along with them without reciting the blessing. In the worst case scenario, one would simply be taking advantage of an opportunity to recite Psalms. Those who insist on publicly conducting themselves contrary to the practice of the congregation only succeed in making fools out of themselves. The unity of a congregation takes precedence at all times.[947]

Whether or not you recite Hallel on Yom Ha'atzmaut is ultimately not a burning spiritual crisis. What is vital, however, is the recognition that this day was indeed ordained by God and is filled with spiritual significance. Whether through Hallel or not, and whether through live music and dancing or not, we must be sure to show our thanks and appreciation to the Creator. We see that God kept His promised to reestablish the third and final commonwealth of the Jewish people and bring about the ingathering of the exiles to the Land of Israel.

SECOND DAY
YOM TOV IN ISRAEL

The first question on the minds of those who find themselves traveling to Israel for the holidays is whether they should observe one or two days of yom tov. You can't really blame them, though – one seder is more than enough for most of us.

The difference in custom[948] concerning the observance of an extra day of yom tov originates from the period before there was a

---

947   See commentaries to Devarim 14:1.
948   Tosafot, Berachot 14a calls it *minhag avoteinu b'yadeinu*. Also referred to as [only] a "custom" in *Teshuvot v'Hanhagot* 3:332.

set calendar. Instead, Jewish months and holidays were proclaimed by the Sanhedrin based on observations of the moon. A new Jewish month would commence upon the sighting of the new moon, which was either twenty-nine or thirty days following the previous one. Unfortunately, those who lived far from Israel could not be informed of the commencement of the new month until the specially dispatched messengers could arrive with the news. This could conceivably have taken more than two weeks, and hence, there was often confusion as to which day to observe the holidays. Accordingly, Jews in those areas would observe an extra day of yom tov just to "be safe." Even when the calendar did enjoy a period of stability and precise reckoning during the period of Hillel, it was decided to continue with a second day of yom tov in fear that the set calendar might one day again be forgotten.[949] Thus the practice of permanently observing two days of yom tov in the exile was born.

What about visitors from the Diaspora who find themselves in Israel for yom tov? Examining the issue from a Talmudic point of view, we find that the Mishna teaches that one should never deviate from local ritual customs.[950] This opens the larger debate as to whether this refers to the local customs of where one has come from, the local customs of where one finds oneself, intentions of where one hopes to reside, or all of the above.[951]

The common conclusion to this debate (as it relates to the issue of keeping one or two days of yom tov) is that if one is merely visiting Israel for the holidays, but intends to return to the Diaspora, one is to observe two days. This is in order to conform with the customs in the place one has come from. Most later halachic authorities accept this ruling.[952]

Nevertheless, when it comes down to practical how-to procedures when in Israel, possibly the most comprehensive overview of this

---

949   Beitza 4b.
950   Pesachim 50b.
951   Pesachim 50b. See as well commentaries on Chullin 18b; Rambam, *Hilchot Yom Tov* 8:20.
952   *Mishna Berura* 496:13, *Aruch Hashulchan* 496:5.

issue comes from the writings of Rabbi Ovadia Yosef.[953] He begins by citing the celebrated view of the Chacham Tzvi, who rules that visitors to Israel should observe only one day of yom tov.[954] He does acknowledge, however, that this is a minority view.[955] The Chacham Tzvi's approach was that all relevant laws concerning local customs depend exclusively on where one presently finds oneself, and not on where one has come from. The *Shulchan Aruch Harav* rules as well that only one day of yom tov need be observed in Israel.[956] This is also the official ruling of the Israeli chief rabbinate. Those who do choose to observe a second day of yom tov in Israel would be well advised to hold their prayer services discreetly amongst themselves. Second day yom tov services are not to be excessively announced or held within the public eye, as is often the case.[957]

An interesting angle to this dispute specifically involves foreign students who find themselves studying in Israel. With regard to unmarried students – as it is common practice among teenagers to come and study in Israel upon completion of high school – Rabbi Ovadia Yosef states that a student who is rather independent and would stay in Israel were he to find a spouse should observe only one day of yom tov. On the other hand, a student who still relies on his parents and would be hard-pressed to just pick up and move should observe two days.

Finally, we come to the opinion of Rabbi Joseph B. Soloveitchik. There is some confusion as to what his view actually was. Some say his opinion was to keep one day in Israel like the locals, while others report his view as being that one should keep what is known as "a day and a half."[958] People should be sure to consult their halachic authority when planning to be in Israel over any yom tov. It is

---

953   *Yabia Omer* 1:40.
954   *Chacham Tzvi* 167.
955   In the words of Rabbi Herschel Schachter, "In recent years, this opinion of the Chochom Tzvi has gained more popularity among the poskim"; cited in "Regarding the Second Day Yom Tov for Visitors in Eretz Yisroel" at http://torahweb.org/torah/special/2003/rsch_ytsheini.html#_edn3.
956   OC 496:11.
957   *Mishna Berura* 496:13.
958   According to this view, one recites the weekday prayers, wears Tefillin, but performs no actual melacha.

interesting to note that in ancient times visitors from the Diaspora observed only one day of yom tov just like the locals. Why should we do anything else in our day?

SPEAKING HEBREW

Within Torah tradition, Hebrew is regarded to have been the first language to be spoken on Earth.[959] In fact, it is even the language that is spoken in heaven. The Midrash teaches that the world was created with the Hebrew language.[960] Thereafter, the heavenly angels,[961] along with Adam and Eve as well as all of earliest humanity, spoke only Hebrew.[962] Adam intentionally named all the animals with the Hebrew language in order to express the hidden meaning of their existence. For example, it is said that dogs are "man's best friend." Could it be a reflection of their Hebrew name, *kelev*, which means "like the heart"?

Hebrew is known as *lashon kodesh* (the "holy language") for a variety of reasons. For one, as mentioned, it is the language of God and the language He used to create the world. Biblical Hebrew is also the only language on Earth that has no words that directly depict the sexual organs or sexual relations. Hebrew is so special and spiritually powerful that it is better to pray in Hebrew even if you don't understand the meaning of the words than to pray in any other language.[963]

Throughout the ages, some sects have urged the restriction of Hebrew to only holy matters, while using other Jewish-flavored languages for day-to-day business. Nevertheless, Hebrew can and should be used when speaking about even the most secular of topics.[964] Although Hebrew can even be spoken in the bathroom, some authorities suggest

959   Rashi, Bereishit 11:1.
960   Bereishit Rabba 18:6.
961   Chagiga 16a.
962   Bereishit 2:23.
963   OC 101:4; but see *Sefer Chassidim* 588 and 785 for a dissenting view.
964   OC 85:2.

not doing so out of respect for the holy language.[965] All efforts to converse in Hebrew as much as possible will ensure one a special place in the World to Come.[966]

Even today, there are enclaves in Jerusalem of extreme Hassidic sects that refuse to use Hebrew outside of study and prayer. Most, however, including the anti-Zionist Satmar, have kept up with Israeli society to at least this extent, and do converse in Hebrew. Make no mistake, Yiddish, Ladino, and even Aramaic[967] are not universal Jewish languages. They were used by specific groups of Jews in specific areas at specific times. The only national Jewish language remains Hebrew to this day. Indeed, in preparation for the imminent messianic era and the mass aliya that will follow, we would be well advised to work on our Hebrew.

Some suggest that it was in anticipation of the exile that the Torah itself began introducing non-Hebrew words into its text. For example, the Torah calls the tefillin of the head *totafot*, a word of Caspian and African derivation.[968] One will also note that Hebrew itself has been often redesigned, particularly in pronunciation, by the various dialects of the places Jews were to be found. It is even questionable whether one may serve as a chazzan in a synagogue whose pronunciation of Hebrew is different from one's own![969]

It is important to note that merely conversing in Hebrew is a tremendous mitzva that cannot be underestimated. The Maharik laments the fact that the mitzva of speaking in Hebrew has been all but ignored in the Diaspora.[970] The famous Torah commentator Rashi derives from the Shema prayer[971] that parents are required to ensure that their child's first words are in Hebrew. The Rambam was known to have said that even speaking languages that resemble Hebrew (e.g., Arabic) has much merit. Let us also recall that there were several

---

965   *Sefer Chassidim* 994.
966   Yerushalmi Shabbat 1:3, 9.
967   It is interesting to note that angels in Heaven don't understand Aramaic; Tosafot, Shabbat 12b. Some say that Aramaic is actually a corrupted form of Hebrew; Rosh, Berachot 2:2.
968   Menachot 34b.
969   Megilla 24b.
970   On Devarim 7:12 cited in the Artscroll Chumash, Sapirstein Edition.
971   Devarim 11:19.

deeds,[972] the strict usage of Hebrew among them, that served as the primary merits of our forefathers being redeemed from Egypt.[973]

Ultimately, however, while *what* language we speak to each other may be important, *how* we speak to each other is essential!

BEIT SHEMESH

Beit Shemesh is our family's newly chosen home city. Beit Shemesh, literally translated as "House of the Sun," was actually the center of ancient Canaanite idolatrous worship of the sun. In fact throughout ancient times, any city where sun worship was common took on the name "Beit Shemesh."[974] Upon entry into the Promised Land, Joshua awarded this area to the tribe of Dan,[975] and it later served as a Levitical city as well.[976] The Amorites frequently made trouble and held their first intifada here.[977]

Conveniently located between Jerusalem and Tel Aviv, with plenty of public transportation, Beit Shemesh is an ideal base for work and play anywhere along the Tel Aviv-Jerusalem corridor. In fact, even in ancient times, Beit Shemesh served as the lip in between the Philistine territory of the coastal plain and the Judean hill country, and even served somewhat as a fortress protecting Jerusalem from unwanted visitors.

Directly across the broad and fertile valley of Beit Shemesh is the town of Tzora, the birthplace of Samson, where a kibbutz by the same name sits today.

---

972   Bamidbar Rabba 20:22; Shir Hashirim Rabba 4:12.
973   Vayikra Rabba 32:5.
974   See for example Yehoshua 19:38, Shoftim 1:33, Yirmiyahu 43:13, Yeshayahu 19:18.
975   Beit Shemesh is first mentioned in Yehoshua 15:10 as being awarded to the tribe of Yehuda. Later in 19:41 it is identified as "Ir Shemesh" and within the boundaries of the tribe of Dan. There are several answers to this apparent contradiction.
976   Yehoshua 21:26; *Divrei Hayamim* 6:59.
977   Shoftim 1:34.

After receiving Divine punishment for having stolen the Holy Ark, the Philistines returned the Ark to Beit Shemesh. They placed it on a cart which was pulled by two nursing cows. The inhabitants of Beit Shemesh then offered the cows as a sacrifice to God. Although it was completely forbidden, some of the curious folks opened the ark to take a peek inside. As a result, a Divine plague killed 50,070 men of Beit Shemesh. In complete hysteria, the Beit Shemeshites sent the Holy Ark nine miles northeast to Kiriat Ye'arim near Jerusalem, where it remained for twenty years.[978]

In all likelihood, Beit Shemesh was a walled city during the era of Joshua, and as such, should observe Purim on the fifteenth of Adar like other walled cities, such as Jerusalem. In reality of course, it does not, and Purim is observed on the fourteenth of Adar just like most of the world. Among the explanations as to why this is so is that the modern-day city of Beit Shemesh is not built directly upon or immediately adjacent to the site of the ancient wall (known as "Tel Beit Shemesh"). Furthermore, unlike in Jerusalem, there are no inhabitants in the immediate area of where the ancient wall once stood, and therefore its official status as a walled city is lacking.[979] It would seem, however, that if a residential community were established adjacent to the site of the ancient wall, Beit Shemesh would once again regain its walled city status and observe Purim on the fifteenth of Adar.

EILAT

Mere mention of the name brings to mind the image of a modern-day, Hebrew-speaking, humus-subsistent Hawaii. A resort and escape, yet a credible force and competitor among the leading Israeli cities. Heck, even Moses himself may have enjoyed a few days on its beaches.[980] As can be seen from its settlement even

---

978   Shmuel I 6:10.
979   For more on this issue see Rabbi David Avraham Spector's book *Beit Shemesh*.
980   Devarim 2:8.

in biblical times, Eilat is actually a very ancient city. Its first visitors were the millions of aliya-bound Jews, after being liberated from Egyptian bondage. Even King Solomon strolled along its beaches long before the IDF.[981] Nevertheless, many people erroneously believe that a visit to Israel is incomplete without a dash down to Eilat, not realizing that it is in fact not part of the original biblical Israel.

Here's something to think about regarding Eilat: We are all familiar with Moses' punishment of not being permitted to enter the Land of Israel.[982] Moses was not even allowed to be buried here. If so, how is it possible that Moses passed through Eilat, and its neighboring Kibbutz Yotvata (home of Israel's finest chocolate milk)? Let's strengthen the question even more: the Torah teaches us that the modern-day State of Israel comprises but a fraction of the land that God promised the Jewish people. "From the Nile to the Euphrates" are the true borders of the ultimate State of Israel.[983]

The answer is, although all the land mentioned above indeed belongs to the Jewish people, it only takes effect following a formal "conquest" and "sanctification" ceremony. For example, when Joshua entered the land, he never "conquered" any land south of Be'er Sheva. A careful look at the verses in the book of Bamidbar will indeed reveal that the division of the land among the twelve tribes included nothing south of Be'er Sheva. Hence, during the period of Joshua (and certainly before it) Eilat was indeed excluded from "Land of Israel" status, and hence, Moses was allowed to travel there. It was only after the conquest of King Solomon that Eilat became a halachic part of the Land of Israel. Furthermore, the various statements throughout the Torah concerning the borders of the land refer to various stages of Jewish history and destiny. The ultimate borders of the "Nile to the Euphrates" are destined to be realized only in the messianic era. Until then, those lands do not merit the status of Eretz Yisrael.

---

981   Melachim I 19:26.
982   Bamidbar 20:12.
983   Devarim 11; Bamidbar 34.

Not all halachic authorities "accepted" Solomon's conquest of Eilat for the purpose of rendering it a part of sanctified biblical Israel.[984] There have therefore been some authorities who advocated observing two days of yom tov in Eilat just like the rest of the Diaspora![985] Additionally, many are of the opinion that Israel's agricultural laws do not apply to produce originating from Eilat.[986]

This has extensive ramifications for the sabbatical year, when working the "Land of Israel" is prohibited. Based on this opinion, it would be completely permitted to work the land surrounding Eilat in the sabbatical year. There are also some segments of the orthodox community who will never travel to Eilat (or south of Be'er Sheva, for that matter) in fear of possibly violating the prohibition of needlessly leaving the Land of Israel.

Regardless of how you personally classify Eilat's halachic status today, one thing is for certain: the Messiah's arrival is imminent, and among his duties, he will bring all Jews from the Diaspora back to the homeland. On that day, the entire land "from the Nile to the Euphrates" will be ours.

GAZA

Israel's national catastrophe known as the "disengagement," the withdrawal from the Gaza Strip, calls for a review of some of Gaza's glorious Jewish history. Unfortunately, many people formulate passionate opinions on the political issues without ever having visited Gaza, nor having any knowledge of its history.

Examining the biblical borders of the Land of Israel as promised to the Jewish people, one will readily notice that this territory

---

984   See http://www.yeshiva.org.il/midrash/shiur.asp?id=701 regarding the halachic status of different parts of Eretz Yisrael.

985   The consensus of halachic authorities is that in Eilat one is to observe only one day of yom tov; *Teshuvot v'Hanhagot* 3:332; *Tzitz Eliezer* 3:23. See also Rambam, *Kiddush Hachodesh* 5:5–12.

986   *Tzitz Eliezer* 3:23.

includes the area known as the "Gaza Strip."[987] The Torah records that the ancient inhabitants of Gaza were the Avvites, a nation no longer living,[988] making Gaza one of the oldest inhabited cities.

Jewish settlement in Gaza began with the tribe of Yehuda, who received that area as part of their tribal allotment in the division of the Land of Israel.[989] Of course, the Philistines also lived in that area, which played a focal role in the life of Samson and Delila,[990] particularly Samson's infamous suicidal destruction of the Temple of Dagon, named for a Gazan fish god. It seems that indigenous Gazans never liked the Jews.[991]

Like the entire Land of Israel, Gaza "enjoyed" its share of conquerors such as the Ptolemies, Assyrian Seuclids, and King Herod, among others. Gaza flourished as a Jewish center throughout the Roman and Byzantine eras, and was a place of regular pilgrimage along with other noteworthy cities of the time. Rulers and empires always sought Gaza due to its location between Asia and Africa, its fertile land, and its value as a seaport. Trade was always a major source of income.

In 635 CE, Arabs overthrew the Byzantines, and Gaza City served as a capital of the Negev. Jewish life was fruitful under Arab rule. Of course, the Crusaders eventually discovered Gaza as well and soon thereafter devastated its Jewish community. It is recorded that in the fourteenth century there were sixty Jewish families living in Gaza, many of whom worked in wine production. The famous Mishnaic commentator Rabbi Ovadia of Bartenura visited Gaza in 1488 and met with Gaza's chief rabbi, an immigrant from Czechoslovakia. Under the Ottomans, Jewish life in Gaza was flourishing and prosperous.

Historically, Jewish life was full of amenities there, including synagogues, yeshivot, and rabbinic courts. By 1641, even the Karaites maintained a synagogue in Gaza. Rabbi Israel Najara, author of the famous "Kah Ribon" Shabbat song, was chief rabbi of

---

987   Bereishit 15; Bamidbar 34.
988   Devarim 2:23.
989   Shoftim 1:18.
990   Shoftim 13–16.
991   Amos 1:6.

Gaza during the seventeenth century. It was in Gaza that the false messiah Shabbtai Tzvi picked up his largest following. Napoleon also arrived for a visit in 1799. Jewish life in Gaza (including Gaza City) continued until the pogroms of 1929, at which time the Jewish residents left for safer cities. In modern times, Gaza was occupied by Egypt at the end of Israel's War of Independence. In 1967, Israel won control of Gaza as a result of the Six-Day War.

It was none other than the Egyptian Department of Antiquities in 1965 that discovered Jewish mosaics along the Gaza seashore, as well as in the vicinity of the Great Mosque of Gaza. There is also evidence that synagogues once thrived all over the area. After 1967, Israeli archeologists continued excavating areas of Gaza and found further signs of ancient Jewish life. The Talmud also mentions its sages who lived in Gaza.[992]

Regardless of what views you hold on this "disengagement," make no mistake – from the historical and biblical perspective Gaza is as much a part of Eretz Yisrael as any other.

THE GOLAN HEIGHTS

The Golan Heights is a dream spot for many Israelis, tourists, and hiking buffs alike. It's the only place in the Middle East where open spaces contain the full gamut of outdoor activities: forests and trails, cliffs and waterfalls, ski sites and hot springs, weaved in between dozens of sites of religious and historical importance on a plateau of creative modern agriculture. The Golan's rich history can be seen in its many attractions: ancient synagogues, fortresses, and settlements. Evidence of the Golan's glorious past is all around.

Contrary to popular belief, the Golan Heights has always been an integral component of the Land of Israel and Jewish settlement. Indeed, Moses himself somewhat consecrated the area and ordained that the Golan Heights should serve as a place of

---

992   Sota 20b.

refuge for those who murdered unintentionally.[993] Upon entry into the Land of Israel, Joshua allotted the Golan Heights to the tribe of Menashe.[994] The "Jewish Golan" actually extends right into downtown Damascus.[995]

The most prominent landmark of the Golan is certainly Mount Hermon. Mount Hermon was already noted in biblical times as a mountain with many summits.[996] Its majestic appearance and impressive structure is frequently cited as a metaphor for God's awesome power.[997] It is thanks to the Hermon mountain that in Israel one can ski in the morning and then head down to Tiberias for an afternoon at the beach.

The campaign of terror that the Syrians conducted between 1948 and 1967 from the Golan upon northern Israel is well documented. The Syrians, however, were not the first to give us trouble from atop the Golan Heights – they stole the idea from the Sidonites and Amorites.[998] It was only in 1967 that we were able to put an end to three thousand years of harassment from the Golan.

Another lesser-known historical episode in the history of the Golan is that of the city of Gamla. Gamla was established in 81 BCE, by then King Alexander Yanai, and was viewed as the capital of the Golan for about 150 years. The city was built on a steep slope of a mountain that had the shape of a camel, hence the name Gamla. In 66 CE, during the revolt against the Roman Empire, Gamla joined the uprising and fought bravely in two battles in a siege that lasted one month.

The fighters at Gamla, outnumbered, defended their city and were forced to retreat to the citadel on top of the cliff. Four thousand Jews were killed in the battle and another five thousand committed suicide by jumping from the cliff. Only two women survived. Gamla is often referred to as the Massada of the north.

993　Devarim 4:41.
994　Yehoshua 17:1.
995　Bereishit 15:2.
996　Tehillim 42:6.
997　Tehillim 29:7.
998　Devarim 3:8–10.

Today, the Golan Heights is the most tranquil area in Israel –
well away from the noise and pollution. It can be enjoyed as a day
trip or as an overnighter. There are options to see the Golan by
foot, jeep, car, boat, or horseback. You don't even need a guide book
– the residents are your best source of information, and are more
than happy to welcome you to the Heights. Sip some wine at the
Golan Heights winery or make a splash at the spring water factory
(visitors get a free bottle!). It's a marvelous place to visit to enjoy a
multifaceted vacation.

L O D

The city of Lod (population 55,000) is a small but indispensable
town in the coastal plain of Israel, ten miles southeast of Tel
Aviv. Lod is actually a very ancient city, first recorded in Thutmose
III's list of towns in Canaan (1465 BCE). According to the Tanach,
it was founded by Shemed, a Benjaminite.[999] In the Hellenistic
period, Lod was outside the boundaries of Judea proper. There is a
minority opinion that the cave in which Rabbi Shimon Bar Yochai
hid when fleeing the Romans was in Lod.[1000] At one time, during
the Maccabean era, Lod was an exclusively Jewish town, but the
inhabitants were all sold into slavery in 43 BCE. In 66 CE, Lod
was burned to the ground by the Syrian consul Cestius Gallus. The
emperor Vespasian may have enjoyed a falafel or shwarma during
his visit there in 68 CE.

Although you may not realize it, you have probably visited
the city several times. That's because Israel's international airport,
named in memory of David Ben-Gurion, is not in Tel Aviv, as your
airplane ticket may show, but is actually in the city of Lod (also
known by its ancient name, Lydda). The original airport was actually
built in 1936 by the British mandatory government of Palestine
(there is a newer wing of the airport that is of more recent vintage).

---

999   Divrei Hayamim I 8:12.
1000 Zohar Chadash, Ki Tavo.

It is the home base for Israel's El Al airlines. Both the airport and Israel Aircraft Industries are important sources of employment for the local population. Other industries of Lod include papermaking, food preserves, electrical appliances, cigarette manufacture and oil refining.

Throughout history, Lod has always served as a major Holy Land player in trades of all kinds.[1001] At one time, Lod even served as the seat of the Great Sanhedrin,[1002] and its resident scholars included Rabbi Akiva and Rabbi Eliezer ben Hyrcanus. It also had a sizeable Christian community at the time of Peter.[1003] In the year 200 CE, Septimus Severus, the Roman emperor, established a Roman city there. Still fairly Jewish, the residents of Lod took part in the revolt against the emperor Gallus in 351 and were severely punished when the coup failed.

By the Byzantine era, the town was predominantly Christian. It is the traditional birthplace and home of St. George, patron saint of England, and there is a church there in his honor. Captured by the Muslims in 636, it served as the headquarters of one of the local provinces. In 1099, the Crusaders occupied the town. According to Benjamin of Tudela, there was only one known Jewish family by the year 1170. After the conquest of Saladin, Jews once again settled in Lod. During the early Ottoman period, there seem to have been no Jews living there at all, though a small Jewish community was reestablished in the nineteenth century. The Jews were once again forced out by the Arab riots of 1921. By 1944, Lod had a population of seventeen thousand Arabs, one-fifth of them Christian. During the 1948 War of Independence, Israeli forces quickly won control of the city. With that, the majority of Arabs abandoned the town.

From a halachic perspective, Lod enjoys an interesting status. That's because the Talmud specifically states that Lod had a wall surrounding it in the days of Joshua, thereby requiring Purim to be observed on the fifteenth of Adar, similar to Yerushalayim. [1004] Interestingly, common custom in Lod is to observe Purim on both

1001 Bava Metzia 49b.
1002 Sanhedrin 32b.
1003 Acts 9:32–35.
1004 Megilla 4a.

the fourteenth and fifteenth of Adar, due to some doubt whether present-day Lod is located precisely where the ancient wall would have stood.[1005] The blessings on the Megilla are recited only on the first day of readings in compliance with the practice of most of the Jewish world.

Today, Lod is a development town populated mainly by Jews (80 percent) who arrived after the establishment of Israel. There is a sizeable Arab population (20 percent) living there as well.

1005 Rabbi Moshe Tukachinsky, *Luach Eretz Yisrael.*

MYSTICAL
AND
SUPERNATURAL

PREDICTIONS

Although most of us pay little attention to newspaper horoscopes, tarot cards, or fortune tellers, such matters have enjoyed some prominence within Jewish thought and tradition. In fact, Judaism is replete with references to the reality of astrological truths and predictions. The Zohar even offers an entire course on reading palms and foreheads.[1006]

Here we will deal with whether one should be concerned with omens, psychics, and other extrasensory predictions. As mentioned, fortune telling, astrology, and other forms of divination have much precedent throughout the Torah. In fact, it was through his astrologers that Pharaoh correctly learned that his dominion over the Jewish people was coming to an end with the birth of Moshe. Pharaoh then attempted to "trick" his fate through his horrendous plan of infanticide, in the hope of drowning the newly born would-be redeemer.[1007] Even our forefather, Avraham, was so well versed in the art of astrology that when promised a son by God, he actually doubted the Divine promise, as he had "seen" in the stars that he was meant to live childless![1008]

In biblical times, no sage was considered fully competent unless he was able to foresee the future through the stars.[1009] Even during the Talmudic era, many sages of the Talmud consulted the stars as part of any important decision.[1010]

What is subject to debate, however, is whether the Jewish people today are subject to mystical merits, astrological predictions, and random fortune.[1011] Some commentators believe that Jews are immune to psychic predictions in the merit of observing the

---

1006 Yitro 78a.
1007 Sota 12b.
1008 Rashi, Bereishit 15:5.
1009 Esther 1:13.
1010 Shabbat 156b; considering that Rav Nachman bar Yitzchak's mother acted based on a psychic's prediction, one can deduce that other contemporaries, including Talmudic sages, relied on other such phenomena as well.
1011 Shabbat 156.

Torah.[1012] In what seems to be somewhat of a compromise, the Talmud concludes that life, children, and livelihood are indeed dependent on *mazal* – (random luck and fortune), whereas everything else in life is provided through a "merit system" between the individual and God.[1013] While the merit system suggestion – that one's lot in this world is commensurate with one's level of observance – does hold some weight,[1014] it must be properly balanced with the Talmudic concept of "there are no rewards in this world for mitzvot performed."[1015]

Any interest in and certainly the practice of predicting the future seems to be in direct conflict with the biblical prohibitions regarding witchcraft and the like.[1016] It appears though that the early Talmudic authorities understood this prohibition as simply opposing the constant involvement of fortune tellers in one's life for all matters, which could then lead one to forget that God is ultimately running the show. Nevertheless, if one were to come across a competent and credible fortune teller – an unlikely occurrence – one would be well advised to take caution from his or her words.[1017]

There were, however, rabbinical authorities who opposed any tolerance for any psychic practices. Leading this outcry was the always rational Rambam. He lashes out against any such practices and pronounces even physical punishments upon those who consider them, declaring them equivalent to idolatry. [1018] We are taught that one who preaches prophesies relating to the Messiah is one who is known to consult demons, play in witchcraft, and is otherwise delusional.[1019]

Interestingly enough, however, the Talmud predicts a person's nature according to the day of the week he was born. For example, children who were born on a Sunday will likely turn out either

---

1012   Opinion of the Ein Yakov, cited in Rabbi Aharon Ross, "Starstruck: The Place of Astrology in Judaism" at http://chaburas.org/astrolog.html.
1013   Moed Katan 28a.
1014   Tosafot, Shabbat 156.
1015   Kiddushin 39b.
1016   Vayikra 19:26.
1017   Ritva, Shabbat 156a, cited at http://www.chaburas.org/astrolog.html.
1018   *Hilchot Avoda Zara* 11:8.
1019   *Sefer Chassidim* 206.

really good or really bad. Being born on a Tuesday may land you a few bucks in life but you'll likely be an unbecoming soul. Brains are given out on Wednesdays. The curious types are usually born on Fridays. The list goes on and on.[1020] The Talmud continues with predictions not only based on the day of the week, but combined as well with which planets were dominant on the day one was born.

The issues concerning psychic practices and predictions continue to find a place in the writings of more recent authorities as well. While some authorities permit it casually, others forbid it completely.[1021] Most, however, are of the opinion that consulting astrologers is a violation of the biblical precept to have faith in God and His decisions.[1022] The Talmud tells us there is not much we can do to improve our lot because this world is really one big wheel – what goes around comes around.[1023] Remember – the challa bread of Rosh Hashana is round!

It would be remiss not to point out that the debates above have little contemporary relevance, as psychic practices today – such as in the form of horoscopes, fortune tellers, and tarot cards – are little more than scams to take your money. The original and professional skills of astrology discussed throughout the Torah and Talmud are no longer known, let alone practiced. Let us recall that "He who trusts in Hashem – kindness shall surround him."[1024] Even with all the above, we should also remember the Talmudic disclaimer: Jews are not subject to mazal![1025]

HALLOWEEN

Those who don't yet live in Israel no doubt feel some discomfort every year towards the end of October, with the much-publicized

---

1020 Shabbat 156a.
1021 See Tur and commentaries to YD 179; Sefer Chassidim 59.
1022 Devarim 18:13.
1023 Shabbat 151b.
1024 Tehillim 32.
1025 Shabbat 156b.

preparations for Halloween. The "holiday" of Halloween derives from the Celtic festival of Samhain, a day on which it was believed that the powers of the devil run strong, and thus an auspicious occasion for the invocation and manipulation of everything spiritually evil. Furthermore, it was also believed that the souls of the dead returned to visit their past homes on this day, and from that, the theme of ghosts, witches, and demons roaming the streets was born. The Catholic Church tried valiantly to fight this pagan phenomenon through the institution of "All Hallows' Eve" as well as "All Saints' Day," which was their alternative for providing their flocks with a more wholesome opportunity to associate with the dead, but to no avail.

For the Jewish people, Halloween was always an evening of bloody pogroms and other attacks on Jews and the Jewish community, especially during the Middle Ages. If you are intrigued by the idea of spirits roaming the streets, however, be on the lookout on Hoshana Rabba night– you may see or hear a few.[1026]

With it being clear that the early origins of Halloween are pagan and foreign, Halloween would appear to be completely off-limits to the Jewish people. This is in contrast to other civic observances like Thanksgiving, which do find some halachic support.[1027] It would be remiss not to acknowledge upfront that the vast majority of Jews who do mistakenly observe or otherwise participate in Halloween festivities are likely ignorant of its true origins and history of terror, and merely dress up in search of candy without any sense of religious duty.

With that being said, it is worth exploring the question of whether a Jew is permitted to celebrate Halloween in any way. In search of an answer to this question, we need look no further than the *Shulchan Aruch* and its commentaries. Based on the Talmud,[1028] the Rema writes: "Practices observed by Gentiles are forbidden to be followed when they seem to stem from an idolatrous source or are without

---

1026 *Sefer Chassidim* 452.
1027 It is reported that Rabbi Yosef Dov Soloveitchik of Yeshiva University would never schedule classes on Thanksgiving in order to allow for families to be together.
1028 Tosafot, Avoda Zara 11a.

logic. [Gentile] customs that are practiced for a logical reason...are permissible."[1029]

It emerges, therefore, that a practice that has its basis in idolatry or some other pagan source is clearly prohibited.[1030] Consequently, the only salvation Halloween would have from a halachic perspective would be if it were a logical observance. Hmmmm... Is collecting candy in costume on an October night logical? With that, on to the next issue.

One may ask, however, whether participating in Halloween by distributing candies to the "goblins" who come knocking at the door is of any halachic concern. On this issue, many authorities are of the position that there would be no halachic concerns based on the Talmudic principle of *darchei shalom*, which is a legal concept referring to the great lengths to which we must go to ensure peace and tranquility with our non-Jewish neighbors. A feeling of animosity would ensue if it were known that all Jewish homes were off-limits to trick-or-treaters and that the Jews were not willing to give candies to non-Jewish children. We would not be seen as warriors of monotheism, but rather, as a selfish and self-centered people, a stereotype we must avoid.

Perhaps as the ideal "trick or treat," drop a copy of this Halloween review onto your Jewish friends who may be unfamiliar with some of the relevant issues of participating in Halloween.

Rabbi Michael Broyde adds:

> Your section on Halloween is correct in that it discourages Jewish children from going trick or treat celebrating, and correctly distinguishes between Halloween and Thanksgiving, which many *poskim* permit to be celebrated as it is a secular holiday.[1031] A simple read of the *Encyclopedia Britannica* recounts the religious history of Halloween as follows:

1029 YD 178.

1030 This would clearly include "St. Valentines Day."

1031 See Rabbi Broyde's article, "The Celebrating of Thanksgiving at the End of November: A Secular or Religious Holiday," *Journal of Halacha and Contemporary Society* 30 (1995):42–66 for more on this.

> Halloween, also called All Hallows' Eve or
> All Hallows' Evening, [is] a holy or hallowed
> evening observed on October 31, the eve of All
> Saints' Day… In ancient Britain and Ireland,
> the Celtic festival of Samhain eve was observed
> on October 31, at the end of summer… It was
> the time to placate the supernatural powers
> controlling the processes of nature. In addition,
> Halloween was thought to be the most favorable
> time for divinations concerning marriage, luck,
> health, and death. It was the only day on which
> the help of the devil was invoked for such
> purposes. The pagan observances influenced the
> Christian festival of All Hallows' Eve, celebrated
> on the same date.

Thus, Halloween, unlike Thanksgiving, plainly has in
its origins religious beliefs that are foreign to Judaism,
and whose beliefs are prohibited to us as Jews.

In order to justify candy collection on Halloween,
one would have to accept the truthfulness of any of
the following assertions:

- Halloween celebrations have a secular origin.
- The conduct of the individuals "celebrating
  Halloween" can be rationally explained
  independent of Halloween.
- The pagan origins of Halloween or the Catholic
  response to it are so deeply hidden that they have
  disappeared, and the celebrations can be attributed
  to some secular source or reason.
- The activities memorialized by Halloween are
  actually consistent with the Jewish tradition.

Since none of these statements appear true, and thus
applying these halachic rules to Halloween leads
to the conclusion that participation in Halloween

celebrations – which is what collecting candy is when one is wearing a costume – is prohibited. Halloween, since it has its origins in a pagan practice, and lacks any overt rational reason for its celebration other than its pagan origins or the Catholic response to it, is governed by the statement of Rabbi Isserles that such conduct is prohibited as its origins taint it. One should not send one's children out to trick or treat on Halloween, or otherwise celebrate the holiday.

The question of whether one can give out candy to people who come to the door is a different one, as there are significant reasons based on *darchei shalom* (the ways of peace), *eva* (the creation of unneeded hatred towards the Jewish people), and other secondary rationales that allow one to distribute candy to people who will be insulted or angry if no candy is given.[1032]

1032 Rabbi Broyde elaborates: Indeed, the question of whether Gentiles are even prohibited from engaging in this kind of pagan practices as a form of secondary worship is most complicated, and is dependent on the various ways one can interpret the words of the Rema found in OC 156:1. This issue (determining what is idol worship for Gentiles) requires a great deal of detailed examination of the contemporary rituals and theologies of various faiths, as well as a clear understanding of what is idol worship according to Jewish law. For an excellent essay discussing this in medieval Jewry, see Rabbi J. David Bleich, "Divine Unity in Maimonides, the Tosafists and Meiri," in Lenn E. Goodmann, ed., *Neoplatonism and Jewish Thought* (Albany, NY: State University of New York Press, 1992), pp. 237–254. This is even more so true when the community is unaware of the halachic problems associated with the conduct, and the common practice even within many Jewish communities is to "celebrate" the holiday. Thus, one may give candy to children who come to one's house to "trick or treat" if one feels that this is necessary.

D E M O N S

"Fantasy is hardly an escape from reality.

It's a way of understanding it."

– Lloyd Alexander

No matter where you go nowadays, there is no avoiding the movie rage and box office sellouts in the world of "fantasy" films. Whether it's *Harry Potter, Jurrasic Park,* or *Lord of the Rings,* the fantasy craze has forced dialogue on the occult, and Jews are no exception to the phenomenon. Have you ever wondered what Judaism has to say about ghosts, wizards, demons, and the like? Below is a short presentation of some relevant Jewish sources on the topic, but as with everything mystical, a grain of salt is advised.

Although the Torah itself makes very little reference to the supernatural, the Babylonian Talmud deals with it at great length.[1033] The Torah purposely left out discussion of angels lest people come to make them into deities and otherwise attribute supernatural powers to them.[1034]

There is support in the Talmud for the limited and controlled existence of ghosts. Spirits of the dead have also been known to affect and interact with the living.[1035] Rest assured, however, that for the most part, they cause no harm, and actually they often try to help. Don't laugh this subject off – not only did your ancestors

---

1033 Interestingly, there is not a single mention of demons in the Jerusalem Talmud. Some commentators suggest that many of the supernatural passages of the Babylonian Talmud reflect the influence of local beliefs of that time. Rav Kook in *Ezrat Kohen* 6 writes that demons were never much of an issue in the Land of Israel due to its holiness.
1034 *Sefer Chassidim* 192.
1035 Shabbat 152b.

believe in this stuff, they even worshipped demons and offered sacrifices to them![1036]

It is recorded that after his death, the ghost of Rabbi Yehuda Hanassi, author of the Mishna, would routinely visit his family in order to recite Kiddush for them on Friday nights.[1037] King Shaul, no less, conducted a séance to call up Shmuel,[1038] and for the record, Shmuel was not too pleased to have been disturbed.[1039] Nevertheless, ghosts are generally considered insignificant within rabbinic literature and Jewish tradition, although it is worth noting that the dead are present at their funerals, and are listening to the eulogies being delivered.[1040]

Demons, the Babylonian Talmud asserts, do exist and were intentionally created by God just like everything else. According to tradition, demons were created on the first Friday of creation towards the evening.[1041] Certainly anyone familiar with Jewish texts would have come across such terms as *sheidim*, *Ashmedai*, and *Azazel*, all of which refer to the esoteric side of Judaism. There is also the infamous Lillith, mother of all demons.[1042] She is known to be grouchy and to sexually harass people, particularly males; Rabbi Hanina forbids men to sleep alone in a house at night lest they fall prey to her.[1043]

The Talmud makes no reservations about its feelings on demons and magic. For example, the Talmud teaches that demons are more numerous than we are.[1044] In fact, according to it there are approximately eleven thousand of them surrounding you as you read this. Indeed, if you have ever gotten tired from walking, or found that your clothes were wearing out rather quickly, it's probably because of those wretched demons rubbing on you and wearing

---

1036 Devarim 32:17.
1037 *Sefer Chassidim* 1129.
1038 Chagiga 4b.
1039 Some commentators suggest that the entire séance was a hoax. See Radak on Shmuel I 28:24.
1040 Shabbat 153a.
1041 Avot 5:8.
1042 Bava Batra 73a.
1043 Shabbat 151b.
1044 Berachot 6.

out your clothes.[1045] No need to panic, however, as demons have a number of other places they prefer to loiter besides among humans. They are also known to hang out on pitchers and other containers of water,[1046] palm trees,[1047] and especially in bathrooms.[1048]

In case you're spooked or scared, just relax. There really is no need to have a demon detector installed in your home. The Jerusalem Talmud and its rabbis all but reject the possibility of the existence of demons. You can also take comfort in what the Rambam has to say on the issue: "Belief in astrology, sorcery, oaths, lucky charms, demons, forecasting the future, and talking to the dead – all these are the essence of idol worship, and are lies…. He who believes in these is nothing but a fool."[1049]

Go figure!

DREAMS

No doubt that at one time or another, you've had a dream – a disturbing dream or maybe even a pleasant one. And then you ask yourself the question of impossible self-evaluation: Could it be prophecy? What about a Divine communiqué of sorts? Has God come down from the heavens to personally address me? Let's see what Judaism has to say regarding dreams.[1050]

Already in the book of Bereishit we see dreams playing a prominent role in various capacities.[1051] Dreams also play a major role in the Torah's development of Yosef, who dreams of ruling over his brothers. While his dream indeed came to pass, with Yosef becoming ruler over Egypt, it must be noted, however, that parts

---

1045 Ibid.
1046 Chullin 105b.
1047 Pesachim 111b.
1048 Gittin 70a.
1049 Rambam, *Hilchot Avoda Zara* 11:11–18.
1050 Based on an article by Rabbi Michael Taubes at http://www.tzemachdovid.org/
      thepracticaltorah/vayeishev.shtml.
1051 Bereishit 18, 28.

of Yosef's dream were indeed inaccurate, as the dream depicted his deceased mother bowing down to him, as well! From here, we see that dreams will always contain components of irrelevance.[1052]

What is the value of those images in dreams that may indeed contain hidden potential or some sort of premonition? Commentators note that not all dreams that the biblical figures ever envisioned were actually recorded, and that is simply because the vast majority of them never came true![1053] So how seriously should we be taking the dreams that we have?

At first glance, the dominant view amongst scholars seems to be that dreams essentially have no validity – at least from the perspective of prophecy. In fact, the Talmud explicitly declares dreams to merely be a reflection of what one has thought about or experienced during the day.[1054] Talmudic commentators further caution those with mystical inclinations not to take their dreams too seriously, and to always remember that anything one has dreamt has no halachic significance whatsoever.[1055] Rabbi Menachem Meiri tells us that dreams are primarily nonsense.[1056]

Those who are convinced that dreams must hold some meaning or authority will be pleased to learn that some of the classical sources do indeed validate dreams as having some spiritual value. Rabbi Don Isaac Abarbanel, basing himself on the Talmud,[1057] declares that a dream is comparable to any other form of prophecy.[1058] There is also a Midrash that defines dreams as "undeveloped prophecy."[1059] Even the Aristotelian and otherwise rational Rambam approaches the subject of dreams in relationship to that of prophecy.[1060] We also can't ignore the many pages of no less an authority than the Talmud that are devoted to offering outlooks and insights to interpreting

---

1052 Berachot 55a.
1053 Chizkuni, Bereishit 37.
1054 Berachot 55b.
1055 Chiddushei Haran, Sanhedrin 30a.
1056 Meiri, Sanhedrin 30a.
1057 Berachot 55b.
1058 Commentary to Parshat Miketz.
1059 Bereishit Rabba 17:7.
1060 *Moreh Nevuchim* 2:36.

dreams.[1061] There were actually several rabbis throughout history who rendered halachic decisions based on what they saw in their dreams.[1062] However, never accept anything that a dead person may tell you in a dream,[1063] unless it's advice on proper repentance for one's transgressions.[1064]

Although Rabbi Chaim Medini seems to side with those who reject attributing significance to dreams, he does say, however, that when danger is predicted in a dream, it should not be dismissed lightly.[1065] In fact, there exist a number of rituals and prayers that one can perform in order to cope with a bad dream; these are known as *hatavat chalom* (amelioration of a dream) and are printed in prayerbooks. These dream rituals are even cited and codified in the *Shulchan Aruch*.[1066] It is even permitted to fast on Shabbat in order to ward off a disturbing dream. Note, however: if you fast on Shabbat due to an upsetting dream, you would also be required to fast another day during the week as a penalty for the sin of having fasted on Shabbat![1067] Another chance of ameliorating your dreams is to recite special prayers during the Birkat Kohanim.[1068]

Bottom line from this writer: if you choose to subscribe to these ideas, then that's great – prophesize away. If you're not one for the supernatural, well, that's fine, too. Regardless of what you believe or which authorities you accept on this issue, all agree that one should not spend too much time delving into such matters, but rather to be sure to focus on Torah and mitzvot above all else.

1061 Berachot 55b.
1062 Taz, OC 585:7.
1063 *Rabbi Yehuda Hachassid* 13.
1064 *Sefer Chassidim* 729.
1065 Sdei Chemed, *Maareches Hadalet* 45.
1066 OC 220.
1067 OC 288:4.
1068 Berachot 55b; *Mishna Berura* 130:3, 4.

MORE MITZVOT

WRITING A SEFER TORAH

"So now, write this song for yourselves, and

teach it to the Children of Israel."[1069]

With this verse, we are assigned the final mitzva of the entire Torah – mitzva number 613. As we will see in greater depth, the precept this verse teaches us is that every Jew is duty bound to write a Torah scroll for him or herself. Well, actually, whether or not women are included in this is a matter of dispute amongst the authorities. Some authorities encourage women to take part in this mitzva as well,[1070] while others exempt them from this mitzva entirely, as women are not required to occupy themselves with Torah study as are men.[1071] Even one who inherits a Torah would still be obligated to have a Torah commissioned and written especially for him.[1072]

Among the many interpretations offered as to the motive for this mitzva, it is suggested that the writing of a Torah and keeping it in one's home will promote and encourage greater Torah study.[1073] Not all authorities accepted this verse as requiring the writing of a Torah scroll. Several rabbinical authorities have suggested that this verse calls merely for the writing of the Torah portion of Ha'azinu, which is referred to as a "song" in rabbinic literature.[1074] Others completely reject the entire notion of having to write anything at all, and seemingly consider this verse no more than poetic prose![1075] Nevertheless, normative halacha accepts this verse as actually obligating the writing of individual Torah scrolls for every Jew.[1076]

1069   Devarim 31:19.
1070   Aruch Hashulchan, YD 270:5, 6.
1071   Rambam, *Hilchot Sefer Torah* 7:1.
1072   Sanhedrin 21b.
1073   Sefer Hachinuch 613.
1074   Rashi, Ramban, Devarim 31:19.
1075   This would appear to be the view of the Behag, who does not address this mitzva.
1076   Nedarim 38a; YD 270.

Among the modern-day authorities who actively promoted the fulfillment of this mitzva was the Lubavitcher Rebbe, Rabbi Menachem Mendel Schneerson. In fact, it was one of Rabbi Schneerson's ten lifelong projects. He felt that it was critical for every Jew to participate in this mitzva, either by commissioning a scribe to write an entire Torah scroll on one's behalf, or even by merely purchasing one letter towards the completion of one. It has been suggested that his urgency in spreading this mitzva derives from a verse in the book of Daniel, which seems to teach that those who have participated in the mitzva of writing a Torah scroll will be saved from future apocalyptic disasters.[1077]

Even one who merely corrects a non-kosher Torah and thereby makes it usable once more is credited with having written the entire scroll![1078] The Midrash relates that prior to his passing, Moshe wrote a Torah scroll on behalf of each and every tribe, and, by extension, every Jew, thereby fulfilling the mitzva on behalf of the entire nation![1079]

Today's application of the mitzva has several manifestations. Considering that this mitzva is intended to further Torah study, many authorities are of the opinion that the requirement to write a Torah scroll is not necessarily literal, and that the mitzva can also be fulfilled by buying Torah books to study from, and this seems to be the dominant view.[1080] Nevertheless, one who participates in the literalist approach by writing a Torah scroll is to be praised.[1081]

We are taught that whoever fulfills this mitzva will merit the blessing of "And everyone who observes this commandment will be blessed, and he and his sons will become wise."[1082]

1077 Ibn Ezra, Daniel 12:1.
1078 Rambam, *Hilchot Sefer Torah* 7:1.
1079 Midrash Rabba, Devarim 9:9.
1080 Tur, Taz, YD 270.
1081 Taz, YD 270.
1082 *Sefer Hachinuch* 613.

TRAVEL

G oing on vacation or otherwise taking time off from our daily routines is an important and healthy part of life. Today, in the twenty-first century, vacations have become fully compatible with a halachic lifestyle. Whether it's Club Med (now with even glatt kosher venues), a cruise (complete with cantorial concerts and Kiddushes larger than wedding receptions) or some other exotic location, any opportunity for time off with a change in scenery is surely appreciated.

Judaism, however, never goes on holiday, and the Talmud and codes of law offer an abundance of customs and practices to be observed with regard to traveling.[1083] Indeed, the Torah itself reminds us to take it along with us when we go on a trip![1084]

To begin with, prior to any trip, you should be sure to give extra charity,[1085] and advise community rabbis of your impending departure.[1086] Although parting is such sweet sorrow, it is considered very inauspicious to cry prior to taking leave for a trip.[1087] There is a popular custom of providing a traveler with money, known as *shaliach mitzva gelt*, which the traveler is to donate to charity upon arrival at his or her destination.[1088] The traveler, now on a mission to donate charity, transforms the entire trip into a mitzva, which is said to confer protection on the traveler.

After actually beginning one's journey, there exists a special traveler's prayer, *tefillat haderech*, which is to be recited. It is short, sweet, and available in any siddur. So important is the recitation of tefillat haderech that disregarding this special prayer is comparable to disregarding the reading of the Megilla on Purim or the ritual hand washing before eating bread.[1089] This prayer is not to be

---

1083 Berachot 29b.
1084 Devarim 6:7.
1085 *Kitzur Shulchan Aruch* 68:6.
1086 *Be'er Heitev* 101:10.
1087 *Rabbi Yehuda Hachassid* 10 (Nosafot).
1088 *Kaf Hachaim* 110.
1089 *Ahalech b'Amitecha* 9:2, cited in Rabbi Eliezer Wenger, *Halichot Mordechai: The Traveler's Companion* (Montreal: b'Ruach HaTorah, 1998). See there for an outstanding and comprehensive review in English of all laws relating to travel.

recited on any routine local drive, but rather when embarking on trips greater than four kilometers in length from the perimeter of one's city of departure. Although ideally it should be recited while standing,[1090] it may be recited while sitting when it is impractical to stand.[1091] Additionally, there does exist an additional prayer to be recited when embarking on airplane travel that has been composed in recent years, although the text is in very limited circulation and not unanimously accepted.

For those who enjoy an alternative approach to applying halacha, it is reported that Rabbi Yosef Dov Soloveitchik would not recite tefillat haderech during his frequent road trips from Boston to New York. He held that the prayer is only to be said on journeys that may arouse some fear or hesitation – certainly not on a routine commute.[1092]

When driving on long road trips, the Lubavitcher Rebbe, Rabbi Menachem Mendel Schneerson, recommended that one should keep a siddur, charity box, and other holy books in the car as Divine protection against accidents. He also encouraged drivers to take a break after every hour of driving and to get out and walk around the car. Although many are lazy, one is well advised to bear in mind that wearing a seatbelt may actually be a mitzva of the Torah.[1093] It is also certainly a rabbinical requirement, and possibly even a biblical one, to keep to the speed limit at all times.[1094] All travels, especially road trips, should preferably be avoided at night.[1095]

Another interesting custom relating to travel has to do with your shoes. Never, but never, polish your shoes on the day of a trip – it's considered bad luck and even dangerous for one's journey.[1096] Additionally, it is considered very inauspicious to return home once having departed, even in order to fetch something forgotten and

---

1090 *Tur* 110:10.
1091 OC 110:4.
1092 Cited in Rabbi Hershel Shachter, *Nefesh Harav*.
1093 Devarim 4:15.
1094 *Teshuvot Chatam Sofer*, CM 44; *dina d'malchuta dina* is a biblical requirement according to many authorities.
1095 Pesachim 2a.
1096 *Rabbi Yehuda Hachassid* 39.

even if needed for your trip.[1097] If your travels will be taking you aboard an airplane or ship, the craft should be boarded with the right foot first.[1098] If taking a cruise for your vacation, you should ensure that the date of departure never falls out on a Wednesday, Thursday, or Friday.[1099] All Friday travel is to be discouraged for fear of possibly having to violate Shabbat.[1100]

Travel to Israel, especially during holiday time, opens up some very interesting halachic debates. For example, if you would be traveling to Israel for Pesach, you may be qualified to observe only one seder and to resume eating bread at the conclusion of the seventh day of Pesach. Issues such as these are subject to a variety of factors and should be discussed with one's rabbi.[1101]

Women will be pleased to learn that a married man is required to bring gifts to his wife upon return from a trip,[1102] and should never return home from a trip hungry.[1103] If one's trip required the crossing of an ocean or desert, or posed any other conceivable form of danger, the blessing Hagomel is to be recited among a minyan, preferably at the Torah.[1104] One should be sure to recite the Hagomel blessing as soon as possible, no later than thirty days after returning from the trip.[1105] According to many authorities women are not obligated in the recitation of Hagomel – certainly not at the Torah – while others suggest that she recite it in front of her husband or other women.[1106]

As with all pleasures in life, Judaism accentuates certain responsibilities when traveling, all intended to help one grow into a more spiritually sensitive person. So the next time you pack your bags for a trip, don't forget to pack your religion.

1097 *Rabbi Yehuda Hachassid* 38.
1098 *Kaf Hachaim* 110:32.
1099 Shabbat 19a; OC 248:1; *Mishna Berura* Introduction, 4, 5, 8.
1100 OC 249:1.
1101 See "Second Day Yom Tov in Israel" for more on this issue.
1102 *Ahalech b'Amitecha* 27:8, cited in Wenger, *Halichot Mordechai*.
1103 Temimei Derech 25b, cited in Wenger, *Halichot Mordechai*.
1104 OC 219:1.
1105 *Mishna Berura* 219:8.
1106 *Aruch Hashulchan* 219:6, 9; *Igrot Moshe*, OC 8:14.

B I R K A T   I L A N O T

One of the lesser-known mitzvot of the spring season is the recitation of a short, simple blessing upon trees in blossom. The basis for this precept is to be found in the Talmud, which declares that "a person who goes out during the days of Nissan and sees trees in bloom recites the following blessing: Blessed are You Lord our God, King of the universe, Who did not leave anything lacking in His universe, and created in it good creatures and good trees, to give pleasure to humankind with them."[1107] Reciting this blessing is so precious that if the deadline for its recitation is nearing, one may take to the fields even on Shabbat to ensure that one does not miss this opportunity.[1108]

Although the wording of the Talmud seems to imply that one may only recite this blessing during the month of Nissan, the consensus of halachic authorities is that the blessing may actually be recited anytime during the blooming season, say, from March to May.[1109] Further substantiation that the "days of Nissan" is more of a figure of speech than a specific directive is that if you live in the southern hemisphere, it would be virtually impossible to ever recite this blessing! You would likely be reciting this blessing in November or thereabouts, when trees blossom in those places. Perhaps one can infer from the wording of the Talmud that it was assumed by our sages that all Jews would be forever living in the Middle East. The real kabbalists, though, seem to insist that the blessing be recited specifically in the month of Nissan for mystical reasons.[1110]

Another point of contention stemming from the wording of this precept is the Talmud's use of the word "trees" in plural. Indeed, some authorities insist that the blessing should only be recited upon gazing at two or more trees in blossom. Most other authorities, however, rule that the Talmud's wording is, again, only

---

1107   Berachot 43b.
1108   *Teshuvot v'Hanhagot* 1:191.
1109   *Mishna Berura* 226:1.
1110   *Kaf Hachaim* 126:1

a figure of speech, and that the blessing may be recited on even a single tree. Some authorities suggest that the blessing be recited on sweet-smelling trees, or trees that produce appetizing fruits, but that reason alone should not delay the performance of this mitzva. One who is blind should go along with a partner to "view" the blossoming trees and have the partner recite the blessing. In this way, the blind individual participates in the mitzva by answering "amen" at the conclusion of the blessing.

An interesting arboreal aside is that God originally intended that both trees as well as their fruit were to be edible by mankind. Unfortunately, the trees did not heed God's will, and provided only edible fruit, rather than completely edible trees.[1111] Nevertheless, we celebrate the tree. Indeed, so beloved is this easy mitzva that many schools in Israel spend a day studying the many details and interpretations behind it, often culminating in a school trip to an orchard, so that everyone can say the blessing together. In fact, it is ideal to endeavor to recite this blessing with a minyan. Women should make an effort to perform this mitzva as well.[1112]

Regardless of how many trees you'll be reciting the blessing over, or whether you'll be reciting this blessing on Shabbat or a weekday, the message is unmistakable: the renewal of nature and our interaction with it is nothing short of an encounter with the Creator. We are told that those who are careful to fulfill this mitzva every year will merit many blessings. Let us bear in mind the biblical teaching that "man is like a tree of the field."[1113] May we merit seeing the true blossoming and flowering of all mankind.

SHECHITA

The mitzva of *shechita* (kosher slaughter) is one that meets us on our plate at every meat meal. Without strict compliance with

---

1111   Rashi, Bereishit 1:11.
1112   *Teshuvot v'Hanhagot* 1:190.
1113   Devarim 20:19.

the laws of shechita, meat consumption is completely forbidden. The mitzva of shechita is perhaps the most significant of mitzvot not explicitly decreed in the Torah, but rather elaborated personally by God to Moses.[1114] As is the case with many other mitzvot, a blessing is recited before commencing the slaughter.[1115] However, unlike most other mitzvot, shechita is actually an optional mitzva that in theory need never be implemented.[1116]

Virtually any Jew can become a *shochet* (ritual slaughterer) – even women.[1117] Oddly enough, even those who are blind are permitted to perform shechita as well![1118] Non-Jews, of course, are excluded from the profession.[1119] Although it is forbidden for a shochet to slaughter while drunk, we need not be too picky if he only had a few drinks.[1120]

Shochtim are requested to arrive at work clothed, but in case of emergency, shechita may be performed no matter what the individual may or may not be wearing.[1121] There are no restrictions on when shechita may be performed – night or day is acceptable as long as the working area is well lit.[1122]

In the event that you'll need to slaughter an animal while on a cruise, you are requested to try to keep it discreet by directing the blood flow down the outer walls of the ship, and to clean up any mess your shechita may leave behind.[1123] According to kabbala, one should not slaughter geese in January or February. Doing so could result in some serious health concerns unless you are sure to eat the goose's liver.[1124]

Although common practice is to use the special shechita knife known as a *chalaf* for kosher slaughter, absolutely any sharp and

---

1114   Taz, YD 1:1/
1115   YD 19:1.
1116   Pesachim 7b.
1117   YD 1:1.
1118   YD 1:9.
1119   YD 2:1.
1120   YD 1:8.
1121   YD 1:10.
1122   YD 11:1.
1123   YD 11:4.
1124   YD 11:4.

smooth object may be used.[1125] There are no minimum width or length requirements for a shechita knife – just as long as it gets the job done.[1126] An embryo found inside a slaughtered animal does not require further shechita and may be eaten as is.[1127] An animal and its offspring may not be slaughtered on the same day.[1128]

While every single aspect of shechita is vital, there are, however, five specific details that are exceptionally crucial.[1129] These five details are:

- *Shechita* – that there be no interruption during the incision
- *Derasa* – that there be no pressing of the shechita knife against the neck
- *Chalada* – that there be no obstruction between the knife and the neck
- *Hagrama* – that the incision take place at the precise site
- *Ikkur* – that there be no tearing of any organs before or during the shechita process

A lesser-known component of the shechita process that applies to fowl and non-domesticated animals is the covering of the blood. That's right – after the slaughter, there is a biblical requirement to take specially prepared earth or sand and to sprinkle it upon any blood pools that may have formed after the slaughter.[1130] This independent mitzva has a blessing of its own.[1131] So important is this component of the shechita process that if one does not have anything to cover the blood with, then it is forbidden to slaughter.[1132] Never urinate or even spit upon dust or earth that was used for this mitzva, as an item used in the performance of a mitzva is to be treated respectfully.[1133]

There is simply no adequate way to convey the importance of shechita. It is the only permissible way, without exception, for a

---

1125 YD 6:1.
1126 YD 8:1.
1127 YD 13:2.
1128 YD 16:1.
1129 YD 23.
1130 YD 28:1.
1131 YD 28:2.
1132 YD 28:21.
1133 *Sefer Chassidim* 824.

Jew to consume meat. One who studies this topic in a little more depth will quickly learn that shechita is actually a very spiritual enterprise.

S H A T N E Z

Although you need not become immediately alarmed, I must caution you, however, that it may very well be a serious sin to wear fine Italian suits such as those manufactured by Hugo Boss, Armani, or Canali. This is because higher end men's suits often have linen inserts in the collar or lapel to give them a stiffer, more executive look. Wearing any combination of wool and linen in a single garment[1134] is a severe prohibition of the Torah,[1135] known as *shatnez*.

Wool and linen attached to each other by any means are forbidden to be worn.[1136] It does not matter whether they are sewn together, spun, twisted, or glued. The prohibition of shatnez applies to all – men, women, and children. The prohibition of shatnez applies not only to mixtures of wool and linen, but also to garments in which even sections of wool and sections of linen are permanently attached.[1137] It is forbidden to wear shatnez even if your body doesn't touch the material, and even if you get no personal pleasure from it. It is also forbidden to dress another Jew, even a baby, with shatnez.

When buying a garment, one cannot rely on the salesperson or even on the label to be sure of a garment's cloth content. This is because manufacturers are not required by law to reveal materials making up less than 2 percent of a garment. Even such a small

---

1134 Wearing one garment of one type underneath one of the other is problematic, as well.
1135 Devarim 22:11.
1136 Kilayim 9:1.
1137 Some authorities prohibit the use of baseball gloves due to an internal shatnez mixture.

amount, however, is prohibited by halacha.[1138] Even if a garment states 100 percent wool on the label, it still may legally contain linen threads such as those used to sew on the buttons, for example.

According to Rashi, the extremely peculiar commandment of shatnez is simply a *chok* – a mitzva with no chance of logical explanation whatsoever.[1139] There are other such seemingly illogical mitzvot as well, such as the prohibition on eating pork, or the process by which the ashes of a red heifer bring purity.

The Midrash suggests that the reason for shatnez stems from the episode of Cain and Abel.[1140] Cain brought God an offering of flax (the source of linen) and Abel brought a sheep (wool). This incident resulted in Cain killing Abel when only the latter's offering found favor before God, and it was thus decreed that never again should the two substances mix.

The Rambam is of the opinion that the rationale for the shatnez prohibition is because ancient pagan priests used to wear gowns of wool and linen weaved together as part of their idolatrous ceremonies.[1141] Additionally, it may just be that the "coat of many colors" that Yakov gave to Yosef, which led to many unfortunate consequences, was crafted from a shatnez mixture.[1142] Oddly enough, there are two exceptions to the shatnez rule: a) the mitzva of tzitzit may be performed with a shatnez garment[1143] and b) the clothing of the high priest was made from a shatnez combination.[1144]

If shatnez is found in a garment, but is successfully removed, the garment may then be worn. In many cases, shatnez can be easily removed from clothing because the wool and linen are not combined in the basic fabric of the garment. Shatnez should not be removed by a seamstress or a tailor, but by a trained expert. Many Jewish communities have full-service shatnez laboratories, with

---

1138 YD 299:4.
1139 Rashi, Bereishit 26:5.
1140 *Pirkei d'Rabbi Eliezer* 21.
1141 *Moreh Nevuchim* 3:49.
1142 Vayikra Rabba 10:6.
1143 See however OC 9:2; *Mishna Berura* 7.
1144 Rambam, *Hilchot Kilayim* 10:32.

trained experts who examine garments for any trace of shatnez. The cost for such service usually runs about ten dollars per garment.

The rabbis have said, "Anyone who is careful to avoid wearing shatnez will merit to be dressed in garments of salvation and a cloak of righteousness."[1145]

Not only must we make sure that our food is kosher, we must ensure that our clothes are as well. Here's a tip to ensure you never run into a question of shatnez: have your suits custom made.

THE BEIT DIN

The secular legal system is actually superfluous for the Torah-observant Jew.[1146] Contrary to popular misconception, Judaism concerns itself as much with worldly and civil matters as it does with the spiritual. This even includes an independent and intricate financial and civil legal code. The fourth volume of the *Shulchan Aruch*, known as the *Choshen Mishpat*, deals entirely with litigation and civil law between Jews.

It is, in fact, a Torah requirement that in the event of a financial dispute between two Jews, the matter must be adjudicated in a beit din, a Jewish court.[1147] Indeed, there is a strict Torah prohibition on summoning another Jew to a secular court.[1148] To do so publicly undermines the value of Jewish law and the competency of our own traditions to resolve disputes.[1149] One who dismisses the institution of the beit din system is considered "wicked" and rebellious against the entire Torah.[1150] Of course, like any chain, the beit din is only as strong as its weakest link. Judges who behave corruptly, let alone

---

1145   Chochmat Adam, *Hilchot Shatnez*, 106:28.
1146   This chapter based on articles by Rabbi Doniel Neustadt available at http://www.torah.org/advanced/weekly-halacha/5762/vayechi.html and http://www.torah.org/advanced/weekly-halacha/5762/shemos.html.
1147   Gittin 88b.
1148   CM 26:1.
1149   Rashi, Shemot 21:2.
1150   CM 26:1.

those who take bribes and act in other dishonest manners, are considered to be among the most wicked people alive. In fact, we are taught that corrupt judges and rabbis are responsible for the troubles that come to this world, and are also the cause of God distancing Himself from the Jewish people.[1151] It is permissible to even engage in deceptive behavior and other shenanigans in order to expose a corrupt judge.[1152]

There are, of course, exceptions to the rule, and there are even times when it may be a mitzva to resolve a dispute in a secular court. For example, in the event that it is known with certainty that the defendant would ignore the call to a beit din, or would not comply with its rulings, it may be permitted to proceed directly to the secular courts.[1153]

Still, it is considered proper behavior to give the defendant a chance and invite him or her to have the dispute resolved according to Jewish law.[1154] If the invitation is rejected,[1155] the beit din can then issue a dispensation for the plaintiff to proceed to the secular court system. Some authorities allow any rabbi to issue this dispensation, not necessarily a beit din.[1156] This last ruling may be especially critical for communities in the Diaspora lacking a beit din that deals in financial matters.

In recognition of a plaintiff making the effort to have a dispute resolved through a beit din, Jewish law awards any expenses incurred by the claimant in pursuing the case in the secular court system to be borne by the defendant.[1157] Often, in a case where one is looking to enforce the collection of a rightfully owing debt, it is permitted to proceed straight to the secular system without seeking permission from a beit din. Similarly, it is permitted to avail oneself of all legal means to ensure that a ruling from a beit din is implemented.

1151 Rashi, Shabbat 139a.
1152 Shabbat 116a.
1153 *Minchat Yitzchak* 9:155.
1154 *Igrot Moshe*, CM 2:6.
1155 Some say that three invitations are required; Bava Kama 92b.
1156 *B'tzel Hachachma* 4:37.
1157 CM 14:5.

Taking this one step further, it is even permissible to ask a secular court to issue a temporary injunction against a defendant's assets in order for the plaintiff to properly prepare and present his case to the beit din.[1158] Similarly, in a situation where, for example, a tenant is not paying the rent and the issue is clear (via lease, etc.) that money is owed to the plaintiff, one may often proceed directly to the secular authorities.

The most vital component of being a first-rate Jew is being a good Jew in the marketplace as well. We must make a continuous effort to make sure that even our seemingly mundane behaviors and decisions are in accordance with Torah law.

THE INTERNATIONAL DATELINE

Notwithstanding that the international dateline is taken for granted by all international bodies and air travelers alike, the same may not necessarily be true regarding its halachic ramifications. Bear in mind that we Jews consider the Land of Israel as the primary focal point of the planet, and by extension, all of creation.[1159] Accordingly, we will see that halacha has its own take on what is to be deemed the international dateline.

In fact, the question of where the international dateline stands has far-reaching consequences for the observance of many mitzvot of the Torah. For example, it will define which day Shabbat is to be observed in various far-flung places around the world. We should realize that geographical and astronomical issues such as these, including familiarity with longitudes and latitudes, were topics well studied in ancient rabbinic circles.[1160]

While from a Torah perspective, a new day commences each evening with sunset, halacha acknowledges the reality of the

---

1158 *Beit Yosef* 47.
1159 Ta'anit 10a.
1160 Eruvin 56a; Pesachim 94b.

civil day, which begins at midnight, as well.[1161] However, as we all know, midnight arrives in different places at different times. When flying westward, for example, one will be fleeing the approach of midnight, thereby encountering it at a later time. To resolve this dilemma, it has been accepted the world over that the dateline and subsequent new day would be at 180 degrees from Greenwich, England. Considering that Greenwich never played a role in Jewish history, its designation has little halachic significance.

The Talmud tells us that the Jewish courts considered the new Jewish month to have arrived when the moon was visible in the Land of Israel before noon on any given day.[1162] If the new moon was spotted after such time, the *next* day was declared to be the start of the new month. The logic of this ruling was to ensure that in at least one place in the world, the new month, known as Rosh Chodesh, would be observed for at least twenty-four hours. Noon in Jerusalem is the latest time at which there is still some location on Earth that has not yet begun the new day. Based on this, many authorities place the halachic dateline 90 degrees east of Jerusalem.[1163] Hence, someone living past this "line" would be observing Shabbat a day later than Jerusalem.

However, not everyone agreed with the 90-degree demarcation. Based on alternative theories, other eminent authorities assert that the halachic dateline lies 180 degrees from Jerusalem.[1164] This latter view is the official position of the chief rabbinate of Israel. Yet others claim that there is no halachic dateline at all,[1165] and that for the purpose of days and dates, one merely follows the calendar in the place where one is presently residing.

As mentioned, this discussion is far from a theoretical one, and there are extensive ramifications for each of these views. For example, when would places such as Korea, Japan, and New Zealand,

---

1161   The Rashbam and others were of the opinion that even from a Torah perspective a new day begins in the morning just like on the civil calendar; Bereishit 1:5, 8. See also the Talmudic Encyclopedia, vol. 22, s.v. "Yom."
1162   Rosh Hashana 20b.
1163   Opinion of the Chazon Ish.
1164   Opinion of Rabbi Yechiel Michael Tukachinsky.
1165   Opinion of Rabbi Tzvi Pesach Frank and others.

which find themselves past the 90-degree line, observe Shabbat and Yom Kippur? According to this view, Shabbat would be observed on Sundays! Such was the dilemma in the 1940s when many European Jews flocked to Kobe, Japan, to escape the Nazis. Believe it or not, some rabbis actually observed two days of Yom Kippur in order to be free of any doubt!

The vacationer to Hawaii is also faced with the issue of when to observe Shabbat. According to one of the opinions mentioned above, Shabbat must be observed on Friday, while according to another opinion, Shabbat is to be observed on Saturday! For your information, the local orthodox community of Hawaii subscribes to the view that declares Saturday as Shabbat.

Whichever opinion you choose to follow, one thing is for certain: there is no escaping being a Jew. It will follow you to the ends of the Earth.

GENIZA

Reverence, dignity, and sanctity are concepts deeply engrained within the Jewish psyche. Not only do such concepts pertain to issues associated with God and Torah, but they even extend to books, papers, and all materials that contain even the slightest references to such sacred matters. Indeed, one who does not relate to holy books with the proper respect is considered as one who desecrates the entire Torah.[1166]

It is a well-known practice within Judaism that Torah scrolls may not simply be tossed in the garbage when no longer usable. They must be buried in a Jewish cemetery, complete with a public ceremony, with specified prayers and readings (these can be found in the book *Ma'aver Yavok*).

The act of reverently disposing of a Torah and similar sacred objects through burial is referred to as placing them in *geniza*,

---

1166 *Sefer Chassidim* 273–276, 916, 918.

which can be translated to mean "in hiding." Not only does a Torah need geniza, but tefillin, mezuzot, and other holy scrolls that are no longer usable must be buried, as well.[1167]

The basis for disposing of holy objects in this way is derived from the biblical prohibition "You shall not do such unto the Lord your God,"[1168] referring to the requirement to destroy all traces of idolatry in the Land of Israel. The Torah is teaching us that destroying idolatry is permitted, but destroying Torah and other similar materials is prohibited.

On the other hand, English Torah materials, or even Hebrew materials that don't quote entire Torah verses, or at least omit the name of God in translation, may be discarded in a dignified manner, such as being respectfully wrapped and placed into a secondary utensil (i.e., a bag).[1169] Synagogue or school newsletters that contain Torah thoughts may therefore be discarded in the household garbage bin after having been wrapped. Similarly, when disposing of "challa" (the required portion of dough to be separated when baking) or tithes from fruits originating from the Land of Israel, the above-mentioned method of disposal may be employed as well.

One would be well advised to distance oneself from possibly violating the aforementioned biblical prohibition.[1170] From here derives the custom that at the top of a letter or other notes, the letters "BH" or "BSD" are written instead of the name of God, as these things are items that are likely to be tossed away after reading. Indeed, the Talmud warns against writing any of the Hebrew names of God on paper that is routinely thrown away.[1171] By contrast, there are ample halachic grounds for writing the word "God" in full on English materials.[1172]

1167 *Igrot Moshe* 4:39.
1168 Devarim 12:4.
1169 See *Bnei Banim* 3:20 on this issue including other solutions to the disposal of holy writings.
1170 See also *Aruch Hashulchan*, CM 27:3.
1171 Rosh Hashana 18a.
1172 YD 179:11; Shach, *Mishna Berura* 85:10.

The concept of ensuring utmost dignity when erasing the name of God has some interesting twenty-first-century applications. For example, would it be permissible to a) record over a tape containing God's name (i.e., a bar mitzva lesson tape), b) close your web browser after having viewed material containing Hebrew verses with God's name, or c) delete Torah-related materials from your hard drive? Questions such as these have been dealt with at length by Rabbi Ovadia Yosef[1173] and Rabbi Moshe Feinstein.[1174] They both seem to permit all these actions, as no physical script is being erased, only electronic material, which is considered insignificant in halacha.

We must always ensure that our reverence for Torah extends right through to written materials that are no longer usable. Indeed, we are taught that even the smashed pieces of the tablets of the Ten Commandments were treated with utmost respect.[1175]

1173   *Yabia Omer* 4:20.
1174   *Igrot Moshe*, YD 1:173.
1175   Menachot 99a.

END OF

LIFE ISSUES

BIKUR CHOLIM

It seems that due to busy schedules and hectic lives, one of the more frequently neglected mitzvot of the Torah[1176] is the mitzva of *bikur cholim*, namely, visiting the sick, infirm, and otherwise shut in.

We are taught that this is one of the mitzvot that God Himself performs.[1177] Indeed, visiting the sick is among nine unique mitzvot whose reward is beyond comprehension.[1178] This latter reward scale may be related to the teaching that one who visits the sick removes one-sixtieth of the ill person's illness. It is a mitzva that can be done countless times each and every day. One should be sure to visit even non-Jews who are sick.[1179] Visiting an enemy, however, is questionable.[1180]

The mitzva of bikur cholim has many different applications, and is not merely a generic "Hello, how are you?" inquiry. Rabbi Akiva would personally clean the room of the sick people he visited and tend to even their most mundane needs.[1181] He used to say that "anyone who fails to visit the sick contributes to their death." To remain with a sick person overnight in order to watch over them and tend to their needs is considered to be an extraordinary act of kindness.[1182]

The halacha states very clearly that for one to fulfill the mitzva of bikur cholim, one must pray for the patient's recovery. We are taught that the Divine presence is at the head of the bed of a sick person, and it is therefore proper that one pray on behalf of the sick individual at the time of the visit.[1183] It goes without saying that one may pray for the sick in any language, as God is a very

---

1176 Regarding whether bikur cholim is a mitzva of biblical or rabbinical origin, see *Sdei Chemed* 1:2:116.
1177 Sota 14a; God went to visit Avraham personally after his circumcision.
1178 Nedarim 39b; Shabbat 127a; *Aruch Hashulchan* 335:2.
1179 Gittin 61a.
1180 Shach, YD 335.
1181 Nedarim 40a.
1182 *Aruch Hashulchan* 335:3.
1183 *Tur*, YD 335.

accomplished linguist.[1184] If one visited a sick person and did not pray for his or her recovery or otherwise provide some substantial benefit, the mitzva is left unfulfilled.[1185]

The Zohar teaches that a person should not sit parallel to the head of one who is ill, because the Divine presence dwells there, nor should one sit parallel to his feet because the angel of death dwells there. A custom deriving from the Talmud is to change the name of the sick individual, which is believed to assist in having any negative decrees on that person annulled.[1186] This is because once someone's name is changed, the individual is considered to be somewhat born anew with a clean slate.

The Rambam has a thorough compilation of all the procedures and obligations of the mitzva of bikur cholim.[1187] He states that no one should think that fulfilling this mitzva is beneath his dignity.[1188] Repeated visits to the sick are encouraged, so long as the visits do not become burdensome to the patient.

It is vital, however, to continually keep in mind the respect and dignity of the patient. Perhaps visiting those with intestinal diseases, severe deformities, and other challenging conditions should be discouraged, lest the patient feel embarrassed. Likewise, perhaps those with severe head illnesses may be better off without visitors, so as not to aggravate their condition. The Rambam also suggests we avoid visiting people at the very start or very end of the day, likely a time when their strength is minimal. It is also inappropriate to visit people immediately upon their taking ill.

How should one behave when visiting the sick? It is suggested that we speak to the patient about daily affairs, trying to get his mind off his troubles. For example, halacha says that if a person who is severely ill loses a relative, we do not inform him of the loss until he himself is healed, lest the news of the death cause him further deterioration. Sadly, there are times when praying for the

---

1184 YD 335.
1185 Rema, YD 335:4.
1186 Rosh Hashana 16b.
1187 *Hilchot Avel* 14.
1188 It is reported that Rabbi Akiva Eiger would visit at least one sick person every single day; *Chut Hameshulash* 207.

speedy death of one who is ill is appropriate, such as in situations where recovery is simply not possible and the patient is suffering terribly.[1189]

The question is asked whether the mitzva of bikur cholim can be fulfilled with a telephone call. This issue is dealt with by numerous halachic authorities, who all seem to conclude that a phone call only suffices in situations where there is no other alternative.[1190]

May the One Who heals bless us all with only good health!

EUTHANASIA

The debate on euthanasia was catapulted to the forefront with the highly publicized case of Terri Schiavo. Although the Terri Schiavo case was one that was comprised of extensive religious, medical, emotional, and legal issues – all of which are completely beyond the scope of this discussion – it would be remiss to completely ignore such a topic, which leaves an effect on all mankind. The preservation and treatment of human life is an area that halacha addresses even to its minutest details.

It's not news that Judaism considers all life sacred, and the preservation of life is an obligation that halacha mandates at virtually all costs.[1191] From the Torah's perspective, there is simply no life that is not worth living, nor can a person's quality of life be properly measured. Similarly, "end of life" requests have little place in halacha, as Judaism does not recognize a person's final directives when they contradict Jewish law. For example, wishes for cremation are to be ignored. Legitimate wishes, however, are to be meticulously followed.[1192]

1189 Ran, Nedarim 40a.
1190 *Igrot Moshe*, YD 1:223; *Yechave Da'at* 3:83; *Chelkat Yakov* 2:128; *Minchat Yitzchak* 2:84; *Be'er Moshe* 2:104; *Shiurim Metzuyanim b'Halacha* 193:1.
1191 Devarim 4:9 and commentaries.
1192 *Sefer Chassidim* 720.

While outright euthanasia is almost always forbidden,[1193] refraining from heroic measures to prolong life is often not. Heroic measures are defined as procedures that are unlikely to provide a cure or significant relief of pain.[1194] Furthermore, it is permitted to pray for one who is terminally ill or otherwise suffering to quickly pass on, although we may not take any active means ourselves to hasten the death.[1195]

According to many authorities, there is no need to resuscitate when a severely ill person suffers cardiac arrest.[1196] Likewise, a fully conscious individual is permitted to decline heroic prolonging measures if he or she so desires.[1197]

A person in a state of imminent death is known in Jewish law as a *gosses*. Imminent is generally defined as a death which is to be expected within three days.[1198] Jewish law compares such a person to a flickering candle, soon to expire.[1199] Other than comfort measures, most other forms of contact are actually forbidden.[1200]

With this background in mind, let us consider the Schiavo case. The issue of Terri Schiavo was complicated by the dispute over whether she was merely severely disabled or actually in a persistent vegetative state – the truth of which may never be known. Keep in mind as well that the Schiavo case teetered on such critical arguments as whether or not intensive rehabilitation could have improved her condition – an opportunity denied her. The result of such questions would have certainly affected the halachic outcomes concerning this case.

One thing is for sure, however: from the perspective of halacha, Terry Schiavo would not have been considered "terminally ill." A terminally ill patient is defined as one who is only expected to live

---

1193 See Shmuel II 1–15 where King Saul takes his own life. Nevertheless there are those commentators who find halachic justification for Saul's actions; see http://vbm-torah.org/archive/halak66/08halak.htm.
1194 *Nishmat Avraham*, YD 339.
1195 Ran, Nedarim 40b, Ketubot 104a, Avoda Zara 18a.
1196 *Nishmat Avraham*, YD 339.
1197 *Igrot Moshe*, CM 7:73.
1198 YD 339:2.
1199 Shabbat 151b.
1200 Semachot I 1:4; see *Sefer Chassidim* 724.

up to a year.[1201] With over a decade behind her in her illness, there was no sign of Terry Schiavo being terminally ill, and certainly not a gosses.

It emerges from the above discussion that Terri Schiavo's "halachic status" would have been equal to that of all other hospitalized patients with disabilities, to whom assistance for recovery would have been a medical and halachic obligation. While we are certainly not equipped with the requisite details to even attempt a halachic ruling on the case in point, one thing is certain – death by starvation is an approach completely beyond any halachic tolerance. The removal of feeding tubes, being a proactive effort to shorten life, has but one categorization from the perspective of Jewish law: murder.

FUNERALS

I have no intention of entering into morbid discussion, nor do I wish to be a bearer of bad tidings, but there are some topics whose time must come. In this case it's death, dying, and specifically – funerals.

The body of one who has died should not be left unburied for even one night.[1202] Indeed, this rule is especially binding in Israel and in Jerusalem in particular.[1203] There is an exception to this rule, however, and that is when the cause for delay is intended to bring honor to the deceased, such as allowing time for close relatives to arrive for the funeral.

One will readily notice that a mourner's garment will always be ripped somewhere in the area of the chest. This custom of ripping a garment is known as *kriya*, and is intended to serve as an expression of one's grief. Common custom regarding the kriya is

---

1201 *Igrot Moshe*, CM 7:73.
1202 YD 357:1.
1203 Bava Kama 82b.

that it is performed immediately prior to the funeral,[1204] although some do so at the time of death. It is is indicative of the importance of the relationship that one should perform the kriya upon the death of one's rabbi as well.[1205] When mourning a parent, the kriya is performed on the left side, for all other relatives – the right side.[1206]

Attending a funeral is a tremendous mitzva whose reward is beyond comprehension.[1207] In fact, we are taught that the well-known directive of "You shall love your fellow like yourself" applies to funerals as well – wouldn't you want a crowd at yours?[1208] When attending a funeral, especially a burial, one should be sure that any outward display of mitzvot, such as one's tzitzit, is hidden so as not to cause the deceased to feel humiliated at the inability to perform any mitzvot.[1209]

Kohanim, as is known, are prohibited from attending any funerals or coming in any other contact with the dead, with the sole exception of attending the funerals of their seven closest kin.[1210] Once the funeral and burial have been completed, the kohanim are forbidden to desecrate themselves any further.[1211] This even precludes future visits to the gravesites such as on yahrtzeits and the like.[1212]

Delivering a eulogy at a funeral is considered to be a tremendous mitzva whose ultimate purpose is intended to cause listeners to appreciate the deceased and learn from their good deeds.[1213] Believe it or not, delivering eulogies at a funeral is actually forbidden on

---

1204   YD 340:1.
1205   YD 340:7.
1206   Taz, YD 340:7.
1207   Peah 1:1.
1208   Rambam, *Hilchot Avel* 14:1.
1209   OC 23:2.
1210   Vayikra 21:2.
1211   YD 373:6.
1212   There does not seem to be any basis for kohanim to visit the resting places of tzaddikim such as at Ma'arat Hamachpela or Kever Rachel. While there are sources such as Mishlei Rabba 9 and *Sefer Hachinuch* 263 which seem to imply that the body of a tzaddik does not defile kohanim, this is not the accepted halacha. See *Kitzur Shulchan Aruch* 202:14, *Yechave Da'at* 4:58.
1213   YD 344:1

days of significance on the Jewish calendar. This includes, for example, Chanuka, Rosh Chodesh, and even the entire month of Nissan. For some reason, this halacha is not properly followed in many places. It is also a mitzva to fulfill all the postmortem wishes of the deceased (presuming they do not contravene halacha, as we've already said).[1214]

So great a mitzva is digging graves for the deceased that those who do so are exempt from reciting the Shema and any other prayers while occupied with this task.[1215] When leaving a cemetery it is customary to pluck some grass and cast it behind you.[1216] Some explain that the purpose of this custom is to remind us that we are but earth as well. Washing your hands upon leaving a cemetery is very important – you certainly don't want to bring any impure spirits into your home upon return![1217] Interestingly, after this washing, one should not dry the hands, but rather allow them to air dry on their own.[1218]

May we merit to see the fulfillment of the verse "Your dead shall yet live...bodies shall arise...awake and sing, you who dwell in the dust!"[1219]

THE DEATH OF THE WICKED

"When the wicked perish there is rejoicing."[1220]

When Yasser Arafat died in November 2004 (and also when Saddam Hussein was hung in December 2006), there was some confusion as to how a Torah Jew was supposed to react. His

---

1214   Gittin 14b; CM 352, 357.
1215   OC 71:5; see also *Sefer Chassidim* 742.
1216   YD 376:4.
1217   Rema, YD 376:4.
1218   *Kaf Hachaim* 4:8; exceptions can be made in the winter.
1219   Yeshayahu 26:19.
1220   Mishlei 11:10.

death was a turning point in both Jewish history and Jewish destiny. This great news was reminiscent of the prayer recited over symbolic foods at our Rosh Hashana dinners: "May it be His will that our enemies be destroyed!"

Arafat was a man who institutionalized, marketed, and perfected hijackings, hostage takings, and school massacres. A man whose resume of terror brings fear to even the most notorious of criminals. What should our response be to his death? Can celebration possibly be in order?

On the one hand, our Western-shaped morality, Jewish guilt, and generations of oppression, combined with the fear of possibly upsetting a neighbor or coworker, are probably all telling us not to be so happy – at least not publicly. You may be thinking to yourself that the death of any human being is no reason to celebrate.

That, my dear readers, is simply not the Jewish approach to the demise of complete evil and wickedness.

While there are abundant scriptural and Talmudic sources, references, and examples authenticating this idea, there is, however, one in particular that articulates this perspective with unmistakable clarity. The Talmud records that as part of Mordechai's reward for having informed King Achashverosh of an impending assassination plot, the king assigned the evil Haman (a barber by day, proto-Nazi by night) to attend to Mordechai's needs.[1221]

Among the ceremonies that Mordechai was rewarded with was to be led through the town square on the king's horse, to be drawn by Haman. As Mordechai was climbing onto the king's horse, we are told that he kicked Haman in the head. At this, Haman asked him: "Doesn't your Torah say that you should not rejoice at the suffering and downfall of your enemies?[1222] Surely your kick was a form of celebrating my misfortune!" To this, Mordechai responded: "The verse you quote refers to a Jewish enemy, and you are actually right![1223] At our Jewish enemy's misfortune we may not rejoice, but

---

1221 Megilla 16a.
1222 Mishlei 24:17.
1223 *Sefer Chassidim* 163.

regarding Gentile enemies of the Jewish people, the Torah says that we are obligated to rejoice!"[1224]

Have no fear, no guilt, and no second thoughts about celebrating the death of those who are completely evil.

Make no mistake: we are not simply celebrating the death of the leader of an enemy nation. Even when President Hafez Assad of Syria died, there were no celebrations. No dancing. No *l'chaims*. No, we are not to behave that way merely at the death of enemy nation leaders. Nor do we celebrate when natural disasters strike enemy states. What we are celebrating is the death of the Godfathers of modern terror. We are celebrating the elimination of people who were evil in its purest form. It should be reflected upon as a blessing not only for Jews but for the entire civilized world.

Arafat is the one who laid the seeds and ideas for all future Islamic-flavored terror. It is from Arafat that Bin Laden got his idea for the most spectacular hijacking of all time. It is from Arafat that Chechen rebels learned how to massacre schoolchildren. It is from Arafat that koranically justified beheadings have become commonplace. Saddam Hussein is a similar case, with his murder of his Kurdish citizens among the many other atrocities he perpetrated upon mankind.

The Palestinian Authority declared forty days of mourning to observe on the passing of Arafat. I couldn't handle so much simcha!!

1224 Based on Devarim 33:29.

OTHER

CRUELTY TO ANIMALS

Not only are we commanded to treat our fellow human beings with decency and respect, but towards animals as well we are taught that kindness and compassion are primary. This idea of compassion to animals, or more specifically, the prohibition on cruelty to animals, is known in halachic literature as *tzaar baalei chaim* ([the prohibition against causing] pain to living creatures). According to some authorities, mistreating an animal is nothing less than a complete violation of Torah law like any other.[1225] Other authorities, while warning cruelty to animals is unconditionally forbidden, consider it to be a rabbinical transgression.[1226] While we may quickly conclude that tzaar baalei chaim applies only to our behavior towards animals, it is actually intended to include our treatment of human beings, both Jews and non-Jews, as well![1227] To cause distress to any person in any way is so severe that one is to be censured for even unintentional occurrences.[1228]

No doubt that on occasion you've come across a cockroach, bee, or spider which for a variety of reasons you chose to kill. Not to worry – exterminating annoying pests is completely permitted.[1229] This is especially true for pests that may be ruining your food, such as when eating in the sukka, or which otherwise may cause pain or annoyance to humans. To properly understand this dispensation, it is important to realize that the parameters of tzaar baalei chaim are such that even though respect must be shown towards animals, there are certain legitimate frameworks where causing pain to animals (such as the annoyance/pain caused in the course of riding upon them) or even killing them (i.e., for food) is permitted in the context of reasonable human needs.[1230] For example, in the event that a bee is buzzing close to one who may have a fatal response to its sting, it is certainly within reason to kill it. The holy Ari, however,

---

1225 Bava Metzia 32b; *Sefer Hachinuch* 596; *Sefer Chassidim* 44.
1226 *Sefer Yereim* 352, cited in Rabbi Shmuel Khoshkerman, *Minchat Shmuel*.
1227 *B'tzel Hachachma* 4:125.
1228 Chagiga 5a.
1229 *Teshuvot v'Hanhagot* 2:726.
1230 *Igrot Moshe*, CM 2:47.

was particular not to kill even under these circumstances. Make no mistake, even when legitimate human needs call for administering pain or death to an animal, it should be done very hesitantly and avoided when at all possible.[1231] Based on what we have just seen, it goes without saying that hunting for sport is not proper Jewish behavior.[1232] It would appear that recreational fishing would also be included in the category of objectionable pursuits.

An infamous challenge to tzaar baalei chaim is the production of foie gras, "glatt kosher mehadrin," no less. Over the years, many observant people have protested that the process of preparing foie gras is extraordinarily cruel to animals and should be banned. Rabbinical authorities have been hesitant to support such a ban, as foie gras was a common staple amongst even the most pious consumers in Europe. It is argued that banning foie gras at this time may retroactively create the impression that our forefathers were not conducting themselves appropriately in their halachic observance.

Exploring the issue of foie gras from textual sources, we find a similar discussion regarding raising veal. Gourmet preparation of veal meat includes with it many cruelties and unnecessary deprivations to the animal. These unnecessary measures do not seem to find themselves permissible under the dispensation of "legitimate human needs" and should be banned according to Rabbi Moshe Feinstein.[1233] It would seem from his words[1234] that he would include foie gras as well, although it is not mentioned by name. It is somewhat disturbing that those rabbis who allow foie gras outright seem to forget the teaching of the Ramban that even when something may be permitted by the letter of the law – it need not be practiced when it appears unbecoming or otherwise not within the spirit of the law.[1235]

1231 Rema, EH 5:14.
1232 Noda b'Yehuda, YD 10.
1233 *Igrot Moshe*, EH 4:92.
1234 Ibid.; "to force feed an animal food it does not enjoy…is forbidden by the Torah."
1235 Vayikra 19:1.

Although tzaar baalei chaim is an important area of halacha to be well versed in, if you're ever in doubt, keep in mind the verse "Hashem's mercy is on all of his creations,"[1236] and you'll surely come to do the right thing.

THE HUMANITY OF SHECHITA

It is taught that the great Rabbi Yehuda Hanassi was a perfectly righteous person, yet he suffered great pain during his life.[1237] When did these troubles begin? It was as a result of a certain misdeed of his. Rabbi Yehuda was once walking through the marketplace when a calf being led to the slaughter ran to him and hid under his cloak for safety. We are told that Rabbi Yehuda turned to the sheep with sharp countenance and said: "Go! It was for this that you were created!" It is from this incident, we are told, that his suffering began.[1238]

Recently, a controversy emerged regarding the shechita practices of certain slaughterhouses. Accusations were hurled implying that not only was the shechita not in accordance with halacha, but was undertaken in a way that was cruel and torturous to the animals. Without delving into the specifics of this story, it was somewhat acknowledged that while the practices in question may have been within the letter of the law, they were certainly not within the spirit of the law.[1239]

The justification for these practices was that according to Jewish law, once the actual slaughter has taken place, the animal is halachically considered dead, notwithstanding that it may take eight to ten seconds before the animal loses consciousness. Occasionally, during this period between the slaughter and death, further handling of the animal takes place – primarily with the

---

1236 Tehillim 145:9.
1237 Bava Metzia 85a.
1238 For an elaborate discussion and commentary on this episode see Rabbi Yitzchak Eshcoli, *Tzaar Baalei Chaim* [Heb.] (privately printed, 5762 [2001]), p. 583.
1239 Statement of Rabbi Sha'ar Yashuv Hakohen of Haifa, among others.

removal of the esophagus and trachea. It is believed that if these two organs are quickly removed, it will actually hasten the animal's death – a practice which appears to be rather cruel in nature.

While it seems that the controversy over this issue has basically subsided, the point of this discussion is to highlight the importance of humanity within kosher slaughter and meat processing. Any procedures in ritual practice that appear disturbing and unacceptable to society should be reconsidered.[1240] Here it is worth reprising the subject of the oxymoronic "glatt kosher foie gras." Although this delicacy may be perhaps technically permissible to eat, it should surely be frowned upon. Being a *menuval b'reshut haTorah*,[1241] namely, following the letter of the law without concern for the spirit of the law, is unbecoming to say the least.[1242]

Make no mistake: shechita is as holy as it is humane. The solution to the problem is not through reevaluating shechita, but rather, reevaluating the shochtim and their procedures. While shechita is an important part of our tradition, it is one that demands reverence. God cares as much for the morality behind shechita as for the ritual,[1243] as evidenced by the idea that it may just be that God's motive and objective in giving us the Shabbat was for no other reason than to allow our animals to enjoy a day of rest.[1244]

I believe the following story perfectly sums up the approach we must have towards the God-given mitzva of shechita.

The Ba'al Shem Tov, in the years that he was a hidden mystic, would make his livelihood slaughtering chickens and cows for Jewish communities before the holidays. When he left this occupation, a new slaughterer took his place. One day, a Gentile assistant of one of the Jewish villagers brought a chicken to the new slaughterer. As the new shochet began to sharpen his knife, the Gentile watched and began to laugh. "You wet your knife with water before you

---

1240 It is suggested the Rabbeinu Gerhsom's well-known ban on polygamy was for no other reason then society at large viewed the practice as unbecoming.
1241 See the commentary of the Ramban at the beginning of parshat Kedoshim for more on this idea.
1242 See Eshcoli, *Tzaar Baalei Chaim*, p. 413 for a halachic analysis of foie gras.
1243 *Sefer Chassidim* 372.
1244 Careful reading of Shemot 23:12.

sharpen it!" he exclaimed, "And then you just start to cut?" "And how else?" the slaughterer asked. "The Ba'al Shem Tov would cry until he had enough tears to wet the knife. Then he would cry as he sharpened the knife. Only then would he cut!"

MUSIC

Music and song occupy a most prominent role within Judaism. Not only is music a part of our history and culture, but in some instances it even comprises an important component of our rituals. The Torah itself is replete with references to song, including the famous "Song at the Sea," which was recited by the entire Jewish nation following the crossing of the Red Sea. The Torah considers it noteworthy that Miriam and the women not only sung praises for the miracle of the Exodus, but that they were even accompanied by tambourines to enhance their praise of God.[1245] King David also made use of every instrument available in his worship of God.[1246]

Musical instruments have existed since the beginning of time. In fact, one of the first industries in history was that of the mass production of musical instruments.[1247] Throughout the course of the Tanach, one can count at least nineteen musical instruments that are mentioned by name.

So important is music within ritual that the Torah may not simply be read as a narrative; rather it must be chanted with the *trop* (the specially ordained cantillation) whenever read publicly. Indeed, it is questionable whether or not a congregation has discharged the mitzva of reading the Torah if their reader omitted the trop, or even chanted the wrong note.[1248] Not only the Torah, but every book of Scripture has its own melody that is to be employed when it is read. We are cautioned to keep the various different trops distinct – we

---

1245 Shemot 14:15.
1246 Tehillim 150.
1247 Bereishit 4:21.
1248 Megilla 32a; *Mishna Berura* 142:4.

are not to use the trop intended for one book of Scripture when reading from another.[1249]

In Talmudic times, music was an integral part of every Temple service. Not only was singing commonplace, but every instrument possible was used to make music to glorify God.[1250] The Temple even employed a maestro-in-residence at all times.[1251] Furthermore, each day of the week had its own song, mirroring that day of creation, a practice still followed today.[1252] It is worth noting that if the singing in the Temple was omitted, it was questionable whether the service was accepted by God.[1253] Even trees, oceans, mountains, and all of creation sing praises to God on a daily basis.[1254]

Trumpets occupied a particularly central role in worship and other ritual events. Indeed, trumpets were required to be sounded during the opening of the Temple doors,[1255] the bringing of offerings,[1256] and even when bringing the first fruits offering,[1257] to name but a few. It is reported that the music in the Temple in Jerusalem was so loud that it could be heard in Jericho.[1258] Even mourning rituals were to be accompanied by appropriate song.[1259]

Synagogues throughout history have employed individuals whose responsibility was to oversee the musical component of services. This distinguished individual was known as the *chazzan*, which actually translates as "visionary." Although a chazzan (who also frequently served as the synagogue caretaker and schoolmaster as well) with a pleasant voice is important, they are not to be hired merely on the merit of their voices, but also by their personability, kindness, and being well suited for the congregation.[1260]

1249 *Sefer Chassidim* 302.
1250 Sukka 50.
1251 Shekalim 5:1.
1252 Rosh Hashana 31a.
1253 Ta'anit 27a.
1254 Psalms 96.
1255 Sukka 54a.
1256 Sukka 53b.
1257 Sukka 47b.
1258 Tamid 3.
1259 Divrei Hayamim II 35:25.
1260 OC 53:4.

Be sure to make music part of your routine. We are told that singing the text when studying holy works assists in better memory retention,[1261] and that it is even considered admirable to sing while you work.[1262] Sorry, I haven't found sources discussing the permissibility of singing in the shower.

RUTH

The book of Ruth, although an inconspicuous book seemingly reserved exclusively for the holiday of Shavuot, actually offers a lot more than meets the eye. Sure, it can certainly be argued that it is most fitting to be read on Shavuot, having been originally written in the same season. It further shares a common denominator with Shavuot in that it similarly deals with acceptance of the Torah. Nevertheless, the book of Ruth is actually the basis for many of the laws found in the *Shulchan Aruch* and practiced on a regular basis. Indeed, most of these laws are applied far more frequently than the one occasion a year the book is publicly read.

First and foremost, of course, are the laws of conversion, which almost completely derive from the episode of Ruth. That's right – many, if not most, of the procedures related to conversions practiced every day by rabbinical courts worldwide stem from that book of Ruth hidden at the end of your Tanach.

The Talmud teaches that prior to Ruth's conversion, Naomi told her: "We have rules as to where we can and cannot walk on Shabbat, rules regarding our dealings with the opposite sex, we even have six hundred thirteen challenging commandments to uphold, and we are strictly forbidden to worship idols."[1263] With these few instructions on how to be a Jew came Ruth's famous response: "Where you walk, I shall walk; where you sleep, I shall

---

1261 Megilla 32a; Tosafot, Sanhedrin 99a.
1262 Sota 48a.
1263 Yevamot 47.

sleep; your people are my people, and your God is my God."[1264] It is from here that the Talmud rules: "We inform prospective converts of a few of the less serious commandments and a few of the more serious commandments. We do not overburden the convert with numerous commandments, nor with their fine details."[1265]

Another halacha derived from the story of Ruth is the practice of greeting one another using the name of God, as Boaz himself did, as it is written: "Boaz came from Bethlehem and he greeted the reapers with 'May God be with you,' and they responded, 'May God bless you.'"[1266] We fulfill this directive today through the greeting "shalom aleichem," and its response "aleichem shalom." Shalom is one of God's names.

Yet another practice from the book of Ruth[1267] is the source for the Talmud's teaching, "One may not leave the Land of Israel to go abroad unless the price of wheat has risen...but if one can still purchase wheat, although somewhat costly, one may not leave." As Rabbi Shimon bar Yochai used to say: "Why were Elimelech, Machlon, and Chilyon, the greatest scholars and leaders of the day, punished? Because they left Eretz Yisrael even though wheat was available, albeit at a high price."[1268] Of course we should take this teaching with a grain of salt, as there are other legitimate grounds for leaving the Land of Israel, which are beyond the scope of this discussion.[1269]

Finally, a most beloved and practiced halacha that few realize derives from the book of Ruth is washing in preparation for Shabbat, along with donning one's finest clothing. As Naomi tells Ruth: "Wash yourself, anoint yourself, and put on your fine clothes."[1270] The Talmud comments on this verse, explaining: "These were her Shabbat clothes. Rabbi Chanina said: A person must have two sets

---

1264 Ruth 1:18.
1265 Ibid.; of course the convert is expected to commit to fully studying and
        practicing Judaism in its entirety.
1266 Ruth 2:4.
1267 Ruth 1:19.
1268 Bava Batra 91a.
1269 See Avoda Zara 13a, Bava Batra 91a.
1270 Ruth 3:3.

of garments, one for the weekdays and one for Shabbat."[1271] Indeed, applying fine perfumes in honor of Shabbat was a custom of even the greatest sages, and is certainly a meritorious custom we should all consider emulating.[1272]

As we can see, the book of Ruth is much more than simply a story about a woman's conversion. As with many of the other "less significant" books of Tanach, it contains fundamental insights on living as a Jew.

RABBEINU GERSHOM

Although the name "Rabbeinu Gershom" may not be a familiar one in regular household usage, Rabbi Gershom ben Yehuda Hakohen was actually responsible for many trailblazing rabbinic enactments that we take for granted today. Born in the year 960 CE in France, he eventually settled and resided in Mainz, Germany, and served as one of the leading rabbis of all Ashkenazi Jewry. In addition to serving as one of the leading rabbis of his day, he also established a yeshiva for advanced study, in which the famous well-known sage and commentator par excellence, Rashi, studied when just a rabbinical student. Although Rashi never studied directly under Rabbeinu Gershom, he nevertheless always referred to him as "Our teacher, may the memory of the righteous and the holy be a blessing, who enlightened the eyes of the exiled, and from whose mouth we all live," which gives just a small taste of the influence Rabbeinu Gershom had in shaping Jewish life.

While there were actually many enactments that Rabbeinu Gershom put into practice, there are three that are most significant and stand apart. Leading this is the prohibition on polygamy, a lifestyle actually permitted by the Torah and previously practiced until Rabbeinu Gershom ended it. Some suggest that the reason for this ban was to parallel the Christian statute which at that

---

1271 Shabbat 113b.
1272 Ibn Ezra, Ruth 3:3.

time also banned polygamy. It is thought that Rabbeinu Gershom felt that if the Jews were to continue with polygamy, tremendous resentment would ensue, possibly leading to pogroms and the like. Others suggest that Rabbeinu Gershom felt that having one spouse was a more moral and dignified lifestyle.

Another well-practiced decree of Rabbeinu Gershom within marital law deals with divorce procedures. While according to the letter of biblical law, a man may divorce his wife without her consent, Rabbeinu Gershom put an end to such a practice, requiring mutual consent for issuing a divorce. Prior to this decree, it would have been theoretically permissible for a man to divorce his wife for any reason whatsoever, even, say, burning his toast. This decree forces second thoughts prior to commencing divorce proceedings.

Finally, a beloved and occasionally disregarded decree of his was the prohibiting and the placing of a rabbinic ban upon anyone who would read someone else's mail or other sensitive documents without permission, including eavesdropping and the like.[1273] This ban, known in Talmudic parlance as a *cherem*, shuns a person from his community in both spiritual and material matters. (There are actually some twenty-four additional offenses that merit being placed in cherem,[1274] although rabbis are strongly discouraged from making use of cherems and the like.[1275] In any event, one should never decree more than one cherem per day.[1276] One should not even live in a place where cherems are common – it means that your neighbors aren't good people![1277])

Rabbeinu Gershom's decrees, including the ban on polygamy, were only binding on Ashkenazi Jews. In theory, Sephardic men are permitted to take more than one wife if they so choose. Also noteworthy is the fact that Rabbeinu Gershom's decrees were originally intended to be in place for only a thousand years. Nevertheless, with minor exceptions, no one has ever seriously

---

1273 Regarding whether or not reading open mail such as postcards is forbidden, see *Aruch Hashulchan* 334:21.
1274 YD 334:43; *Sefer Chassidim* 43.
1275 See Rambam, *Hilchot Talmud Torah* 7:13.
1276 *Sefer Chassidim* 143.
1277 *Sefer Chassidim* 106, 410.

even considered the idea of eliminating any of the practices he put into place.[1278]

The end of Rabbeinu Gershom's life was full of trauma, including the forced conversion of both his wife and son to Christianity, which led to him "sitting shiva" for fourteen days. This son, his only one, later died in his father's lifetime. It was also during Rabbeinu Gershom's life and leadership that King Heinrich II issued an edict of expulsion against the Jews of Spain.

THE NEW SANHEDRIN

In ancient times, questions of nationwide religious concern were settled by a seventy-one-member rabbinic tribunal known as the *Sanhedrin*. The Sanhedrin was the supreme political, religious, and judicial body of the Jewish people, and was entrusted with safeguarding and interpreting the Oral Torah. It even survived after the destruction of the Holy Temple into the fifth century. The obligation to ensure such a rabbinical system is a mitzva of the Torah.[1279] There is even an entire tractate of the Talmud that deals with the Sanhedrin and all its laws.

With minor exceptions as we will discuss, this body no longer functions, nor are there any remnants of its existence. There is, however, a tradition that the Sanhedrin will return, in a seemingly natural fashion, immediately prior to the messianic era to teach and judge the Jewish people.[1280] Furthermore, the tradition continues, the proclamation of the return of this body will take place in the holy city of Tiberias which sits on the Sea of Galilee. The Rambam discusses in detail how this tribunal is to be reestablished.[1281]

Equipped with this piece of introductory information, it is now worth discussing the modern attempt at reestablishing this

---

1278 See EH 1:10 regarding polygamy today.
1279 Bamidbar 11:16; Devarim 16:18.
1280 Yeshayahu 1:26.
1281 Rambam, *Hilchot Sanhedrin* 4.

Sanhedrin. Indeed, recently a movement has sprouted taking upon itself responsibility for recreating the Sanhedrin, and has even found and appointed seventy-one rabbis to fill its ranks. The proclamation and launch of this Sanhedrin took place in a hotel in Tiberias in October of 2004. No similar attempt at such an undertaking has been made in the last sixteen hundred years, with the last attempt having been tested in the holy city of Tzfat. Due to the opposition of other leading rabbis of the time, however, the Tzfat tribunal was quickly shut down.

One of the "signs" organizers have relied upon for undertaking their task at this time is the tradition that the Sanhedrin will be restored after a partial ingathering of the Jewish exiles, which is to precede the rebuilding of Jerusalem.[1282] As can be imagined, this move is somewhat controversial in both religious and secular circles, and has not been unanimously accepted. In an additional move to register their intentions and convictions as well as follow in the ways of old, this group ascended the Temple Mount, after having immersed in a mikva and other halachic preparations, in order to tour and prepare for their seats in the soon-to-be-built Holy Temple.[1283] Fearing a riot upon the Arabs seeing seventy-one bearded men preparing to begin the rebuilding of the Temple, the police often limit these pilgrimages or even ban them altogether.

Also on this new group's agenda is the desire not only to establish the Great Court of seventy-one members, but the smaller courts of twenty-three members as well. The courts of twenty-three can be referred to as "local" or "mini" Sanhedrins, which were seated in cities outside of Jerusalem, and dealt with matters in those places. I was both perplexed and honored to have been invited to join this ever-growing rabbinical council in its Beit Shemesh branch. For a variety of reasons, I respectfully declined the invitation. I'm content watching the progress of this endeavor from the sides.

Fanatical zealots or the beginning of the messianic era? For now, let's wait and see.

1282 Megilla 17b.
1283 Note: visiting the Temple Mount is a controversial issue with some rabbis forbidding it while others encourage it. One should consult a rabbi before deciding to visit the Temple Mount.

SPICES

B elieve it or not, spices occupy a prominent place in Jewish literature and even ritual.[1284] Our rabbis teach us that the Torah is compared to salt, and the Mishna to pepper.[1285]

Although the Torah itself only mentions four spices, the Talmud enumerates dozens. In fact, the rabbis of the Talmud ordained a blessing to be recited upon the smelling of pleasant spices,[1286] as is done during the Havdala ceremony. Smelling spices regularly is credited as an omen for inspiring devotion to God.[1287] Great rabbis are actually compared to sweet-smelling spices.[1288] In fact, Rabbi Yosef Karo, the author of the *Shulchan Aruch*, sold spices for a living.

In rabbinic literature, saffron is considered to be the most prestigious of spices. Saffron is a spice that has been as prized as gold for thousands of years. Saffron grows around the Mediterranean area, including in Israel. The three kinds of wild saffron that grow in Israel today are actually government-protected species. The cost of saffron in ancient times could have run up to one hundred times the price of most other spices. The Talmud says that a profitable crop is one that includes saffron.[1289]

Saffron is known as *charkom* in Hebrew, and was one of the eleven spices (along with marijuana[1290]) that made up the incense offering that was burned during the daily Temple service.[1291] Saffron was used extensively as a dye, as well.

Saffron has a very early connection to Judaism. It is mentioned among other spices in the Song of Songs: "Spikenard and saffron,

---

1284 This chapter is based on an article by Rabbi Steve Gindi archived at http://www. milknhoney.co.il/.
1285 Sofrim 15:8.
1286 Berachot 43b.
1287 Arizal; compare the "Azamer b'Shvachim" poem sung Friday nights.
1288 Shir Hashirim 3:6.
1289 Bava Metzia 109a.
1290 There are compelling arguments that the "Kaneh Bosem" of Shemot 30 was indeed cannabis. See *Igrot Moshe*, YD 3:35 on the permissibility of using marijuana.
1291 Rambam, *Klei Hamikdash* 2:4.

calamus and cinnamon, with all trees of frankincense; myrrh and aloes, with all the chief spices."[1292] These sweet spices are characteristic of the "garden of lovers," referring to the loving relationship between God and the Jewish people.

Prior to bestowing the blessing of the firstborn upon his son Esav, Yitzchak asked him to prepare an elaborate and succulent lunch. Our sages teach us that the stew Yitzchak requested was to be properly spiced with oil, salt, pepper, saffron, and cumin.[1293] Taste was especially important for the then-blind Yitzchak, who could not enjoy the appearance of food.

Some other interesting facts on saffron include its halachic flexibility. You see, should you desire to add saffron to your holiday meals, you will be pleased to know that you can grind it on yom tov, an otherwise forbidden activity.[1294] Also, according to the Mishna, menstrual blood can be distinguished from other blood due to its resemblance to red saffron threads.[1295]

According to the Talmud, saffron also has medicinal properties. In the event of diarrhea, simply suck on a little saffron for relief.[1296] It is also promoted as an inexpensive and readily available treatment for male erectile dysfunction when diluted with red wine.[1297] Additionally, when mixed with acacia gum (gum arabic) and liquid alum, saffron can also serve as a birth control agent as well as an abortion stimulant.[1298]

The Talmud also recommends brewing beer with saffron. Drinking such beer regularly is known to keep one healthy.[1299] Beer drinking is regulated, however – it should not be drunk at night.[1300] Spices are an important part of adding flavor and zest to our lives.

1292 Shir Hashirim 4:14.
1293 Midrash Sechel Tov.
1294 Beitza 14a.
1295 Nidda 19a.
1296 Gittin 70a.
1297 Ibid.
1298 Shabbat 110a.
1299 Ibid.
1300 Shabbat 140b.

The ultimate spice, however, is the Torah, known as "the spice of life."[1301]

MEDICINE

Although I wouldn't trade in my physician for a rabbi, it's worth noting that the Talmud and its rabbis are full of medical advice. The Talmud even contains many insights into biology and anatomy. An example of the latter would be the design of our bodies. We are taught that the pinky finger was designed to fit into our ears in order to block ourselves from hearing forbidden speech, such as gossip, slander, and the like.[1302] Long before x-rays were on the scene, the Talmud suggested that a heart has at least two chambers,[1303] how many bones are in a human,[1304] and even how to treat gum disease.[1305]

Even something as simple as blood is dealt with at great length in the Talmud, particularly its color. Although you may readily dismiss the color of blood as being "red," there is actually a heated debate in the Talmud as to what is considered to be the true red color.[1306] Reflexology is also discussed by the Talmud – squeezing your big toes may cause your eyelids to close.[1307]

Maintaining good health is important in Judaism.[1308] In fact, the Rambam states that if we are not healthy, then it's impossible to have any understanding or knowledge of God.[1309] To this end, the Talmud actually prohibits Jews from living in a city without

---

1301 Kiddushin 30b.
1302 Ketubot 5a.
1303 Chullin 45b.
1304 Bechorot 45a.
1305 Avoda Zara 28a.
1306 Nidda 19.
1307 Shabbat 151b.
1308 For Talmudically prescribed healthy eating habits see Shabbat 33a, Gittin 70a, Kohelet Rabba 1:18, Pesachim 114a, Shabbat 152a, Berachot 54b, Sanhedrin 101a.
1309 *Hilchot De'ot* 3:3, 4:1.

a physician.[1310] The next time you feel ill, though, don't rush to phone your doctor immediately. Sometimes a self-diagnosis is just as reliable as your doctor's.[1311]

Psychiatrists will be pleased to learn that the Talmud puts mental health on a par with physical health.[1312] Chiropractors should be aware for the sake of their patients that proper bowing during prayers will ensure a strong spine.[1313] Eye examinations in Talmudic times were slightly different than the common letter charts used by eye professionals today; if you were able to see twenty cubits, then your eyesight was considered excellent.[1314] Although you may have thought that sugar was the culprit, it is actually leeks that are bad for your teeth.[1315]

Take care of your eyes – walking quickly and taking large strides can damage them,[1316] as can salt.[1317] Picking your nose is considered so unbecoming that it is recommended that one who does so should have his hand cut off.[1318] Taking care of your kidneys will ensure that you become wise.[1319] Got pimples? Simply wash your face in some beet juice.[1320]

Here are some Talmudic prescriptions for common ailments: for stomachaches, simply take three hundred long pepper grains and drink a hundred of them in wine every day.[1321] To stop nosebleeds, take a root of clover, a piece of rope, saffron, and a palm branch, burn them all together, and put it in your nostrils.[1322] For toothaches, you can take earth from around an outhouse mixed with honey and eat it, or drink garlic mixed with oil.[1323] I won't even go into

---

1310 Sanhedrin 17b.
1311 Yoma 83a.
1312 Ibid.; Shabbat 128b; Tosafot, Shabbat 50b.
1313 Bava Kama 16a; perhaps prescribe davening to your patients.
1314 Sukka 2a.
1315 Shabbat 110a.
1316 Shabbat 113b.
1317 Eruvin 17b.
1318 Shabbat 108b.
1319 Rosh Hashana 26a.
1320 Shabbat 134a.
1321 Gittin 69b.
1322 Gittin 69a.
1323 Ibid.

headaches. Even dermatology, gynecology, and urology are dealt with at great length. Although modern-day medical drugs may be more effective in fighting off common ailments, one should use them sparingly, lest one's body become addicted.[1324] Medicines are best taken between the holidays of Pesach and Shavuot.[1325] In any event, most medications will have some sort of negative side effects.[1326]

I'll admit it – most of the recommendations above don't really work, but that doesn't matter. Our sages teach us that medicine will always be an advancing field, and we are required to discard ancient remedies, even those of our holy Talmud, when our own university-trained physician advises us so. Science and medicine do not contradict Torah, they complement it. *Eilu v'eilu* – they are both works of the living God.

1325 Shabbat 147b.
1326 Eruvin 54a.

APPENDIX

TALMUDIC QUOTES TO LIVE BY

Be flexible like a reed and not rigid like a cedar.[1327]

The loss of one's temper leads to Hell.[1328]

Becoming angry is like worshipping idols.[1329]

Two scholars who live in the same city but cannot agree or cooperate on halacha arouse God's anger.[1330]

More people die from overeating than from hunger.[1331]

One's character is judged through three things: the manner in which one conducts business, one's behavior when drinking wine, and the caliber of one's conversations.[1332]

1327 Ta'anit 20b.
1328 Nedarim 22a.
1329 Pesachim 66b.
1330 Ta'anit 8a.
1331 Rashi, Yoma 80b; see Rambam, *Hilchot De'ot* 4:15.
1332 *Avot d'Rabbi Natan* 31.

Who is rich? He who is happy with his portion.[1333]

Anyone who does not teach his son a skill or profession is regarded as one who teaches him to rob.[1334]

Food should be appetizing as well as nourishing.[1335]

A person is led in the path he wishes to follow.[1336]

Greet everyone in a friendly manner.[1337]

Someone who judges his fellow favorably will be judged favorably in Heaven.[1338]

Receiving guests in one's home is greater than receiving the Divine presence.[1339]

1333 Avot 4:1.
1334 Kiddushin 29a.
1335 Yoma 74b.
1336 Makkot 10b.
1337 Avot 4:15.
1338 Shabbat 127a.
1339 Shabbat 127a, *Sefer Chassidim* 56.

He who does not return a greeting is called a robber.[1340]

———————————————

A Jew who sinned is still a Jew.[1341]

———————————————

Jews are characterized by modesty, mercy, and benevolence.[1342]

———————————————

The only ones who are poor are those who lack knowledge.[1343]

———————————————

Knowledge leads to wealth.[1344]

———————————————

If you have no work to do, then find something to do.[1345]

———————————————

One who works for a living is greater
than he who fears God.[1346]

———————————————

———————————————

1340 Berachot 6b.
1341 Sanhedrin 44a.
1342 Devarim Rabba 3:4.
1343 Nedarim 41a.
1344 Sanhedrin 92a.
1345 *Avot d'Rabbi Natan* 11.
1346 Berachot 8a.

*On judgment day, a person will have to give an accounting
for every good thing that his eye saw but did not enjoy.*[1347]

---

*There is a replacement for everything
except the wife of your youth.*[1348]

Love your wife as yourself but honor her more.[1349]

---

*Those who have the ability to eliminate a wrong and do
not do so bear the responsibility for its consequences.*[1350]

---

*Whoever raises his hand to another Jew is called a
wicked man even if he did not slap him. One who
slaps a Jew is as if he slaps the Divine presence.*[1351]

---

*Every person has three names: one his parents gave him,
one people call him, and one he acquires himself.*[1352]

1347 Yerushalmi Kiddushin 4:12.
1348 Sanhedrin 22a.
1349 Yevamot 62b.
1350 Shabbat 54b.
1351 Sanhedrin 58a.
1352 Kohelet Rabba 7:1.

Jerusalem was destroyed because the children were in the streets and not in the schools.[1353]

Be sure not to give a child a gift before informing the parents.[1354]

What was created on Shabbat day after God rested? Peace of mind, rest, contentment, and quiet.[1355]

Who is wise? He who learns from everybody.[1356]

If a person desires to become pious, let him study the laws dealing with monetary matters and ethical guidelines.[1357]

Don't try to evade paying taxes, for if you're caught, they will take from you everything you own.[1358]

1353 Shabbat 119b.
1354 Beitza 16a.
1355 Bereishit Rabba 10.
1356 Avot 4:1.
1357 Bava Kama 30a.
1358 Pesachim 112b.

ABOUT THE AUTHOR

Rabbi Ari N. Enkin fulfilled his lifelong dream of making aliya in July 2004 after serving seven years as a congregational and community rabbi in Montreal, Edmonton, and Winnipeg. He received his semicha from the Yeshiva Gedola of Montreal and from the late Rabbi Pinchas Hirshprung, and has recently received Yadin Yadin ordination as well. He holds a master's degree in Informal Adult Education from Athabasca University in Alberta, Canada.

Since making aliya, Rabbi Enkin continues to teach in a number of institutions of Torah learning, generally focusing on halacha studies in addition to *shiurim* and public speaking engagements by invitation. Rabbi Enkin also serves as the general editor of the highly acclaimed Hirhurim website and as rabbinical advisor to judaism.about.com. He is also a frequent contributor to a number of publications, primarily on halachic topics.

Rabbi Enkin is married to Shayna and they have three children: Shira, 8; Eitan, 4; and Tehilla, 2. They currently reside in Ramat Beit Shemesh. Rabbi Enkin's preferred area of study and teaching is, of course, halacha.